W9-APL-957

COLOR IN SPINNING

DEB MENZ

COLOR IN SPINNING

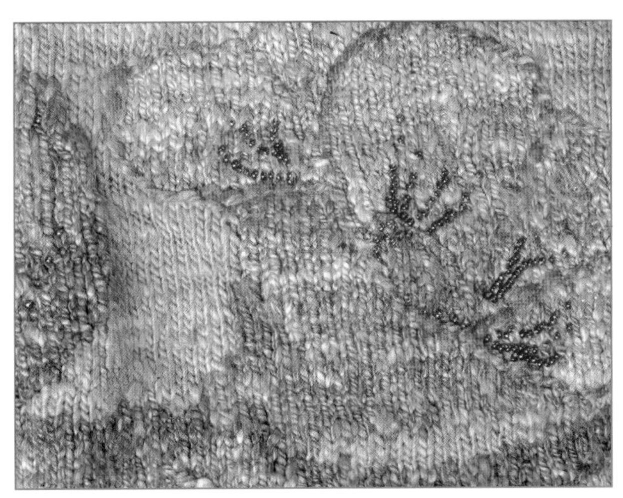

DEB MENZ

INTERWEAVE PRESS

Cover design, Elizabeth R. Mrofka
Illustration, Susan Strawn Bailey
Still photography, Joe Coca
Process photography, Jim Wildeman

Interweave Press
201 East Fourth Street
Loveland, Colorado 80537
USA

Printed in Hong Kong by Sing Cheong

Library of Congress Cataloging-in-Publication Data

Menz, Deb, 1954-
Color in spinning / Deb Menz
p. cm.
Included bibliographical references and index
ISBN 1-883010-37-3
1. Spinning. 2. Color in textile industries. 3. Hand spinning.
4. Spun yarns. I. Title
TS1480.M461997
667'.3—dc2 197-43428
CIP

First Printing: IWP—7.5M:1297:CC

To Buzz, Celia, and Nathan

Acknowledgements

I've discovered that writing a book is not just the work of the person listed as the author. This book is the culmination of three years of work with the help, support and assistance of many, many folks. Without them, it could not have happened.

Where do I begin to say thanks? I'll start with the folks who encouraged me, who believed in my work and my ability to explain what I do to others, especially my students from workshops across the country. Thanks to my teachers: Michelle Wipplinger for encouraging me to write and teach and for teaching me more than she'll know; Priscilla Gibson-Roberts for giving me the confidence to continue with this project when it was not easy; and Celia Quinn for teaching me so much and being a good friend and supporter when I needed it.

I am honored that Linda Ligon had enthusiasm for this book when it was only a passing thought. Thanks go to everyone at Interweave Press for being so supportive and positive. Rita Buchanan provided insight, editing, and encouragement that made me think the book really could be finished. Judith Durant's talent and hard work made the book better than I imagined possible. Thanks to Susan Strawn for her patience and long phone calls to make the artwork turn out "just right" and to Joe Coca and his talent for capturing colors and fibers on film. My in-town photographer, Jim Wildman, gets an "A" for his good cheer and willingness to do all the process shots in my small space in the basement.

I want to thank Patricia Emerick, Celia Quinn, Don Weiner and Paula Simmons Green for proofreading various chapters for readability and accuracy. Their insights were invaluable. Paula Simmons Green and Patrick Green also provided me with equipment when needed and have believed in what I do. Noel Thurner donated combs for color research when I began Chapter 7. Lani Belch of LaniCombs produced a hackle to my specifications for the colorwork in Chapter 7. Jan Louet created another kind of hackle specifically for the methods in Chapter 7. Magnus Drudik made sure I received my long-awaited wheel in time to spin all the samples for the illustrations.

The afghan in Chapter 8 would not have been possible without the talented assistance of the following students: Lindsey Cleveland, Sue Flynn, Lynda Heiple, Joleen Joslin, Stacy King, Holly Leeds, Celia Menz, Min Moore, Celia Quinn, Lynn Ruggles, Marta Sullivan, Sharon Ward, Melissa Williams, and Karen Wisdom.

My list would not be complete without the mentioning of support I received from family and friends. I have a circle of friends, none of whom spin or are remotely interested in fiber, who have been there for me in so many ways these three years: Barbara, Kirby, Stacy, Richard, Terri, Karl, Ann, and Mike, I am genuinely lucky to have you guys in my life! Then there are the folks I literally run with: Lynee, Charlie, and Darrell. You listened to me day in and day out about this project—I promise the book is a dead subject.

Last, but not least important, is my family—Celia, Nate, and Buzz. They have gone over and above during this time to make the project possible. Buzz agreed to do all the cooking, cleaning, and grocery shopping while I wrote the book. He thought it would be a year. He hung in there for three. Thank you so much for that vote of confidence and your willingness to do whatever it took to make the book happen. The kids have been patient and have picked up my slack without much complaint when I said,"Not now, after the book." Well, kids, it's now after the book, and we can take time. Thanks for seeing me through this, Celia and Nate!

contents

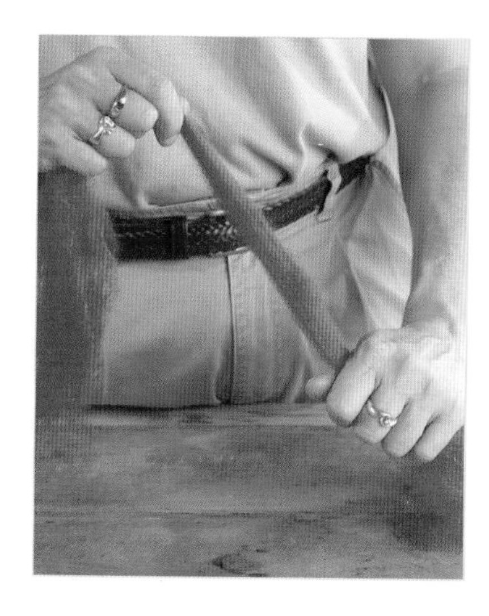

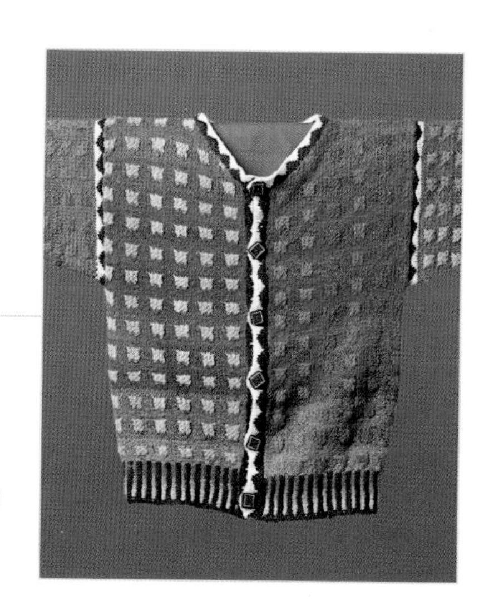

Introduction

The book you are reading is the accumulation of more than twenty years of playing with color, fiber, and equipment. I have come a long way from balancing Paula Simmons's *Spinning and Weaving with Wool* on my lap as I tried to treadle and draft at the same time.

Fiber preparation for me began as an afterthought to spinning, and it was drudgery at best. I had always tried to spin with the least amount of fiber preparation—until I attended my first spinning workshop which was taught by Bette Hochberg. She showed us that one cannot spin well without well-prepared fibers. By the end of that three-day workshop, I believed her.

I bought my first drum carder without written information on how to use the darned thing, but that didn't stop me. I learned a lot by trial and error and by carefully watching the batts. For entertainment's sake, I added dyed colors to the batts while carding. One thing led to another and I found myself creating yarns that combined lots of colors. At first those colors were muddy and subtle. Learning how to keep the colors clear in the final yarn is the result of several years of experiments, which included more failures than successes! Gradually, I discovered which techniques were successful and how to reproduce them. Once I understood color and drum-carding, I wanted to conquer luxury-fiber blending. And I wasn't content with just natural colors, so I learned to dye luxury fibers, too. After many more months in the basement with my equipment and color—*voila!*—it worked! I moved on to painting rovings, then to using combs; I wanted to include many colors using any fiber preparation technique. None of this happened overnight; it evolved over a long period of time.

The yarns I create are those that industry does not produce at any cost. I want to create any yarn I need and not be limited by a preparation technique. My yarns range from subtle heathers to outrageous multicolored, multi-fibered yarns, and for all of them, preparation is the most important aspect. At first I didn't think other spinners would be interested in my techniques because they are so labor-intensive. Then Michele Wipplinger, editor and founder of the *Color Trends* series saw my work and encouraged me to keep records and teach others about using color with fibers. Since then, my students have inspired me to organize my techniques and my records, and this book is the result.

One thing I have learned over the years: There are no short cuts!!! All the short cuts I have tried (and I've tried most of them) turn out to be shortcomings instead, and the resulting yarns have been disappointing. Besides, most of those "short cuts" didn't actually save much time, anyway. They were just excuses for sloppiness.

This book is about how to use and interpret colors in your handspun yarns. I enjoy working with colors intuitively and don't want to be tied to rigid percentages in order to control mixes. I encourage you, too, to experiment with the techniques. Work with your heart and the fibers will be your own. There is no substitute for hands-on practice.

I hope you enjoy using this book as much as I have enjoyed creating it.

chapter chapter chapter

1

Understanding color principles most useful to spinners

— 1 —

Understanding color principles most useful to spinners

Using color is the largest stumbling block for most people who work with fiber. Spinners often feel that to use color well, they need a talent bestowed from above and beyond. Wrong! Few are born with the skills needed to work easily with color.

Instead, using color is like any other subject or skill that you can master with study and practice. Reading this chapter, you'll see that a few main principles about color interactions keep cropping up over and over in different contexts. Once you've learned these basic concepts, you can easily adapt them to your own work. But what matters most is approaching color with an open mind. Be ready to experiment and take color chances. Practice, practice, practice, and above all, have fun! The only way to learn to use color effectively is by actually using it.

DESCRIBING COLORS AND COLOR RELATIONSHIPS

There are three main variables in color: hue, value, and saturation. Being able to look at a color and describe it in those terms is much more helpful and accurate than describing colors with names such as tomato red or lemon yellow; names like that means different things to different people. *Hue* denotes a wedge-shaped area on the color wheel, sometimes

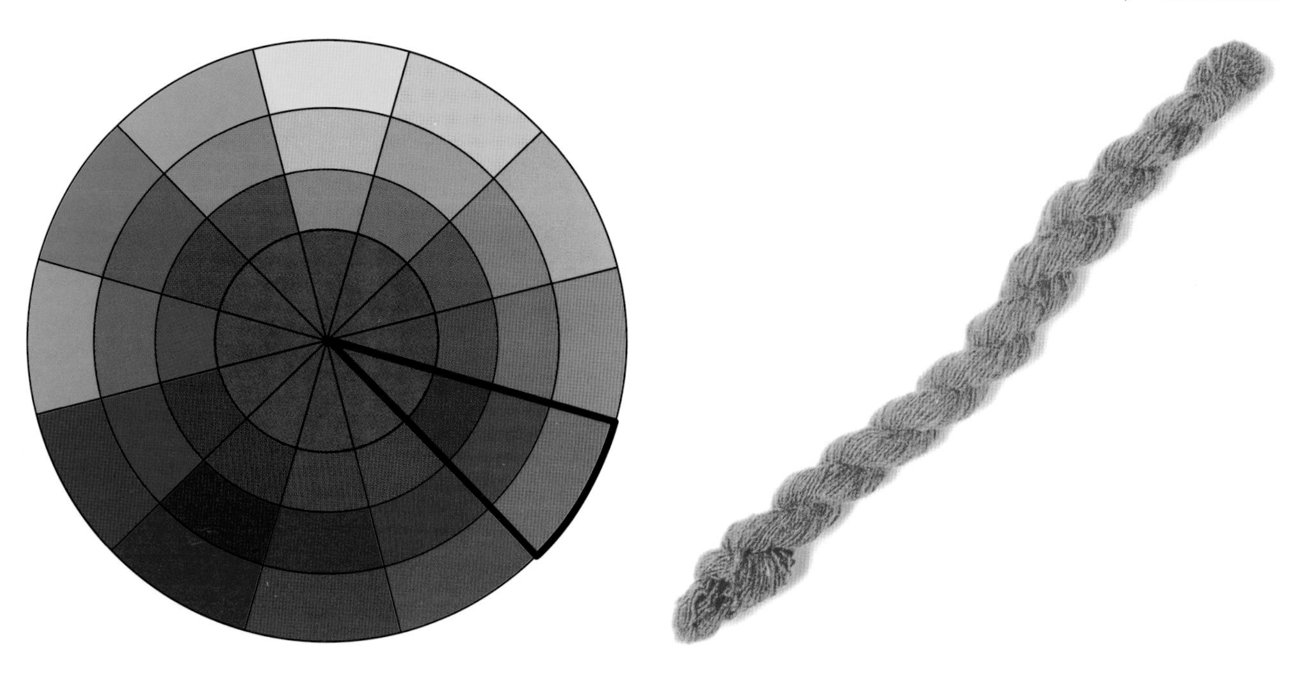

Twelve-hue color wheel. This example starts with the most saturated color in the family on the outer ring and then proceeds through mixtures with the color's complement, ending in the center with neutral gray. The highlighted wedge is the hue family the yarn belongs to.

Value scales.

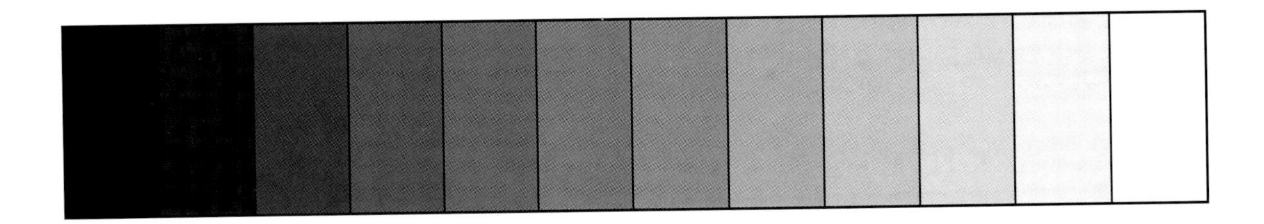

A 12-step black-to-white value scale.

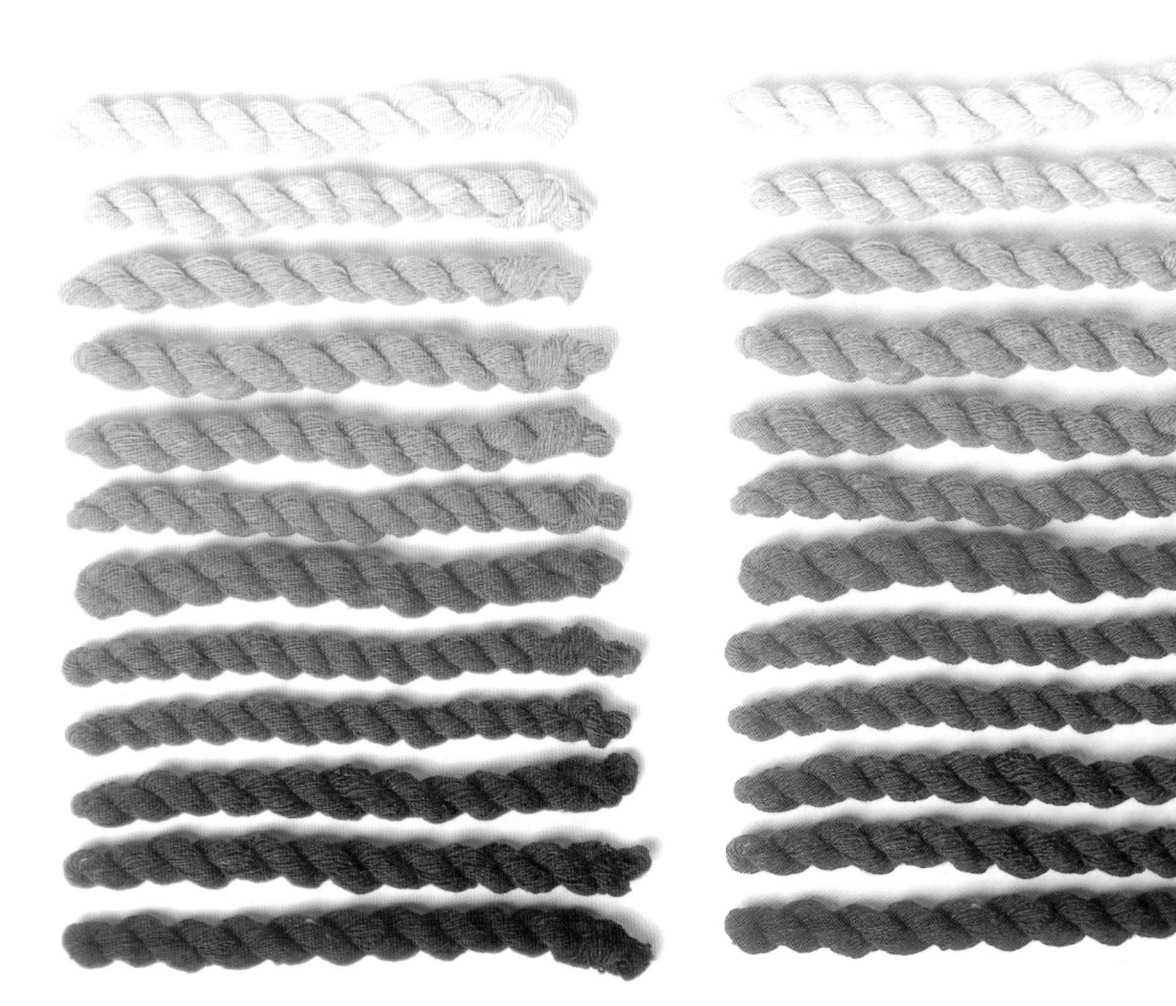

A value scale shown in yarn, both in color and in black and white. The top five skeins are tints (white added) of the original color, the sixth skein is the original color, and the bottom six skeins are shades (black added) of the original.

This black-and-white version shows the relative value of the original color and its tints and shades.

called a hue family or color family. A hue can be any variation of a color within that family. *Value* is the relative lightness or darkness of a color, as compared to a gray scale. *Saturation* or *intensity* is the relative brightness or dullness

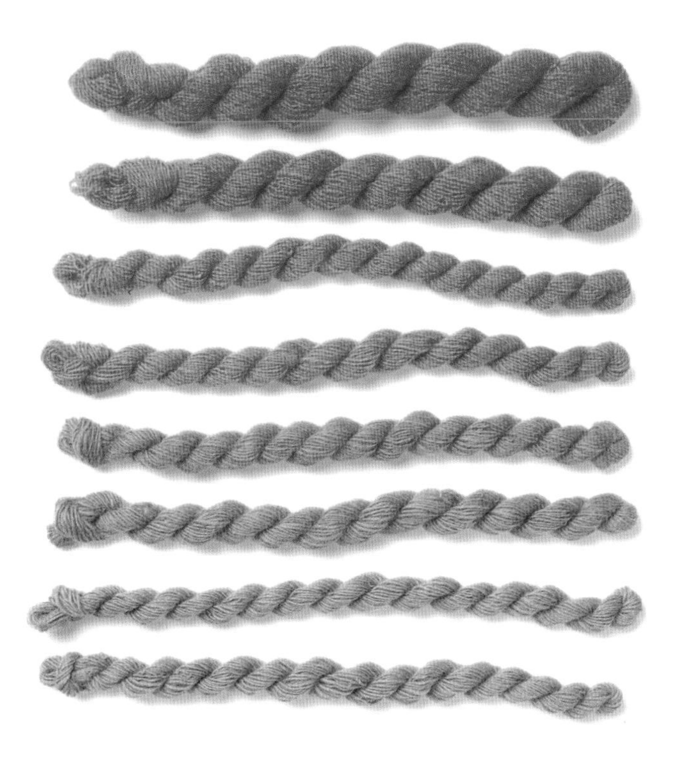

Saturation. The top skein is the most intense color and the rest of the skeins were progressively dulled by adding gray.

of a color, or the amount of pure hue in a color, by comparison to neutral gray.

With a little practice, you can learn to describe the hue, value, and saturation of any color. It takes more practice to predict how these variables will change when you mix dyes or blend dyed fibers to make new colors. Although we can talk about hue, value, and saturation as separate variables, in truth they are closely interrelated. For example, when you try to change a color's value, you may change its saturation, too. This may seem confusing at first, but as you do more dyeing and blending, you'll become more and more comfortable with these terms and the ideas they represent, and more familiar with how dyes and colors behave.

Looking at a color wheel is the best way to identify three main kinds of colors. A twelve-hue color wheel includes three primary, three secondary, and six tertiary colors. The *primary colors* are red, yellow, and blue. These are the basic colors that cannot be obtained by mixing. *Secondary colors* are made by mixing primaries. The colors in this group are orange (made by mixing red and yellow), purple (from red and blue), and green (from blue and yellow). On the color wheel, each secondary color appears midway between the two primaries it is mixed from. *Tertiary colors* are made by mixing a primary color with an adjacent secondary color. The tertiary colors are yellow-orange, red-orange, red-violet, blue-violet, blue-green, and yellow-green.

The color wheel also shows relationships between colors. *Monochromatic colors* fit within a single hue family, or one-twelfth of the color wheel. *Analogous colors* can include the whole range of colors between two primaries or colors from three adjacent families, and fit within one-fourth of the color wheel. *Complementary colors* come in pairs, and are located opposite one another on the color wheel.

With a hue family, there are countless variations of colors. Looking at value, colors can be light or dark. *Tints* are lighter hues, made by adding white to a color. *Shades* are darker hues, made by adding black to a color. Looking at saturation, colors can be bright or dull. *Tones* have the same value as the original color, but they have been made duller or less saturated. (Later, you'll learn that there are several ways to dull a color.)

Finally, colors are described in terms of *temperature*. The colors on one-half of the color wheel are considered *warm,* with orange as the warmest. The range of warm colors goes from yellow-green to red-violet. The other half of the color wheel, going from red-violet to yellow-

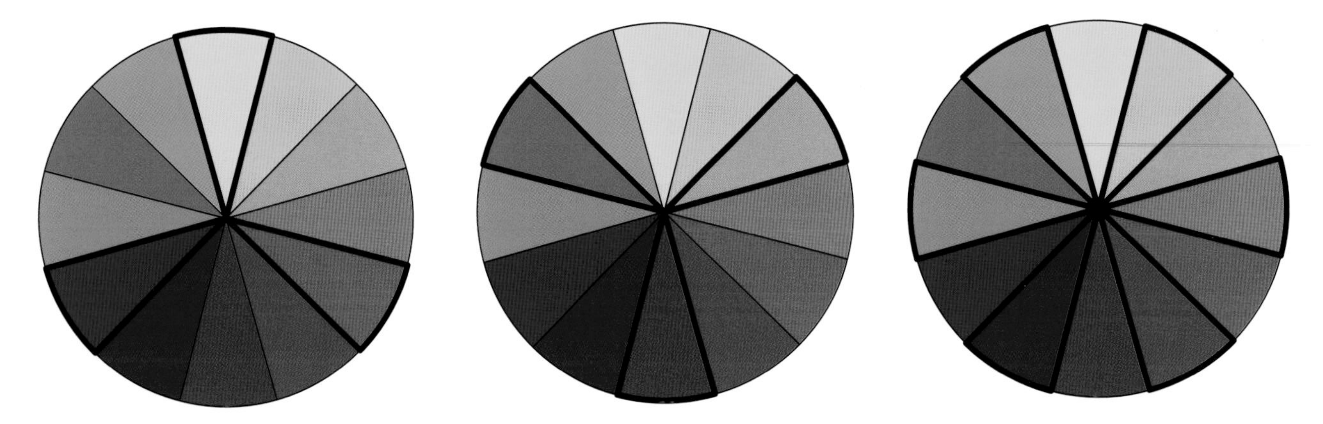

Primary, secondary, and tertiary colors. From left to right: primary colors highlighted; secondary colors highlighted; tertiary colors highlighted.

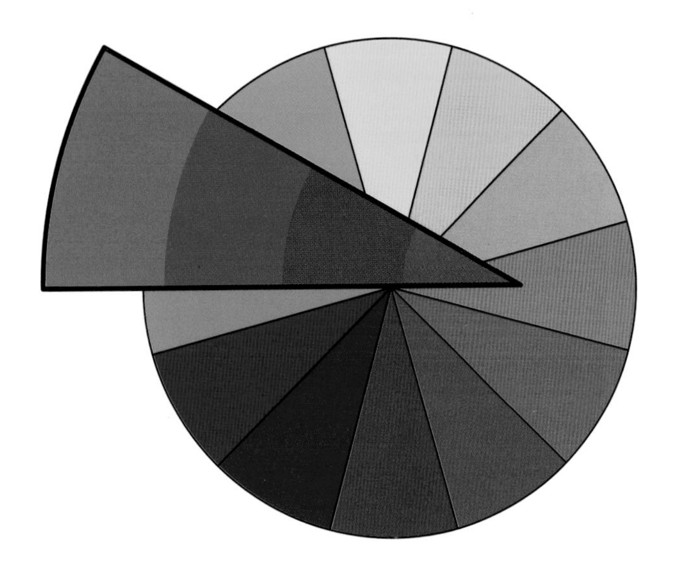

Monochromatic colors. These are any colors belonging to one hue family.

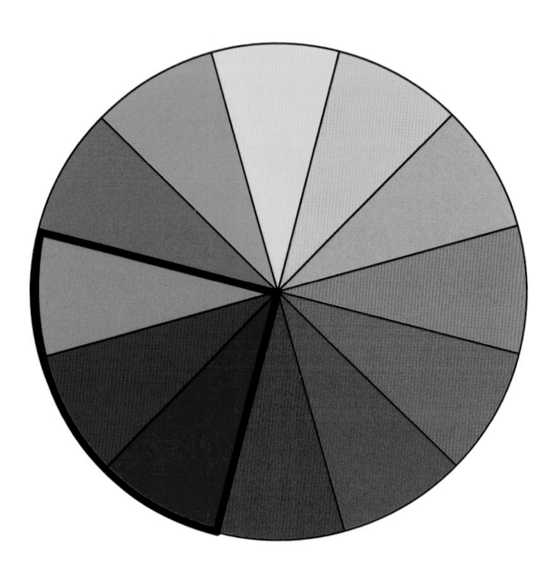

Analogous colors. These are colors that fall within the same quarter of the color wheel.

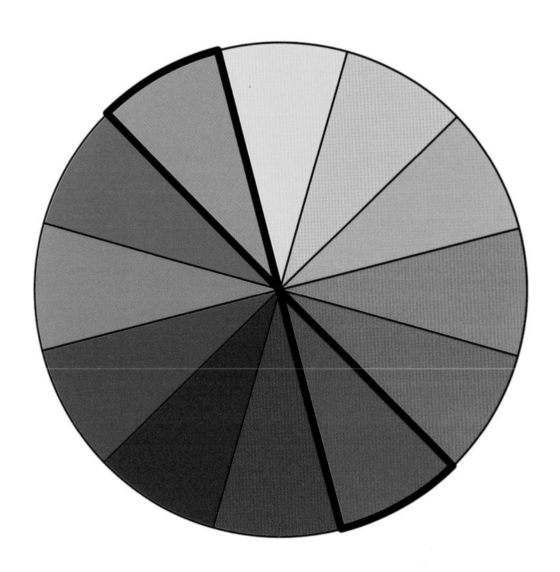

Complementary colors. These are pairs of colors located across from each other on the color wheel.

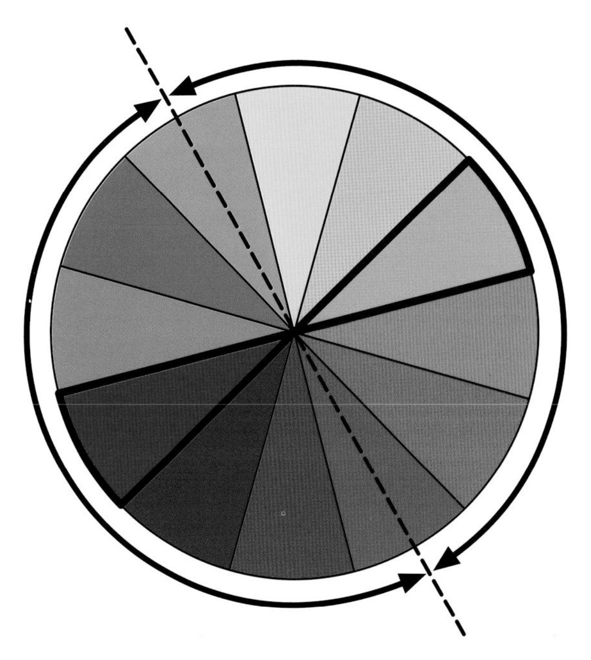

Warm and cool colors. Orange is in the middle of the warm half of the color wheel. Blue is in the middle of the cool half of the color wheel.

green, is the *cool* half of the color wheel. The coolest color is blue.

THE COLOR PRINCIPLES MOST USEFUL TO SPINNERS

Spinners work with different types of color principles, depending on the scale of their work, the distance from which the piece will be viewed, and the amount and type of color blending or color designing used for each instance. The two most common principles used by spinners are *color mixing* and *optical mixing*.

Color mixing

This is the intimate mixture of colors that happens when two or more colors of dyes are combined. Mixing makes completely new colors. The original colors may not be evident in the final mixture.

When dyeing, you need to understand how to choose colors to obtain desired and predictable results. I do not approach mixing dyes in strictly traditional ways. I try to understand the essence of colors and their relationships and mix dyes accordingly. My approach is intuitive and specific to the needs of each project.

In actual practice, dyes do not react the same as colors do in theory. Dyes have impurities that make them somewhat eccentric. I'll cover the specific quirks of each dye and variables to consider when you're choosing and combining dyes in Chapter 2; here I'll introduce the basic concepts.

Choosing primary colors of dyes

When creating your own color palette, there are several possible primaries to start with. The obvious choice would be the standard red, yellow, and blue. That would be perfect if all the primaries were pure. But no primary dye color is 100% pure. All dye colors have *undertones,* or subtle, underlying tendencies of warmth or coolness. For example, a bright yellow with an undertone of orange is warmer than a bright yellow with an undertone of green. Reds can have a cool blue undertone or a warm orange undertone. Blue, the coolest color, can have undertones of yellow or red. It's hard to say which is warmer or cooler, but I usually label the undertones going toward green or yellow as warmer blues and undertones going toward violet or red as cooler blues.

Paying attention to undertones is a very important aspect of mixing colors, so instead of using three primaries, I use six primaries: a warm and a cool yellow, a warm and a cool red, and a warm and a cool blue. To mix the brightest and most intense colors, I choose the primaries with undertones going toward the desired color. For example, to mix the brightest green, I use a blue with a green undertone and a yellow that is going toward green as well. (If you wanted to make duller greens, you could use the other combinations of blues and yellows.)

Another possibility is using the printer's primaries: magenta, yellow, and cyan. Two-color mixtures from these primaries are brighter than those from the red, yellow, and blue triad. The printer's triad can be combined with the red, yellow, and blue triad. Again, this gives six primaries to choose from, instead of the traditional three.

Starting with different primaries results in different sets of mixed colors. Which primaries to choose depends on what colors and qualities you want for any specific project. That is one advantage of dyeing your own colors.

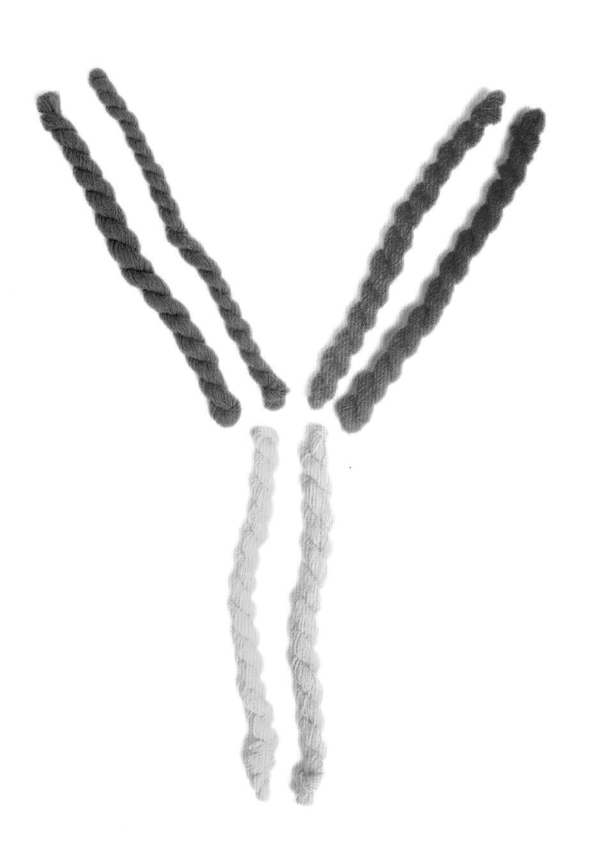

Six primary colors. From top left: warm blue, cool blue, cool red, warm red, warm yellow, cool yellow.

Choosing which primaries to mix. Clockwise from top right: warm yellow; cool yellow; warm blue; cool blue; warm yellow and cool blue mixed; warm yellow and warm blue mixed; cool yellow and cool blue mixed; and at center is the brightest mix—cool yellow and warm blue.

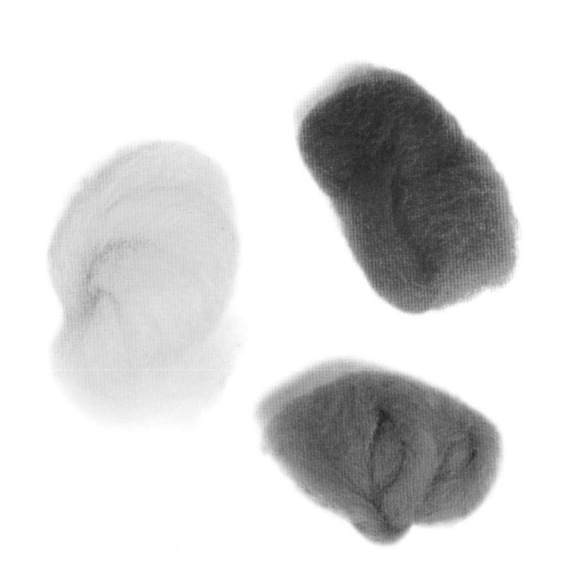

Printer's primary colors. Yellow, magenta, and cyan.

Hue gradations around the color wheel

Many colors fall between the primary colors on the color wheel. To mix one of these intermediate hues, locate it on the color wheel; the two primaries it falls between are the ones to use in the mix. The proportions will depend on the color. Which primary is closest? Use more of that one, and less of the other. It takes some practice to get proportions right, but the more you work with dyes, the easier this becomes.

Value progressions for each hue

Value progressions are changes in the relative lightness or darkness of a color. Painters add either white or black to the color to lighten or darken it. In dyeing, value progressions are usually created by varying the amount of dye being used for whatever weight of fiber is being dyed.

Using less dye makes *tints,* colors that are lighter in value. An undertone of a color is easier to see in a tint than in a shade. The subtle characteristics of a color show more clearly in a tint.

Adding black to a color produces a *shade,* which is darker in value than the original color. Warm and cool colors differ widely in how they react when mixed with black or gray. Warm colors tend to change hue personalities more significantly than cool colors. For example, adding black to yellow produces a range of olive- to khaki-greens that do not look like yellow. Adding black to orange makes a range of browns that could be mistaken for a mix of all three primaries. On the other hand, adding black to blue just makes a darker and duller blue. Again, practice will help you anticipate and understand how colors change when you mix them.

Intensity or saturation progressions

Changing a color's intensity can be accomplished in several ways. In painting, you can

Hue gradations using dye. Dye formulas are the same on both sides. From top to bottom: 100%, 80/20, 60/40, 40/60, 20/80, 100%. The skeins at left are yellow and scarlet; those on the right are gold and magenta 338.

Mixing black with colors. Dye formulas used in all three sets are the same proportions. From bottom to top in each: 100% hue, 85% hue/15% black, 70/30, 55/45, 40/60, 25/75, and 10/90.

Yellow changes to khaki with the addition of black to the dye formulas.

Orange changes to brown with the addition of black to the dye formulas.

Blue gets duller with the addition of black to the dye formulas, but the hue doesn't change.

add black, gray, white, or the color's complement. In dyeing, the same is true, except instead of adding white, you use less dye.

Adding more or less of a color's *complement* (the hue on the opposite side of the color wheel) yields a range of browns and grays that show the dominance of one color or the other. There will be one mixture, though, that will be a true neutral gray. Colors made by mixing complements are much less bright than either of the original colors, but they are more interesting than colors produced by adding black to reduce the saturation of the color.

How can colors mix to form a neutral gray? A neutral gray mixture appears when all three primary colors are present in the mixture in the right proportions. Look at the pairs of complementary colors on the color wheel. Each pair includes all three of the primary colors. Violet is a mixture of blue and red, and yellow is its complement. Voila—blue, red, and yellow. Blue is a primary and orange is a mixture of red and yellow. Again, all three primaries are present. This is true for all complementary pairs.

Let's take this a step further. If you have an orange that has been mixed from red and yellow and you want to tone it down, what do you add? Add a touch of blue to the mixture. What if you've mixed a red-violet that is too bright? Yellow-green is red-violet's complement. Chances are you do not have yellow-green all mixed up, so either mix some up or think a little more. Blue is already in the red-violet mixture and yellow-green is made up of yellow with a little blue, right? So, just add a

Mixing complementary colors. Dye formulas from right to left: 100% green, 85/15, 70/30, 60/40, 30/70, 15/85, 100% red. The skein in the middle, 60% green and 40% red, is a neutral color.

little yellow and a little more blue to the red-violet mixture and you have a quieter version of the original color.

How and why to use more than two colors in a mixture

The subtleties of a palette come from using small amounts of several colors to achieve a pleasing result. For example, you might use more than one hue of the primary colors. To mix a rich but subtle green might take three or four colors—a warm and a cool yellow (the cool yellow to make the color clearer and the warmer yellow to tone it down a touch), and a turquoise (warm) blue and a royal (cool) blue (the turquoise to make the mixture clearer and the royal blue to give the color depth).

Now, take that idea a step further. To make a deep, forest green, you could use the same four colors, but use less of the cool yellow and warm blue than last time. Use more of the warm yellow and cool blue to accentuate the dullness of the final green. To further tone down the overall color, add a small amount of the complement of green, which is red. If that color is still not dark enough, add a touch of black to deepen and dull down the overall effect. See the logic?

Instead of mixing colors in terms of complements, another means to the same end would be to work with a *triad* of colors, such as a red, a yellow, and a blue. An almost limitless number of colors can be mixed using these three colors in various proportions. Colors mixed using all three primaries appear more complex,

Using a triad of colors in dye formulas. The tufts of fibers show the pure primary colors used. The skein in the center uses equal amounts of all three colors. The other skeins surrounding are in various proportions of all three colors.

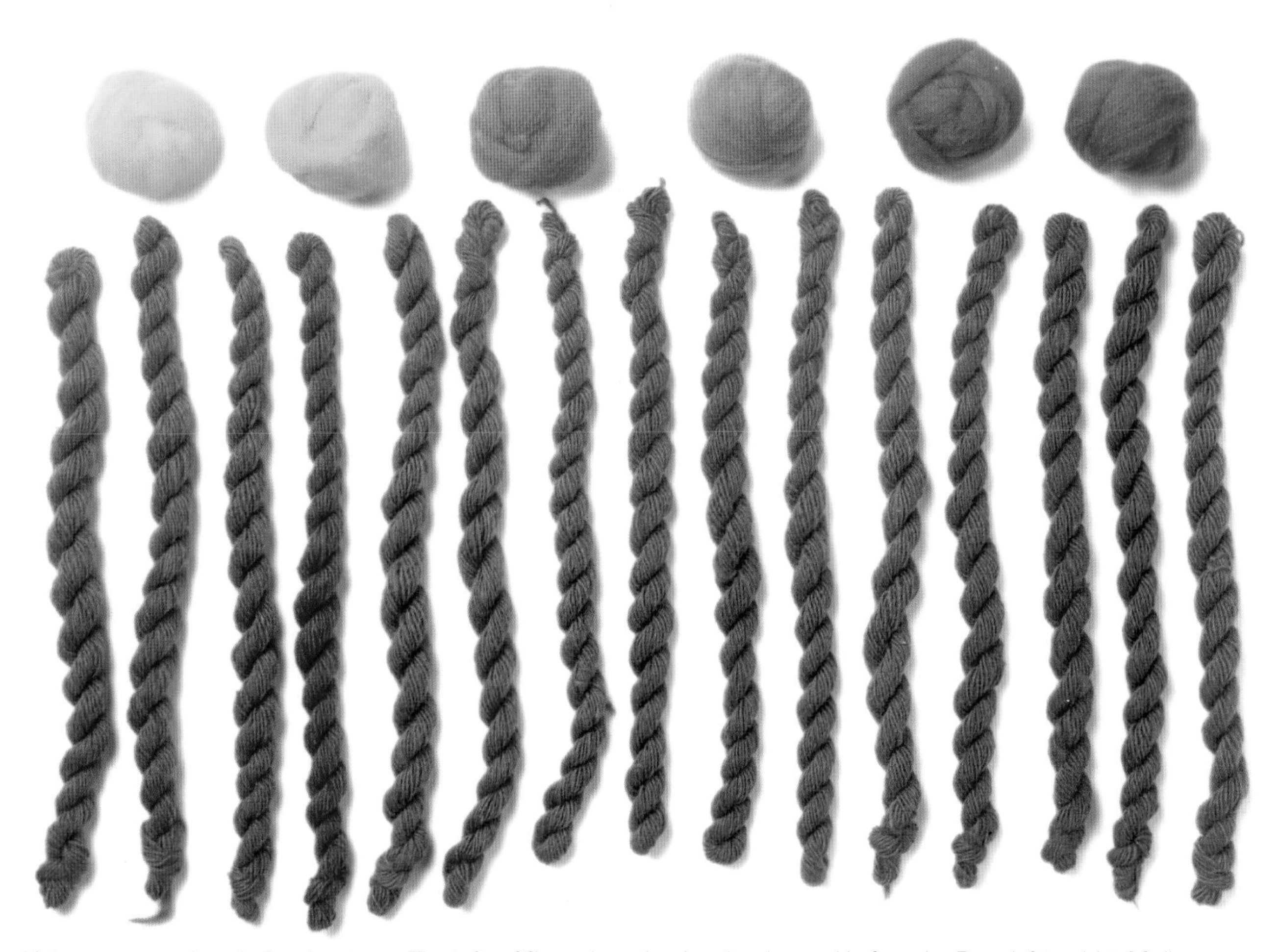

Using a warm and cool of each primary. The tufts of fibers show the six primaries used in formulas. From left to right: (Y)ellow (cool), (G)old (warm), (M)agenta 338 (cool), (S)carlet(warm), (B)lue (cool), and (T)urquoise (warm). Formulas from left to right: 60Y/30M/10T; 60G/30M/10T; 10G/60S/30B; 10G/60M/30B, 30Y/10S/60B; 30Y/10S/60T; equal amounts of all six. The last eight are all 33% of each of three primaries, but primaries change: Y/M/T; G/M/T; Y/S/T; Y/S/B; Y/M/B; G/M/B; G/S/T; G/S/B.

are less bright, and more closely imitate vegetal-dyed colors than two-color mixes.

Optical mixing

When you place small quantities of two or more distinct colors side by side, it looks from a distance like a single new color. If you look closely, you see that the original colors remain separate, but when you stand back the colors seem to mix. The impression of a new color is created from the interaction of the dots of color, and this new color varies depending on the size of those dots.

Understanding the principle of optical mixing is essential when you design multicolored handspun yarns. The main variables to consider when making color choices for multicolored yarns are the same as those made when describing a color: hue, value, and saturation. Another consideration of optical mixing involves the *size of the dots* of colors in the final yarn. How do you control that? Easy. When you blend two or more colors of dyed fibers, the more times the fibers are carded or combed together, the smaller the dots of color appear in the final yarn. To keep the dots larger, card or comb the fibers fewer times. For larger dots of colors in multicolored carded or combed yarns, use fewer colors and thicker areas of each color. For larger dots in painted-roving yarns, keep the painted stripes longer and use fewer rovings in a yarn. All these topics will be covered in depth in Chapters 3 through 7.

Optical mixing.

A multicolored sweater that employs optical mixing. From a distance, the background color almost looks solid. The yarns were created using painted rovings.

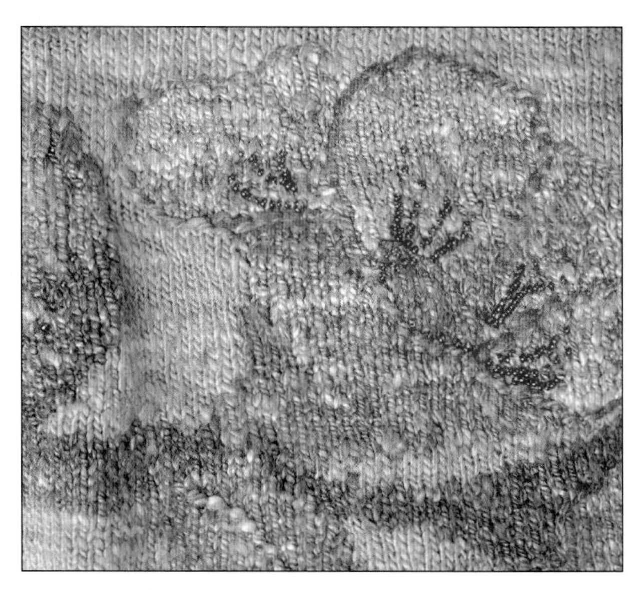

A close-up of the sweater shows more of the dots of colors in the yarns.

The same six colors were used in both swatches. The sample on the right was carded more, so the dots of colors are smaller and the yarn looks duller. The sample on the left was not carded as much, so the dots of colors are larger and the yarn appears brighter.

Optical mixing. The same eight colors and preparation were used for both samples. The sample on the left was spun thicker and the colors appear bolder. The sample on the right was spun thinner and the colors appear more subtle.

The *distance from which the yarn will normally be viewed* is another important variable in optical mixing. If the yarn will be closely examined, the dots can be small and still be distinct. If the yarn or final piece will be viewed from farther away, the colored dots must be larger to successfully create the desired color mix. (At some distance, the colors will no longer read as an optical mix, no matter what the size or color of the dots. At that point, the values of the colors are more readily perceived than the hues themselves.)

In a multicolored yarn, the *thickness of the finished yarn* determines the size of the largest dot. The dot cannot be larger than the yarn itself. The thinner the yarn, the smaller the dots of color, and the closer you need to look to fully appreciate their optical mixing.

USING THE PRINCIPLES OF CONTRAST TO CHOOSE COLORS

You can either work with a single color in isolation or with a group of colors in a design. Placing one color beside another creates an interaction between the colors that affects how each is perceived. Putting several colors together creates interesting contrasts and interactions. Historically, colorists have observed and described specific ways that colors relate or contrast with one another when used together. Theorists such as Goethe, Bezold, Chevreul, and Itten have identified seven contrasts that are unique enough in artistic value and in visual effect to be analyzed individually and understood.

Each contrast can be easily interpreted in fiber work. Individual contrasts are most effective if only one variable exists at a time. In other words, keep the other characteristics of the colors consistent, except for the contrast being studied. The contrasts can be used for choosing palettes of colors for yarns or for the design of finished pieces. They can be considered and interpreted however you see fit. Don't feel you have to adhere to them rigidly, but use them as a reference to spring from. Working with color is fun when you understand its interactions well enough to play with them without too many surprises or frustrations.

Contrast of hue. Clockwise from top left: skein and swatch using maximum hue contrast of red/yellow/blue; blue/yellow/violet; and red/yellow/blue with black and white.

Contrast of hue

This is the use of at least three distinctly different hues in a single design. "Distinctly different" means that the colors have minimal hues in common. The most extreme use of contrast of hue comes from using the three primary colors—red, yellow, and blue. None of those colors has hues in common. Using strong contrast of hue results in yarns that appear "wild". But remember that a dull yarn results from thoroughly blending all three primary colors. Too much carding or combing can transform bright colors into browns or grays.

Another example of contrast of hue would be a combination of yellow, blue, and violet. There is not as much contrast between blue and violet because both have the hue blue in their make up.

Using contrast of hue works best when all the colors have the same saturation or intensity. Black and white can be included to dramatize the overall effect. This is often seen in folk art.

Contrast of value

This is the range of light to dark values of all the colors in a single design, as compared to the neutral gray value scale. It is one of the most important contrasts to consider in designing because, from a distance, it is the contrast of values, not hues, that you see first. It is also value contrast that provides a "feeling" to a yarn or a finished piece.

You can create a value scale for any hue family. Begin by finding the gray value of the fully saturated hue. From there, lighten the hue by using less dye to obtain the tints. To complete the scale, add black to obtain the shades of the hue.

Different fully saturated hues fall in different places on the gray scale. A fully saturated orange has a different value than a fully saturated blue. The value of saturated warm colors on the color wheel fit on the lighter (higher) end of the gray scale. Saturated cool colors are darker and fall on the lower end of the value scale. That is why some ranges of values of colors are easier to find and work with than others. When a fully saturated color is dark, it is hard to find colors in the same hue family that are darker. The reverse is also true. It is hard to find colors lighter than a saturated color that falls high on the value scale.

Paying attention to value is very important. You must consider it when devising dye formulas or choosing colors to blend by carding or combing. The range of values chosen for a single multicolored yarn will greatly affect the yarn's final impression, as will the range of values of yarns combined in a project. The untrained eye can perceive from five to ten shades of gray between white and black. The more you study value and train your eyes to see subtle differences, the more values you will know and the more effectively you can use color.

Viewing colors and their relative values can produce the same sort of emotional response as listening to music. *Value keys* are specific value relationships among colors that can produce predictable emotional responses. There are seven value keys, and they fall into two categories, called major and minor in reference to musical terms.

Major keys

Major keys include the whole range of values from white or almost white to black or almost black. As in music, major keys are strong, positive, well balanced, and assertive. Yarns using the major key as the design element appear multicolored, wild, and active, because such a wide range of values is combined.

The difference among the three major keys is the dominant value: light, mid-range, or dark. The effects vary depending which value is dominant. When very light and very dark values are placed side by side, the light values make the dark ones look darker and the dark values make the light ones look even lighter. This makes a striped or barber-pole effect in the yarn, and a speckled or salt-and-pepper effect when you knit with the yarn.

Contrast of value. A range of colors that are all at the same saturation. Notice the difference in the relative value of these colors.

High major. Light values are dominant in the high major key. Other values are represented, but in smaller amounts than the light values. The impression this key gives is lightness. In a yarn, light colors would dominate with accents of medium and dark values. Some barber-pole or salt-and-pepper effects occur because of the wide value differences.

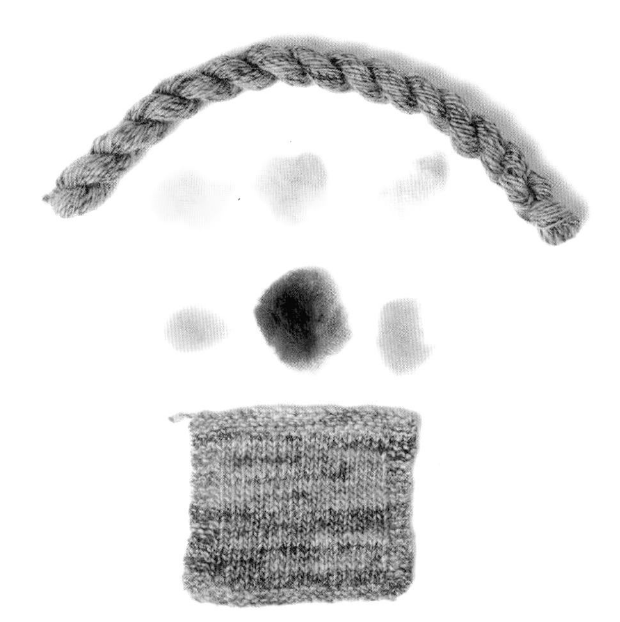

High major key.

Middle major. Middle values dominate in this key. Again, the whole range of values is represented, but the middle values are in the majority. Designs using this key appear stable and well balanced. A yarn using this key would have a medium-value color such as red as dominant, with accents including a very light color and a very dark color. Of the three major keys, this one has the least obvious contrasts because the dominant middle values bridge the light and dark accents.

Middle major key.

Low major. Dark values are dominant here, with medium and light accents. This key gives the impression of being dramatic, theatrical, or very somber. A yarn in this key could begin with a very dark shade of blue, with greens for medium-value accents and yellows for light-value accents. The light-value accents will stick out and look like specks or the "salt" in the "salt and pepper".

Low major key.

Minor Keys

Minor keys have a much narrower value range, and include smaller areas of the gray scale. Because they have less value contrast, the minor keys are much more subdued and subtle than the major keys. Quieter yarns are designed using minor keys. Such yarns are actually multicolored, but can be used as solids in knitting or weaving designs. The results look much richer than what you get with solid-color yarns. There are four minor keys.

High minor. Only values in the lightest third of the value scale are used—this means pastels or tints of colors. Medium or dark values are not included. This key gives the impression of peacefulness and can appear very subtle and delicate.

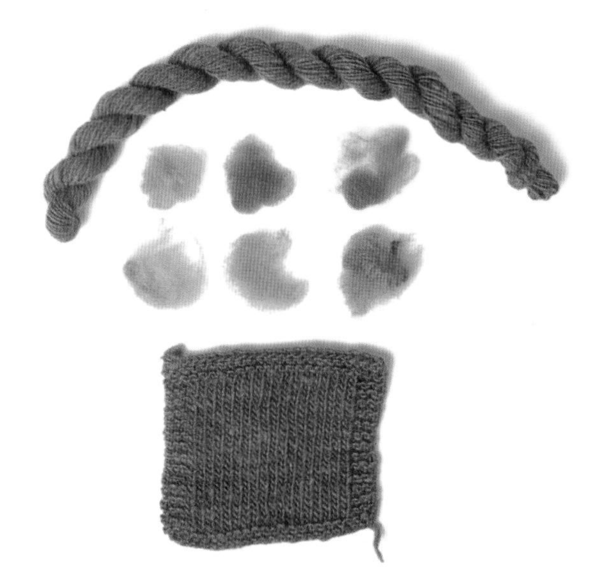

Middle minor key.

High minor key.

Middle minor. Only values in the middle third of the value scale are used. No really light or really dark values are included. This key can have a dreamlike quality and be strong, but serene. There are many possibilities for designs in this key. The yarn will appear very quiet if dull or desaturated colors are used. It will be lively if you use saturated colors that are close in value.

Low minor. Values from only the lower third of the value scale are used with no medium or light accents. This key produces designs that are very quiet, gloomy, and almost sinister, effects that can be high-

Low minor key.

lighted by the hues chosen. An example would be very dark, neutral browns and grays with accents of dark shades of purple and blue and red.

Extended middle minor. This key is an extension of the middle minor key. Instead of just the middle third of the scale, the range of values is slightly wider, falling between middle major and middle minor. This key gives an impression that is a little harder to pin down; it can be somewhat surrealistic. Many effects are possible here, depending on the hues and saturations chosen.

Extended middle minor key.

Warm/cool contrast

As mentioned before, the color wheel can be divided into halves: warm and cool. Any warm color includes yellow or red in its makeup, ranging from yellow-green through red-violet on the color wheel. Any cool color includes blue, ranging from red-violet to yellow-green.

Warm and cool colors react differently when combined in a design. The warm colors appear to pop out and come forward and the cool colors seem to recede and stay in the background. This is because saturated warm colors have higher values than saturated cool colors. To achieve a harmonious composition, it takes a larger proportion of cool colors to balance the warm ones.

The relative warmth or coolness of a color is affected by the colors that are placed next to it. A color will appear warmer when placed next to colors that are cooler than it is. The same color will appear cooler if placed next to colors that are warmer than it is. By carefully choosing each color for a yarn, you can control the color of the final yarn. Think about temperature when you want to add an accent color that will make the other colors in a yarn stand out or fade into the background. For example, if you've chosen an analogous range of red-violets to blue-violets and the combination seems too quiet, what will liven it up? The main colors are on the cool half of the color wheel, so add a warm color—any color from yellow-green to red—for contrast. The further the accent color is from the main range of colors, the more contrast there will be in the finished yarn.

Remember that all colors have undertones, or subtle underlying tendencies to warmth or coolness. Colors are more compatible when their undertones match. For instance, imagine choosing an analogous color palette that goes from yellow to red-orange on the color wheel. Since the range is warm and incorporates the warmest color, orange, the colors used will work more smoothly together if all their undertones are warm. The choices can be as follows: a yellow with a red undertone, a yellow-orange with a red undertone, an orange with a yellow undertone, and a red-orange with a yellow undertone.

Complementary contrast

This technique employs opposite colors on the color wheel in a single design, including any of the tints, tones, and shades of each hue as well as any mixture of the two hues. Complementary colors are fascinating to work with because they react differently under different circumstances. When complementary colors are thoroughly mixed as dyes, they create a range of dull, subtle browns and grays. When

Warm/cool contrast. Top skein: yellow yarn with lavender (a cool color) as an accent. Bottom skein: violet yarn with orange (a warm color) as an accent. Tufts of fiber are colors used in adjacent yarn.

Warm/cool contrast and undertones. The skeins that form the inner circle have cool undertones. The skeins that form the outer circle have warm undertones.

yarn is thoroughly blended at the combing or carding stage, a similar range of dull colors results, but the original colors are still present when viewed at close range (see optical mixing on pages 25–27).

A different interaction takes place when complementary colors appear side by side in a yarn or design. Then the colors intensify each other. The most intense interaction takes place when both colors are of equal saturation. This is a very good way to liven up yarns that would otherwise be dull. It does not take much of the complement to add spark to a yarn.

Each pair of complements has its own idiosyncrasies. Yellow and violet have an extreme value difference. Orange and blue have the biggest difference in temperature. Orange is the warmest color and blue is the coolest color. When equal amounts of saturated orange and blue are placed side by side, the orange tends to dominate. Red and green have evenly matched values if each color is at its highest saturation. For that reason, this is the easiest pair of complements to work with.

Simultaneous contrast

This technique makes use of a color's ability to shift perception of a second color toward the first color's complement. What does that mean in English? When looking at a large area of color, your eyes project that color's complement

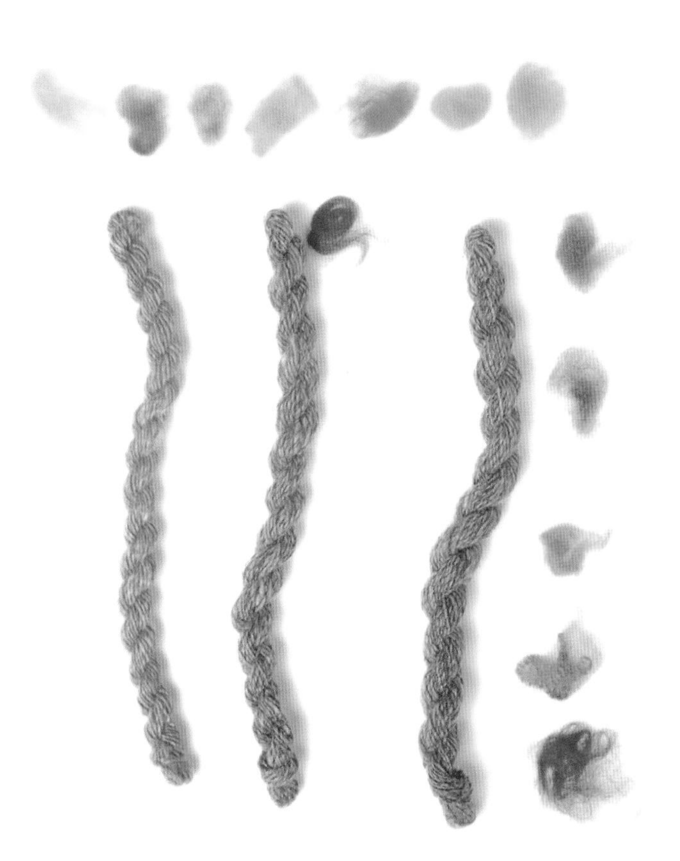

Complementary contrast. The green skein at left includes all seven greens, the middle skein adds only one red to accent the greens, the skein at right adds more red so it appears to be half red and half green.

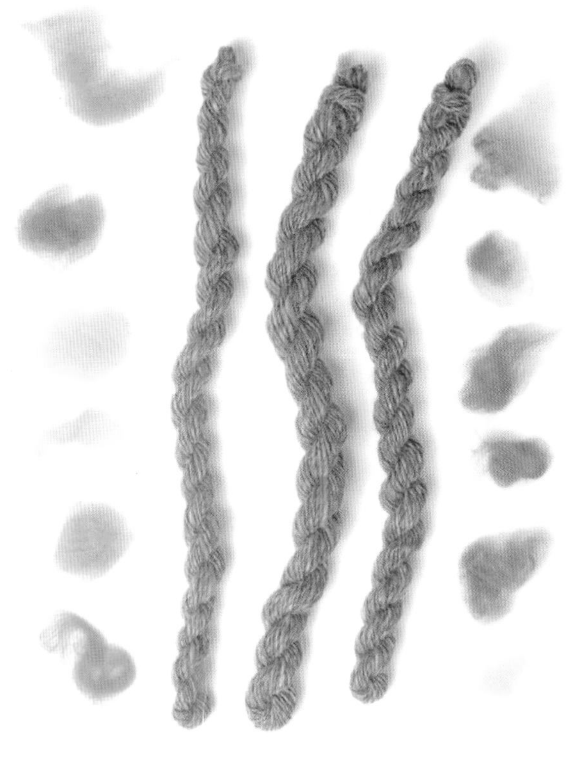

Complementary contrast. All three skeins use orange and blue. The skein at left is predominantly orange with blue accents, the center skein is half of each color family, and the skein at right is predominantly blue with orange accents.

onto the other colors beside the one you are looking at. For example, if you are looking at a large area of green with small spots of violet throughout, your eyes will automatically project red, the complement of green, onto the violet spots, making them appear slightly redder than they really are. This phenomenon can be used in designing to enhance the colors chosen.

Several variables can exaggerate simultaneous contrast. Saturation is an important consideration. The strongest contrast will occur when the saturation or intensity is the same or similar for both colors.

Using similar values of both colors will also optimize simultaneous contrast. If values are too different, the value contrast will become the dominant contrast and the simultaneous one will be unimportant. Simultaneous contrast is most effective if the colors chosen to interact are *not* complements. Complementary colors do not "shift" each other's hues, but intensify them. (Simultaneous contrast is why complementary colors intensify each other when placed side by side. Each color is projecting its complement onto the color beside it, reinforcing and intensifying the contrast.)

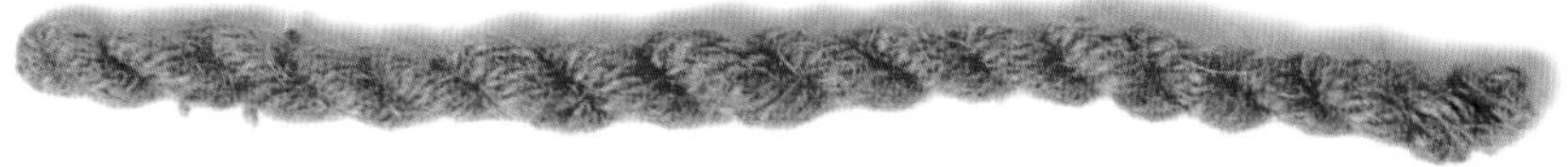

Simultaneous contrast. The violet dots are the same color as the violet skein below. The dots on the swatch appear a little redder than the skein.

Simultaneous contrast. The same violet is added to both the blue-green yarn and the red-orange. The violet looks warmer in the blue-green swatch and cooler in the red-orange swatch.

In simultaneous contrast, the proportion of each color affects the result. For optimum contrast, surround the color you want to change with a larger amount of the second color. In a yarn, think of the predominant color as the stable color and the accent color as the one you try to "change".

Contrast of saturation

This is the use of several saturations or intensities of color in a single design. As mentioned earlier, there are several ways you can change the saturation of a color. Using less dye creates lighter colors or tints. Adding black creates darker colors or shades. Adding a color's complement makes colors that are duller or less saturated than the original color, but which look interesting, rich, and complex. Another way to desaturate a color is to tone it down by adding a gray of the same value.

Defining a color as either saturated or dull is a matter of comparison. Any color looks brighter when placed next to a color that is duller, or duller when compared to a color that is more intense. At the same time, the bright color makes the dull color look even duller, and the dull color makes the bright color look even brighter. It is all relative, so do not judge your color selection for a yarn until you have placed all the colors side by side to see how they "get along".

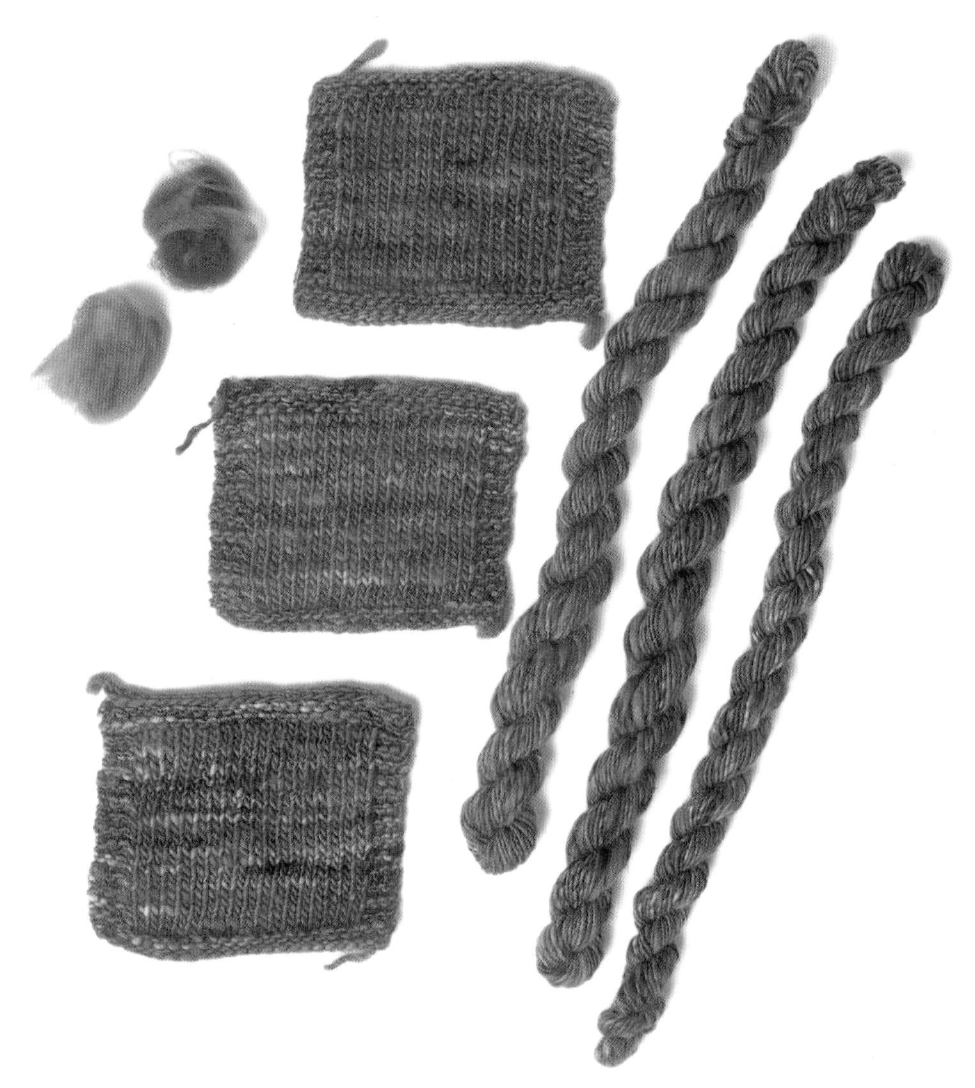

Contrast of saturation. Two sets of fibers (bright/warm and dull/cool) were spun together in different proportions. In the top sample and skein the bright is dominant with a little dull, the middle sample and skein have equal amounts of bright and dull, and the bottom sample and skein are predominantly dull with bright accents.

Contrast of proportions

This refers to the amount of each color used in a design in relation to the other colors in that design. Colors differ in their ability to catch and hold your attention. Because of these differences, colors must be used in different proportions to achieve balance. The main features of a color that determine its dominance are value, temperature, and saturation. Warm colors with light values easily stand out in a yarn. These colors can be used in small quantities and still appear to be in balance. Cool colors with darker values can be used in larger amounts and still appear balanced. This effect is most obvious when all the colors in a design are at full saturation.

The color theorist Goethe assigned a number to each hue family to determine what proportions of colors would give a balanced result. The numbers he assigned to each color are:

yellow :	orange :	red :	violet :	blue :	green
3 :	4 :	6 :	9 :	8 :	6

You can use these numbers in ratios to decide the amounts (measured by weight) of each color to combine in a design. For example, for a two-color yarn using orange and violet, the ratio of orange to violet would be 4:9. Less orange is used than violet, because it takes less of a warm color and more of a cool color to appear balanced in a finished piece. Using these numbers enables you to estimate how much of each color to combine for a pleasing result. It's not a hard and fast system, but it does give you proportions to start with.

Did you ever wonder why yellow "takes over" a yarn so quickly? Look at yellow's number—3, the lowest number for any hue. A saturated yellow has the highest value of all the hues. On top of that, yellow is a warm color. That means it takes less yellow for a yarn to seem balanced. To combine yellow and green for example, there should be twice as much green in the yarn as yellow because green's number is 6.

Goethe's numbers can also be used for combining more than two colors. For example, to make a yarn that includes yellow, orange, red, and blue (with saturations being equal), you would use three parts of yellow, four parts of orange, six parts of red, and eight parts of blue.

The principle of proportion applies to complementary colors, too. Here are proportions for mixing some of the complementary pairs: Use three parts violet to one part yellow, one part orange to two parts blue, or equal parts of red and green. The differences in proportions are due mainly to the value differences of the fully-saturated hues.

Contrast of proportions. The skein on the left uses equal amounts of yellow and green, and yellow dominates. To make the colors seem balanced, the proportion should be 3:6, the proportion employed in the skein on the right.

Contrast of proportions. This skein uses yellow, orange, red, and blue. To make the colors look balanced, the proportions are 3:4:6:8. In grams that figures to 2.1 yellow, 2.9 orange, 4.3 red, and 5.7 blue for a 15-gram skein.

COLOR HARMONIES

To put colors together, you can follow guidelines or recipes for some of the common color relationships, called color harmonies. Again, the reference to musical terms means color harmonies can produce emotional responses. Color harmonies act in fiber as chords act in music.

Each harmony is based on a balanced combination of two or more hue families. You can use any number of colors from each hue family, and one or another family can dominate the harmony—they don't have to be used in equal proportions.

Complementary. This harmony uses two hue families which are complements, located opposite each other on the color wheel. This relationship was covered earlier in this chapter.

Split complementary. This harmony uses three hue families. Chose a color on the color wheel, then choose the hue families on both sides of its complement. When these colors are placed side by side, they react like complementary colors, but not as strongly. I use this harmony frequently in yarn design. Having a third color family to work with allows many more color interactions in the yarn.

Double split complementary. There are five hue families in this harmony. Choose a hue family, then choose two hue families on both sides of its complement. This harmony can work even better than the split complement for multicolored yarns because there are two additional hue families to work with. Very subtle and complex effects can be achieved and the

Complementary harmony.

Split complementary harmony.

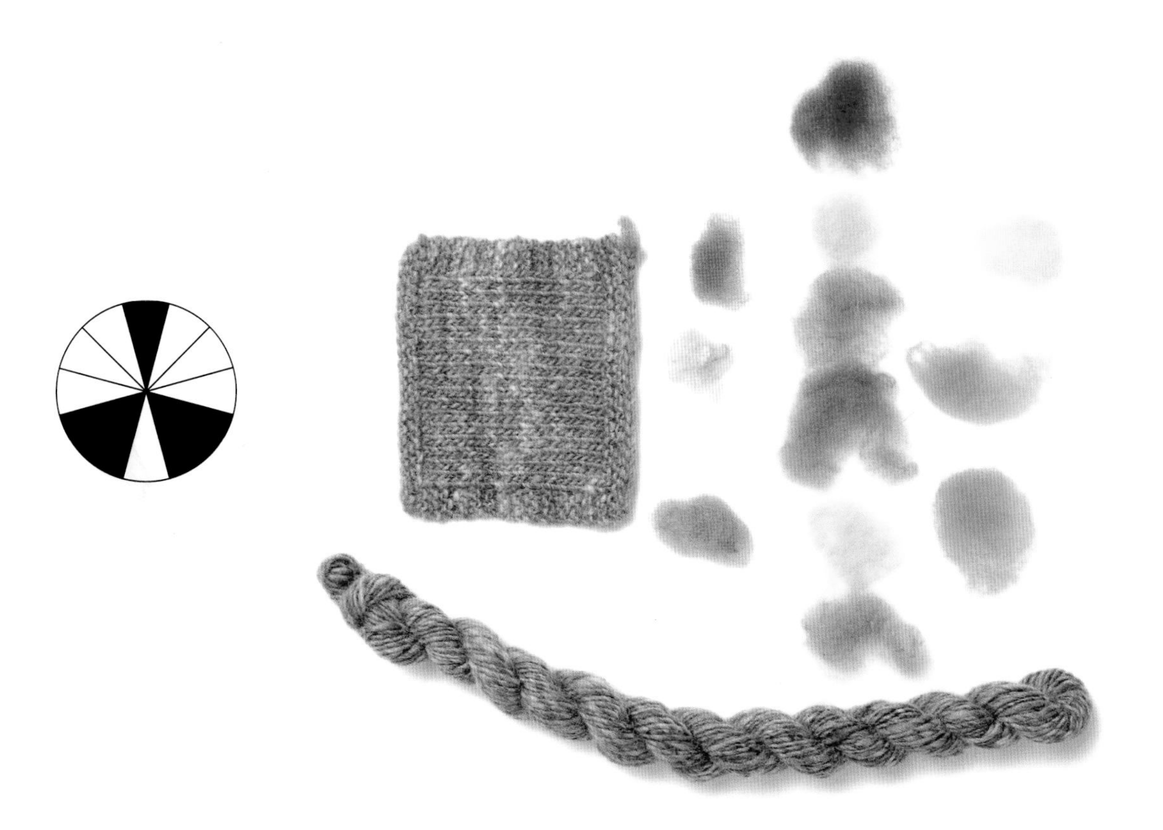

Double split complementary harmony.

"barber poling" that often occurs in simpler yarns is less likely with so many colors present.

Triad. This harmony includes three hue families, as its name implies. Three equidistant hue families, such as red, yellow, and blue, form a triad. On a twelve-hue color wheel, there are four possible triads. Multicolored yarns that range from very subtle to outrageously wild are possible, depending on the value and saturation choices made.

Double triad. There are six hue families in a double triad. Using a twelve-hue color wheel, you choose a triad of colors, then choose three more colors that are one step left or right of the first three. There are eight possible double triads. Very rich yarns are possible with this harmony, and the design options can go on and on when you vary the values, contrasts, and saturations.

Tetrad. A tetrad includes four hue families—two pairs of complements that form a rectangle on the twelve-hue color wheel. The

Triad harmony.

Double triad harmony.

Tetrad harmony.

relationship of complements is being used, but in a slightly different context. You are working with the complementary relationship and with the relationship *between* the pairs of complements, basically a warm/cool relationship. Yarns using this harmony are more complex than ones that employ only one relationship at a time.

Square quadratic or double complement. Again, there are four hue families, but here the two sets of complements are as far apart on the color wheel as possible, like opposite opposites. It's like superimposing a square onto the color wheel. This harmony almost guarantees a lively yarn because the contrasts are so large. Take advantage of that contrast and choose colors to maximize the effect.

Hexad. A hexad uses six hue families—three sets of complements equidistant on the color wheel. On the twelve-hue color wheel, that turns out to be every other hue. Every spinner at one time or another wants to create a rainbow yarn. This harmony is the one to use. The hues in the harmony are equally spaced all around the color wheel. Because adjacent colors are not used, the colors combined seem clear and distinct.

Square quadratic or double complementary harmony.

Hexad harmony.

OTHER SOURCES FOR COLOR INSPIRATION

The color wheel is not the only place to find color ideas. In fact, it's only one of many. Look around you—ideas are everywhere! Take the time to be more aware of your surroundings. Doing this enhances your life and makes a hectic schedule seem a little saner.

For example, nature is a constant source of color inspiration. You can get color ideas from beach shells, rocks, bird feathers, insects, landscapes, or leaves and flowers. Look for color inspiration at the nearest museum. Paintings offer a wealth of ideas. Examine a painter's color choices, record what pleases you, then try combining those colors into a skein of yarn. Photographs are a similar source for color inspiration. Another wonderful place to spend time with color is a fabric or upholstery store. Or visit bookstores—books of all kinds can trigger wonderful color ideas. Just keep your mind and eyes open to what you see around you. Color ideas can even come from such mundane sources as magazine ads. The search for inspiration means your time spent in waiting rooms or grocery lines will always be worthwhile.

Whenever you observe color combinations that you find attractive, record them for future reference. Keep a notebook that describes in words what you observed, or use colored pencils or paper to make swatches of the colors. Taking photographs is another way to keep track of ideas. I keep a notebook that combines all these things. It doesn't matter how you remember or keep track of your ideas, just do it! Translating them into actual yarns will be covered technique by technique in the following chapters.

Pottery used as color inspiration. At right the pot is shown with paper swatches of all the colors found in it. Twenty-eight colors of fiber were used to create five multicolored batts for the roving.

Fabric as inspiration. I isolated five shells from the fabric and used colored pencils to record the colors of each. I came up with twenty-nine colors to create five batts and spun yarn from each. For the long swatch I used one batt at a time with white and black. The swatch below the long one uses all five batts together with white and black, and the swatch on the left uses all five batts together without white or black.

SELF-STUDY EXERCISES

Doing these exercises will help you become more comfortable with using color and understanding color relationships. Depending on the exercise, you will use paints, papers, dyes, or fibers.

1. *Describing hue.* Use colored papers, dyed fibers, or dyed yarns. Pick out as many colors as possible that belong to a single hue family. Arrange them in an order that seems logical to you. *Purpose:* to become aware of different colors within the same color family, to learn to perceive subtle differences, and to arrange colors in some order.

2. *Describing value.* Use paints. Create an equal twelve-step value scale from white to black. Cut out one- by two-inch pieces and mount onto cardboard to use as a reference tool. *Purpose:* to make a value scale for use in deciding the relative values of colors. This will also teach you to be more aware of subtle value differences.

3a. *Describing saturation.* Use paints. Choose one color and mix six new colors by adding gray to the color in progressively larger amounts until you reach a neutral gray. *Purpose:* to see how a color is affected by the addition of gray.

3b. *Describing saturation.* Use fibers, yarns, or colored papers. Choose a bright color, then choose colors that are in the same hue family, but duller. *Purpose:* to train your eye to detect subtle differences in saturation.

4a. *Mixing secondary colors.* Use paints or dyes. Mix two primary colors in varying amounts to obtain a range of colors that fall between the primaries. *Purpose:* to see the relationship between the primary colors, and to see how colors fit together on the color wheel.

4b. *Mixing tertiary colors.* Use paints or dyes. Choose a secondary color and one of the primaries next to it. Mix them together in varying amounts to obtain a range of colors. *Purpose:* to see the relationship of colors as they proceed around the color wheel.

5. *Mixing tints.* Use paints or dyes. Choose a color, then mix a range of six to eight new colors by adding varying amounts of white to the paint or using progressively smaller amounts of dye. *Purpose:* to see what happens to a color with the addition of white, and to see how pale a color can be and still be perceptible.

6. *Mixing shades.* Use paints or dyes. Choose a color, then mix six to eight new colors by adding progressively larger amounts of black. *Purpose:* to see what happens to a color with the addition of black, and to see how dark a color can become and still be perceptible.

7. *Mixing tones.* Use paints or dyes. Choose a color, then mix six to eight new colors by adding progressively larger amounts of gray to the color. The gray must be approximately the same value as the original color. If using dyes, gray is obtained by adding small amounts of black. *Purpose:* to learn that the gray you use makes a difference, and to see that a color can be made duller without changing its value.

8a. *Mixing complements.* Use paints or dyes. Choose a pair of complementary colors and mix them in different proportions to produce a series of seven colors between them. *Purpose:* to see what colors result from mixing a pair of complements in various proportions.

8b. *Intensifying complementary colors.* Use colored papers or fibers. Choose a color, then find the color's complement in a matching intensity. *Purpose:* to train the mind's eye to see the complement that will make both colors "sing". That happens when the colors are complementary and of the same intensity.

9. *Warmth or coolness of a color.* Use papers, paints, or fibers. Choose a color. Mix or find six colors that are warmer than the color chosen. Next, mix or find six colors that are cooler than the color chosen. *Purpose:* to teach your eyes to recognize and compare the relative warmth or coolness of colors.
10. *Making a color wheel.* Use paints, papers, dyes, or fibers. Find or mix a twelve-hue color circle by starting with the primary colors, adding the secondary colors, then adding the tertiary colors. Repeat with the tints of all twelve colors, then repeat with the shades of all twelve colors. Arrange in a circle. *Purpose:* to design your own color wheel and fully understand the relationships between colors.
11. *Contrast of hue.* Use fibers. Choose or mix three or four hues with strong color contrasts. Combine them to create a multicolored yarn. *Purpose:* to learn how the contrast of hue can work in a yarn.

12a. *Contrast of value.* Use paints or dyes. Choose a color, then by using less dye, adding white paint, or by adding black, try to match the values on the value scale you made in Exercise 2. *Purpose:* to learn the real relative values of colors and how to create them.

12b. *Contrast of value.* Use papers or fibers. Choose a color. Choose another color of a value that will make the original color look darker. Next choose a color of a value that will make the original color look lighter. *Purpose:* to learn how to knowingly choose the value of the color that will do what you want in a yarn.

13. *Value keys.* Use papers or fibers. First work only with the black-to-white value scale—no colors—and create a yarn or design for each of the seven major and minor keys. Now repeat the exercise, using colors. *Purpose:* to understand how important the choice of values is and be able to consciously design with specific values in mind.
14. *Warm/cool contrast.* Use fibers. Choose four warm colors and four cool colors that are approximately the same value and saturation, and combine them in a multicolored yarn. *Purpose:* to learn what happens when warm and cool colors are put together in a yarn.
15. *Complementary contrast.* Use fibers. Choose a pair of complementary colors. Use the colors plus their tints, tones, shades, and mixtures to design a multicolored yarn. *Purpose:* to observe how complements and their mixtures work together in a single yarn.
16. *Simultaneous contrast.* Use paints, papers, or fibers. Choose a color, then find another color that will make the original color appear warmer when the two are placed side by side. Repeat, but this time find a color that will make the original color appear cooler. *Purpose:* to learn to see how colors affect one another.

17a. *Contrast of saturation.* Use fibers. Choose a color and combine it with any of its tints, shades, or tones in a single yarn. *Purpose:* to see how the colors interact when several saturations of a color are combined in a single yarn.

17b. *Contrast of saturation.* Use paints, papers, or fibers. Choose a color. Then find another color that will make the original color appear brighter. Next find a color that will make the original color appear duller. *Purpose:* to learn to see how colors can affect the brightness or dullness of the colors surrounding it.

18. *Contrast of proportion.* Use papers or fibers. Choose several colors. Combine them using Goethe's proportion numbers to make a collage or yarn that looks balanced. *Purpose:* to learn how to combine pleasing proportions of colors.

19. *Color harmonies.* Use paints, papers, or fibers. Study the color harmonies one at a time. Use each harmony to create a palette of colors for a yarn, keeping all the contrasts in mind while choosing the colors. *Purpose:* to learn to use the color wheel as a design source for color combinations in yarns.

20. *Using a picture as a design source.* Take a photograph or picture and look carefully at it. With paints or colored papers, make a palette of colors that matches the palette in the picture. Combine those colors for a single yarn. *Purpose:* to utilize a color idea source and to become more aware of what you see.

chapter 2 chapter chapter

Step-by-step immersion dyeing

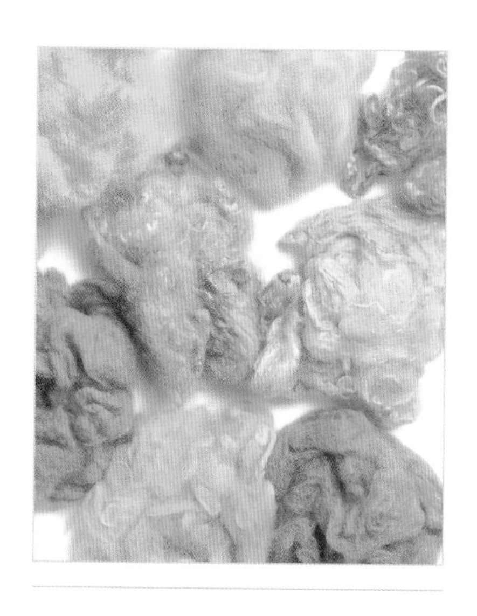

–2–

Step-by-step immersion dyeing

Like many people, you may have doubts or reservations about dyeing fibers. Relax. You don't need a chemistry degree to be successful. Fiber dyeing is not a complicated process. Anyone can master it when the procedure is broken down step-by-step and the purpose of each step is understood.

Some people hesitate to try dyeing because they're afraid that the colors may turn out streaky or blotchy. Although that can be a problem when you dye yarn or fabric, it isn't when you dye fiber. Spinners have a big advantage here. It's okay if the color is uneven on fiber because fiber is not an end product. It must still be carded or combed, then spun and possibly plied, and any unevenness will disappear during those steps.

Concerns about health and safety keep some people from dyeing. Don't worry. If you observe simple precautions, dyeing is a safe and creative way to obtain unique results with fibers. Finally, you may think that dyeing takes too much space or equipment. Actually, it isn't hard to set up a workspace suitable for dyeing, and little special equipment is needed.

There are several good reasons to take the time and energy to dye your own fibers. The first is to obtain specific colors and ranges of colors that are not commercially available. For the most part, it seems that only fashion-oriented colors of yarns and fibers are available to the fiber artist. If you want a full range of color-wheel colors, finding them from a single supplier will be difficult at best. But if you dye your own colors, you are limited only by the dyes and your imagination. Doing your own dyeing means you can create a personal palette. Using distinctive colors will further identify your work as uniquely yours.

Most spinners keep only a limited amount of fiber on hand. They can't afford to buy a mountain of commercially-dyed fiber and wouldn't have space to store it all anyway. By dyeing your own colors for each project, you need only keep and dye as much fiber as you need for a piece. Or, you can save time by dyeing a year's supply of fiber in a full range of colors. Then you can concentrate on color, designing within your palette, and not have to take time out to dye for each project. Also, it's easy to explore color combinations if you have a wide range of dyed fiber ready for experiments.

CHOOSING DYES FOR NATURAL FIBERS

There are two ways that fiber can be colored with dyes. One method, immersing fiber into a dyepot with dye, chemicals, and water, will be explained thoroughly in this chapter. Chapter 3 will explain the other method, which is painting dyes directly onto fiber. Either way you apply the dye, the procedures will make more sense if you understand how dyes work. I don't want to get too technical because I know you don't want to get bogged down with chemical jargon, but let's start with some basic information about dyes and fibers.

First, a dye is a substance that is used to permanently color a fiber. It is a specific material that has been chemically created for that purpose. Dye molecules have three parts that each do different jobs. One part is the "color" in the dye. That part of the molecule varies with each color of dye. Attached to the "color" part of the dye molecule is the part that bonds with a suitable kind of fiber (different dyes bond with different fibers). This part determines how intense the color will look on the dyed fiber. The third part of the dye molecule enables it to dissolve in water. Without this, dyeing could not take place.

Although each kind of dye has special requirements, the various dye processes have many basic features in common. With all dyes, how much dye to use depends on how much fiber you are dyeing and how deep or intense a color you want. Starting with a certain number of dye colors that you purchase, you can mix an infinite number of new colors. All dye processes require some kind of chemical assist (a compound such as salt or acetic acid). Water, dyes, and chemical assists are combined to make a dyebath, where the dyeing takes place either at room temperature or heated to simmering temperatures. After dyeing, you always have to rinse the fibers to remove any excess dye.

If you take the time and trouble to do your own dyeing, you want to be sure that the colors will last. *Fastness* refers to a dye's ability to keep color after it has been applied to the fiber. *Colorfastness* is a general term that means the dye remains the same color as when it was applied. *Washfastness* means the color stays the same after repeated washings. *Lightfastness* means the color remains the same despite exposure to direct light for long periods of time. Fastness varies among different dyes, colors, and fibers.

The main groups of natural fibers

Natural fibers are obtained from two main sources: plants and animals. The two types of fiber have very different chemical makeups and characteristics. Knowing the properties of each group helps you dye them successfully. (For more information about kinds of fiber, see pages 129–132 in Chapter 4.)

Cellulose fibers come from plants or plant byproducts. Examples include cotton, flax, ramie, hemp, and rayon. Although their molecular structures are complex, all cellulose fibers are chemically similar, so they all react similarly with dyes. Cellulose fibers are very tolerant of alkaline solutions and high temperatures; in fact, cotton yarns can be strengthened by boiling them in an alkali solution. By contrast, cellulose fibers deteriorate when exposed to strong acids.

Most *protein fibers* are hairs from an animal, such as wool from sheep, angora from rabbits, or mohair and cashmere from goats. (Silk, from silkworms, is an exception.) They are called protein fibers because their chemical makeup includes some or all of the twenty-six amino acids. Protein-fiber characteristics vary depending on the number and proportion of amino acids present. In general, strong alkalis destroy bonds in protein molecules and can weaken or actually dissolve protein fibers. Even mild alkali solutions can damage protein fibers. Heating the solution, even to temperatures as low as 120°F, intensifies the reaction and increases the damage. Even without the presence of alkalis, protein fibers can be weakened by prolonged exposure to high temperatures such as boiling in a dyepot. On the other hand, protein fibers are tolerant of acid solutions.

Although *silk* is a protein fiber, it differs from the others because it is secreted from the silkworm and the resulting fiber is a continuous filament. Also, silk shares some of the chemical properties of protein fibers but in other ways behaves more like cellulose fibers. It tolerates both acid and alkaline conditions and can be dyed with either group of dyes—those designed for protein fibers or the ones used for cellulose fibers. Excess heat should be avoided, however. Exposing silk to temperatures higher than 185°F reduces its luster. When dyed, silk is not as lightfast as other protein fibers.

Dye classes

Dyes are grouped into classes according to the way the dye molecule attaches to the fiber and the chemical assists needed to complete the process. Some classes of dyes work better than others on specific fibers. Knowing the characteristics of each dye class lets you choose the best one for a fiber. Note that each class of dyes includes a range of colors which you can mix to make many more colors. Not all colors within a class behave exactly the same, but with practice you soon learn to anticipate and compensate for their variations.

Fiber-reactive dyes

This class of dyes was designed to be used on cellulose fibers. In the dye process, the dye molecules form a chemical bond with the fiber. Because of this strong bond, fiber-reactive dyes tend to be very washfast. An alkaline environment (pH 10.5) is recommended for best results.

Various kinds of fiber-reactive dyes differ in the size of the dye molecule, the speed with which the dye bonds to the fiber, and the temperature at which the reaction takes place. With "cold" type reactive dyes such as Procion MX and Sabracron F, the dye reaction takes place at room temperature; heat is not required. Other fiber-reactive dyes do require heat.

Fiber-reactive dyes work in two phases or steps. In phase one, salt and dye are added to the dyebath, followed by the fiber. Then the dye molecules migrate to appropriate sites on the fiber to complete the phase. (In fast-acting fiber-reactive dyes, some dye may react with water in the dyebath before getting to the fiber.) Phase two begins when soda ash is added to the dyebath. Soda ash raises the dyebath pH to the point that permanent bonding takes place. After the soda ash solution is added, the dye stops moving onto the fiber, and whatever dye is already there becomes bonded. Any dye that has reacted with the water simply sits on the fiber's surface, without bonding to it. That excess dye must be thoroughly rinsed away.

Fiber-reactive dyes have bright color ranges and can be easily mixed. They are relatively inexpensive and easy to use. The hardest part is being patient enough to complete the rinsing process. Fast-acting fiber-reactive dyes cannot be left in a dyestock solution for any length of time because the dyes react with the water and make the dyestock solution useless. Slower acting fiber-reactive dyes can be left in a stock solution for a month or two without any ill effects.

Acid dyes

This class of dyes works best for protein fibers, with the optimum pH ranging from dye to dye. Several different kinds of acid dyes are available to home dyers. They differ in the size of the dye molecules, the ease of producing even or level (not streaky) results, and colorfastness. In every case, heat is a necessary part of the dye process. Acid-dye colors will not be fast unless heat has been applied.

Leveling acid dyes, usually known simply as "acid dyes", are one type in this class. Kiton dyes are an example. These dyes work best in an approximate pH range of 2 to 3. Sufficient heating over a long enough period of time is needed to complete the dye process. The dye molecules are small so it is easy to achieve level dyeing. Kiton dyes are not as colorfast as others in this class. They are lightfast when exposed to indirect sunlight and have good fastness to dry-cleaning, but when you wash the dyed fiber, some dye tends to migrate back into the water, fading the fiber over time. The colors available are very bright and clear, are somewhat mixable, and are relatively inexpensive. To ensure true colors, dye different protein fibers one at a time. Depending on the fiber, each dye color attaches or "strikes" at different times. All colors of Kiton dye do not work equally well on silk.

Super milling acid dyes are another kind of acid dye. Examples are Washfast Acid dyes, Gaywool dyes, One Shot dyes, Country Classics dyes, and Jacquard dyes. These dyes work best in a more neutral pH range of 5.5 to 7. The name "super milling" comes from industrial dyes used on fibers that are to go through further washing processes, where it is important for the dyes not to run. The molecules of super milling dyes are much larger than those of leveling acid dyes; the colors are more washfast, and more have very good lightfastness, too, but it's harder to get even, level results. There's a tradeoff between levelness and fastness—it's impossible to get both in one dye.

Premetallized dyes

These dyes include metal ions that help them stick to or bond with fibers. The dye process takes place most efficiently in a slightly acid to nearly neutral environment. Premetallized molecules are large, so the dye is very washfast and colorfast, but level results are hard to achieve, and the dye process takes longer than with other acid dyes. Premetallized dyes can dye more than one kind of protein fiber in a single dyebath with relatively consistent results for all. They work well with silk. Again, heat is needed to produce fast colors. The colors obtained from premetallized dyes are not as bright as the colors obtained from leveling acid dyes.

The dyes used in this book

The many dyes available to fiber artists today each have advantages and disadvantages, but it gets confusing if you try using them all. After a lot of experimentation, I now use only two kinds of dyes: Sabraset for protein fibers, and Sabracron F for cellulose fibers and silk. I've chosen these two on the basis of the fibers they dye, the range of colors they provide, their fastness, safety, ease of use, price, and availability. These are the dyes I recommend in this book. They provide all the colors you want on any kind of natural fiber.

Sabraset dyes

Among the newest dyes available to fiber artists, Sabraset combine a premetallized dye and a "hot" temperature fiber-reactive dye. They can be used on any protein fiber, including silk. Because the dye molecules are large, the colors are very colorfast, lightfast, and washfast. Also because of the molecule size, the dye process takes a while to complete and it's harder to achieve level results. Heat is required to fix the dye onto the fiber.

Sabraset dyes are produced and sold in a highly-concentrated powder form that must be measured and dissolved in a dyestock solution before use. The dyestock solutions are relatively easy to mix and can be stored in a dark, dry location for at least six months. The stock colors are bright and have very similar dyeing strengths, characteristics that make it possible to mix a wide range of clear, subtle colors. For all these reasons they are great dyes to use. (If you're familiar with Lanaset dyes, Sabraset are the same product under a new name.)

Sabracron F fiber-reactive dyes

Like Sabraset dyes, Sabracron F dyes are sold in highly concentrated powder form. This kind of fiber-reactive dye was introduced in 1978 as a successor to the Procion MX dyes, and there are several differences between the two. Molecules of Sabracron F move slower in the dyebath, so a dyestock solution can be kept for up to two months; Procion MX dyestocks could be kept for only seven days. Sabracron F dyes were designed for use on cellulose fibers but can also be used on silk.

GETTING SET UP FOR DYEING

Equipment

Dyeing equipment is not rare or expensive. You can find most items at local hardware stores, thrift shops, or yard sales. It's okay to raid your kitchen for dye equipment, but never use the equipment for food after using it for dyeing. Scales, graduated cylinders, pipettes, and other measuring devices calibrated in metric units may be hard to find locally. If you live in a large city, check the Yellow Pages for laboratory- or scientific-supply companies.

Equipment needed to begin dyeing.

Otherwise, order these items by mail—see the appendix for addresses of suppliers.

Apron to protect your clothing.

Assorted jars and bowls of various sizes, plastic or glass, to mix dyes in.

Buckets for soaking fiber in water before dyeing. The size depends on the amount of fiber to be dyed at one time. Usually one- to five-gallon plastic buckets work fine.

Calculator for determining amounts of dyes and chemicals to use.

Candy thermometer to monitor the temperature of the dyebath. A candy thermometer's range exceeds any temperature used for dyeing.

Dyepots. Dyepot material is important. Choose either stainless steel or enameled pots (like the kind used for canning). The metal of any other pot can react with the dyes and affect the final product. Stainless steel are the most durable and the most expensive. Enameled pots cost less, but don't last as long—if you accidentally chip the enamel, the pot rusts and becomes useless.

What size dyepot to choose? It's handy if you can afford to have a variety of sizes, but that is not always practical. Whatever pot you use must be large enough for holding the water and submerging the fiber, but not too heavy for you to lift. For example, a large canning pot is big enough for dyeing a pound of fiber, but it weighs almost forty pounds when full of water.

Funnel (plastic) to use when pouring dyestock solutions into jars or jugs for storage.

Jugs to store dyestock solutions. Glass or plastic beverage or milk jugs work fine. They must have tight-fitting lids.

Metric measuring containers to measure large amounts of dyestock and dyebath water. Get three sizes: 250-, 500-, and 1000-milliliter. They can be glass or plastic.

pH meter to measure the pH of your water and dyebaths (optional).

Protective mask to ensure your safety and minimize any possible allergic reactions to dyes. Inexpensive paper masks are adequate to protect you from dye powder. I use an industrial-type mask that has replaceable filters for particles or vapors. This type is more expensive, but worth the investment if you do much dyeing.

Rubber gloves are a must for protecting your hands from dyes and chemicals. Gloves also limit your exposure to water and keep your hands from getting dried out when you do a lot of dyeing. I use the blue "heavy duty" gloves when working with hot fiber, and thinner gloves for more dexterity when measuring dyes.

Scales to weigh fiber, dye, and any dry chemicals needed for the dye process. There are several kinds of scales and balances at a wide range of prices. Triple-beam balances or electronic scales work fine. Get one that can measure amounts accurately to a tenth of a gram.

Spoons and stirring sticks for mixing and stirring dyes. Either plastic or stainless steel spoons are okay. For mixing dyestocks, I use a set of wooden paint sticks, one for each color of dye, and employ the same stick for the same color each time. I use half-inch dowel rods to lift and turn fiber during the dye process. You could use a large stainless steel spoon instead.

Syringes or pipettes to measure small amounts of dyestock and liquid chemicals. I prefer syringes, and use three sizes: 3-milliliter capacity that measures in 0.1-milliliter units, 12-milliliter that measures in 0.2-milliliter units, and 35-milliliter that measures in 1.0-milliliter units. Metric pipettes work well, also.

Facilities

Simple facilities are sufficient for dyeing. First you need a heat source. This can be a regular stove, but preferably not the one in your kitchen. Outdoor gas grills or propane stoves are fine. Propane "lobster pot" stoves also work great for outside dyeing and are not very expensive. Hot plates are inconvenient because they typically do not get hot enough, or take too long to get hot. Be sure your heat source is safe: don't use a Coleman stove in the basement or plug a hot plate into an overloaded circuit.

Water is necessary for all dye processes. It is wonderful to have both hot and cold running water nearby when you dye! That saves a lot of time carrying water from another location. Having sinks in your dye area is even better.

Good lighting helps you see the wonderful colors you are creating. Ventilation keeps fresh air moving through the area. Locating the dye space outside takes care of that issue. If you work inside, open a window or turn on some type of exhaust fan.

Counter space is important, but it need not be fancy. My counter tops came from the junk pile of a neighborhood remodeling job, so the price was right. Old doors or plywood laid on saw horses work fine, too.

Secure storage space is essential. Dyestock solutions store best in cool, dark, dry conditions. Because dyestocks look tempting, be sure to store them out of sight and reach of children and animals. I store mine on shelves near the ceiling of my basement dye studio.

Safety

The dyes recommended in this book are no more hazardous than normal household chemicals but can be harmful if used improperly. Follow these personal safety precautions. First, always wear a mask when working with dye powders. Dust-fine, they're the most hazardous part of dyeing. Second, wear an apron while dyeing and take it off when you leave the dye area in order not to transport stray dye. Third, wear rubber gloves. Dyes and chemicals can be easily absorbed, but not if your hands are protected by gloves. Fourth, never eat or drink in your dye area. You don't know what stray particles may end up on your doughnut or in your coffee.

Be neat. If you spill something, clean it up immediately. When measuring dye powder, use disposable paper to catch any spillage and discard it afterward. Wipe the area with a damp

A dye studio. This setup in the author's basement has all of the essentials for safely dyeing fiber.

cloth or paper towel after measuring. When you finish work, be sure to stow all the dyes and chemicals where no one can get at them. Don't leave anything lying around where someone can accidentally bump into it.

Using metric measurements

The metric system is not complicated or hard to understand. In fact, it's a simpler and more accurate way to measure than the U.S. method. Knowing and understanding metrics can really simplify your dyeing life. Metric equipment is much more exact but no harder to use than a set of teaspoons. With metrics, you can easily do all your dyeing calculations with a calculator—and no one has to be a math whiz for that!

You need only remember one set of numbers to convert U.S. weights into metrics: 1 ounce = 28.4 grams. Once you know that, everything else follows. For example, if you want to dye 8 ounces of fiber, you multiply 8 by 28.4 to get 227.2 grams.

Using the metric system is especially convenient when you're figuring dye formulas, preparing dyestock solutions, or measuring out the desired amount of dyestocks or chemical assists for a particular weight of fiber. For example, common table salt is used with Sabraset dyes at 10% of the weight of fiber (WOF), so for 300 grams of fiber, you would use 30 grams of salt. It's a lot easier to make such calculations in grams than in ounces.

In general, you weigh dry materials such as powdered dyes in grams and measure the volume of fluids in milliliters (often abbreviated to ml). For example, the first step in dyeing is dissolving the dye powders in water to make dyestock solutions. A standard 1% solution contains one part dye and ninety-nine parts water. You measure the dye in grams and the water in milliliters. This works because the metric system is set up so that one gram of water equals one milliliter of water. Isn't that handy? (Actually, the equivalency is precise only for pure water. With dyestocks and other dyeing solutions, one milliliter of solution will weigh approximately but not exactly one gram. Still, that's close enough for practical purposes.)

MIXING COLORS ACCORDING TO DYE FORMULAS

Usually the colors you dye do not come from a single dyestock solution. The end color is, instead, a mixture of two or more dyestocks. The recipes for mixtures are called *dye formulas* and are expressed in terms of percentages of the total volume of dye for the dyebath. Using dye formulas makes it possible to mix up the same color over and over with consistent results, no matter the quantity of fiber being dyed.

A dye formula states the percentage of each color that is used—for example, a formula for orange might call for 85% gold dye and 15% red dye. Dye formulas also take into account the depth of shade (DOS). The intensity of a dyed color is determined by the ratio of dye to the weight of fiber. The more dye you use, the higher the DOS and the more intense your color. I'll speak more about DOS later.

The typical dye formulas I use with Sabraset and Sabracron F are listed on pages 82–84. If you want even more recipes to follow, you can buy books of color samples and dye formulas. As you do more dyeing, though, you'll want to design your own formulas. This is not difficult. Approach it the same way you do cooking recipes—with a sense of fun and adventure! A little knowledge and some hands-on dyeing experience will provide all the colors and formulas you can imagine.

I approach mixing colors a little differently from some dyers, who do color studies using two colors of dye at a time in a series of standard proportions. My approach is more painterly and intuitive. Instead of limiting myself to two- or three-color mixes, I use as many colors as necessary. This way I obtain a much richer, more complex palette of colors.

I don't dye lots of samples for their own sake, but I do keep extensive records as I design palettes of colors for particular projects. Over the years I've accumulated a large number of formulas to work with. For easy reference I keep them in notebooks along with samples.

Designing your own dye formulas

When dyeing, you need to know more than just color theory to be successful in mixing predictable colors. You must understand the particular dyes you have chosen, their specific characteristics and underlying subtleties, and the way each color reacts in a mixture. This knowledge comes with practice, from trying various combinations and observing how they turn out.

Ask yourself three basic questions each time you create a dye formula:

What is the hue family of the desired color?
What value do you want?
How bright or how saturated should it be?

Once you have answered these questions, you can follow a five-step approach to choosing the right dyestock colors and figuring what proportion of each color to use in your formula. Here are the steps to follow:

1. *Look at the color wheel and estimate where your color fits in.* In Chapter 1, you learned how to describe a color. That is what you are doing when you plot your dye on the color wheel. Think about hue, value, and saturation, then place the color on the wheel with those qualities in mind. Do the best you can to estimate where the color belongs.
2. *Find the primary colors on either side of your desired color.* They must be included in the dye formula. Choosing which *undertone* of a primary to use makes a big difference in how the mixed color looks (see page 20). Remember that all colors have an undertone, a subtle essence of warmth or coolness, within their hue. Sometimes the undertone can be seen only by comparison to another color within the same hue family, but it's important to look for undertones and take them into consideration when choosing colors to mix.

   Normally, instead of using three primary dye colors, I use six—two for each hue. This makes it possible to mix a wide range of clear, bright colors. To mix the brightest colors, I use the primaries with the undertones closest to the final mixed color. For example, the brightest oranges are made from yellows with red undertones mixed with reds with yellow undertones. Many other oranges are possible—you could mix cool yellows and warm reds or warm yellows and cool reds—but these mixtures are not quite as bright as the first. The same principle applies to mixing any color.

   Using both the warm and cool undertone of a primary is another good idea. For example, you could mix a warm and cool yellow together and use that mixture as the yellow in the formula. That way the qualities of both yellows appear in the mixture, which makes the final color appear more complex and rich. The technique of using more than one undertone of each primary to achieve rich results is called *color loading*. You can mix equal amounts of two undertones, or use different amounts so the warm or cool undertone dominates. Color loading extends the range and kind of colors you can mix from a given palette of primaries.

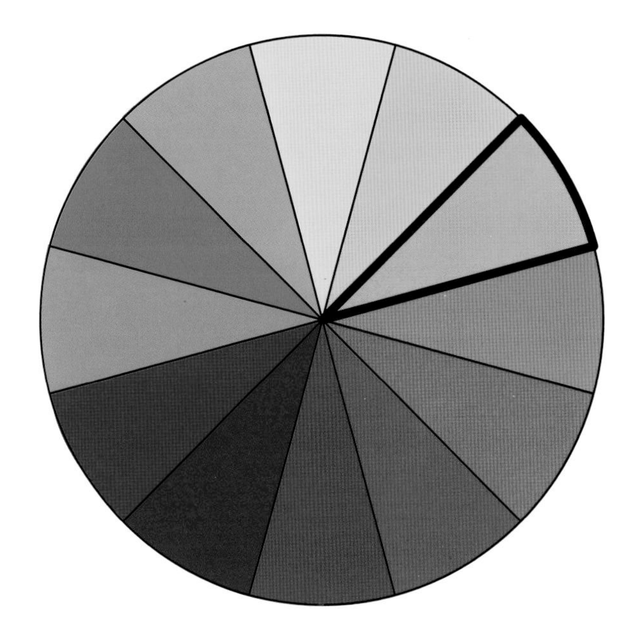

Choosing primaries to mix. This color wheel shows where the color to be mixed is located, between yellow and red. To get the "right" orange, use the yellow and red with the desired undertone: warm yellow (gold) and cool red (magenta 338).

3. *Estimate the percentage of each dye color to use by the location of the mixed color on the color wheel.* Figuring out dye formulas would be easy if dyes performed in reality the way colors appear on the wheel, but unfortunately they don't. This is where you need to know your dyes' characteristics. All dye colors do not behave equally. Some colors in a range of dyes are stronger and more dominant, while others are weaker. You need to know the relative strengths of the dye colors you are going to work with. Here are things to think about:

What is the *strength* of each color of dye in comparison to other colors of that kind of dye? If a dye color is strong, you do not need to use as much of that particular color in a formula to achieve the desired results. If a dye color is weak, you need to use more than theory indicates. Working with actual dye colors will make this obvious, and you'll soon learn how different colors behave.

What is the relative *value* of each dye color in comparison to the others? Knowing the relative value of a dye color is important because it takes a larger quantity of a light-value dye to dominate a mixture. Light-value colors are weaker than dark-value colors. When estimating percentages, plan on using larger amounts of lighter colors such as yellows. It always takes more dye for light colors to "hold their own" in a formula. For example, with Sabraset dyes, a good orange formula is not 50% yellow and 50% red, but is 70% yellow and 30% red.

What is the *intensity* or saturation of each pure dye color in a mixture? If the dye color is not bright by itself, it will never be bright in a mixture. A mixed color cannot be brighter than the colors that go into it. In fact, the more colors in a dye formula, the duller the final color will be.

After you have considered all of these dye characteristics, look again at where your desired color falls on the color wheel. To mix that color, you'll use whatever primaries are appropriate, adjusting the percentage of each primary on the basis of its strength. These percentages will be estimates, but as you gain more experience with dyeing—especially if you keep records in your dye notebook!—your estimates will become more accurate.

4. *Fine-tune the formula.* Consider the intensity of the desired color. Is it bright or dull? If you want a bright color, a two-color mix works well. But if a two-color mix looks too bright, you can dull it down by adding either a small amount of its complement or black. These give different results. Adding the complement makes a lively, interesting mixture. Adding black simply darkens a color without providing richness.

   To tone down a color just a little, add 2% of the complement or black. This may be enough to give the desired result; if not, you can always add more. Remember that mixing complementary colors forms a range of browns and dulled hues with various undertones, depending on the amount of each complement in the mixture. At some point, the mixture turns a neutral gray.

5. *Choose a depth of shade (DOS) number.* DOS relates the amount of dye to the weight of fiber being dyed. The more dye you use, the deeper or more intense the color of the dyed fiber. Low DOS numbers produce pale or pastel colors. Higher numbers produce rich, dark, more intense colors. As you gain experience with dyeing, you'll learn how to choose a suitable DOS number for whatever color you want to make.

   Following these five steps, you can make any dye formula you want. The color won't always turn out exactly as you expect, but that's why you keep a dye notebook. Developing formulas becomes easier the more you work with dyes. There's no substitute for hands-on practice.

Keeping a dye notebook

If you plan to do any amount of dyeing, keeping a notebook is well worth the effort. It serves as a record of the formulas for all the colors you have dyed, with samples. Not having to blindly recreate the same or similar colors again and again will save you lots of time.

For my dye notebook, I use 8½-by-11-inch plastic slide holders that fit in a three-ring binder. You can get slide holders at photo or office-supply stores. Each sheet holds twenty slides or dye samples. The spaces are just big enough for a tuft of fiber and a square paper label, on which I write the dye formula and

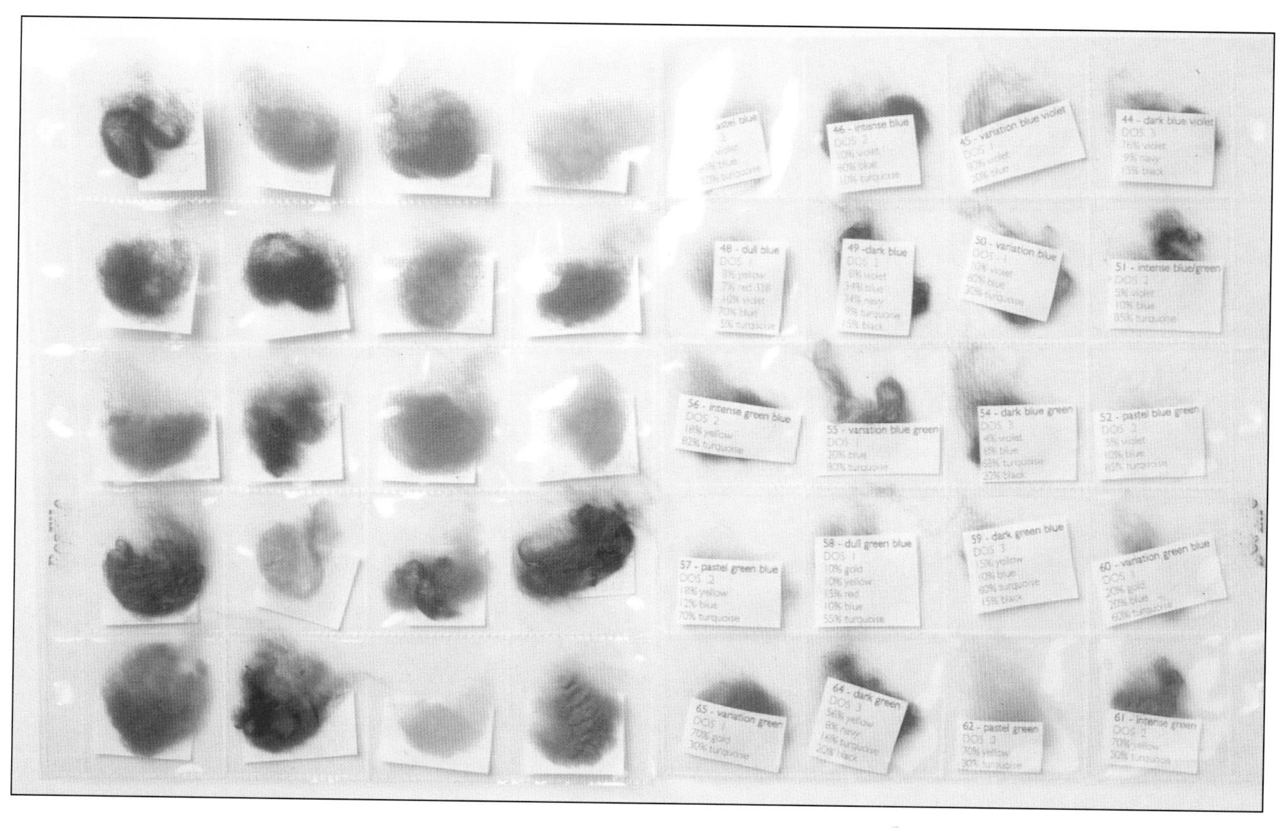

Dye notebook records. You see the tufts of fiber on one side, and when the page is turned you see the paper with the dye formula and DOS. Formulas are arranged by hue families.

DOS, and the color's name (if I want to name it). If you look at the front of the sheet, you can see all the colors. Flip the sheet over, and you can read all the labels. I arrange my sample sheets according to color families.

USING SABRASET DYES

Sabraset dyes are designed for dyeing wool and other protein fibers. They come in several colors that you can mix to make many more colors. The powder from these dyes is very concentrated. One ounce of powder can dye seven pounds of fiber to a medium hue, or up to seventy pounds of fiber in a pastel color.

Mixing the dyestock solutions

The first step is mixing the dye powder with water. There are two reasons for this: safety and accuracy. Inhaling dye powder can cause health problems. Once the powder is dissolved in water, the risk is greatly reduced. Also, measuring a dyestock solution is more accurate than weighing out tiny amounts of dye powder.

Mix dye powder into a 1% solution, using ninety-nine parts of water for every one part of dye. In metric terms, this means you mix ninety-nine milliliters of water with one gram of dye. Using these proportions keeps the math very easy.

Making Dyestock Solution

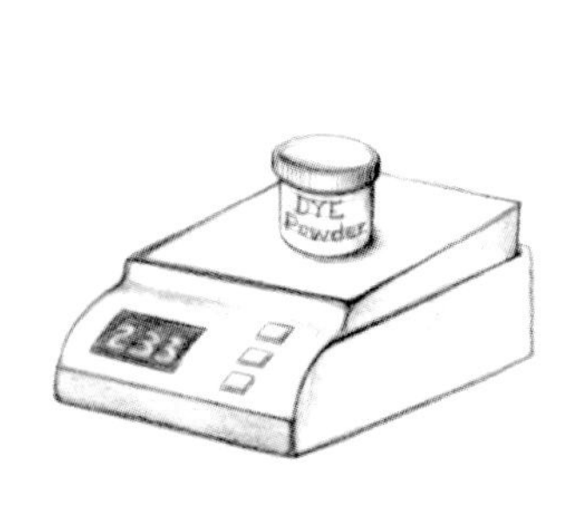

Weigh dye powder in grams.

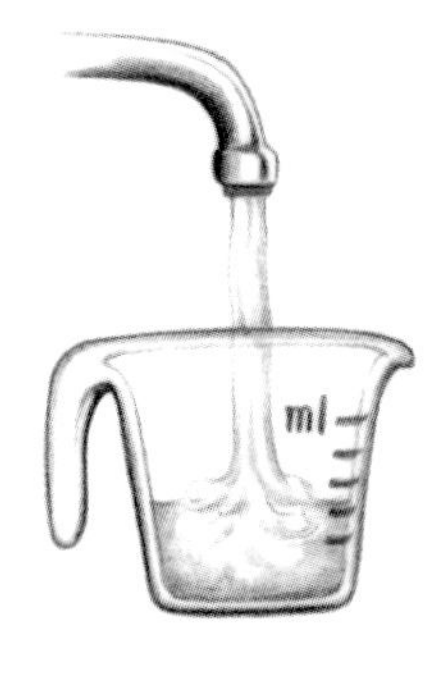

Measure hot water to add to powder.

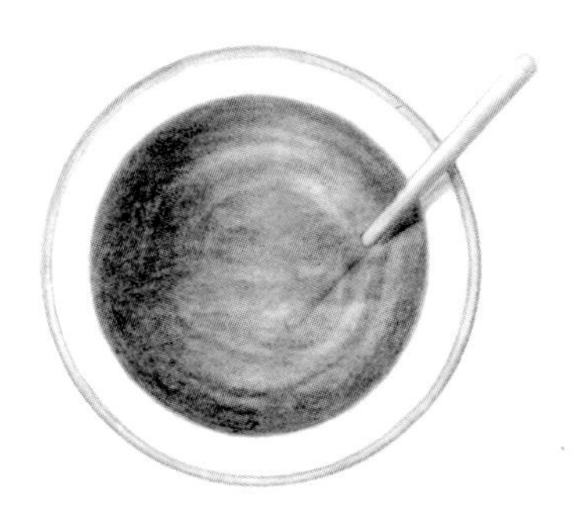

Mix the powder and water together until the powder dissolves.

Store in sturdy plastic or glass jugs.

Once your powder is weighed, pour it into a heatproof, nonreactive container such as a glass or stainless steel jar or bowl. To figure the amount of water you need for a 1% solution, use this equation:

(weight of dye powder × 100) – (weight of dye powder) = amount of water to use (ml)

Measure a small amount (50 ml) of the total water needed. This should be hot water from the tap. Pour a little onto the dye powder and stir to make a paste. While stirring, continue pouring the rest of the 50 ml into the paste. Next, measure all but the last 100 ml of the water needed. This water should be boiling hot. Stir the boiling water slowly into the paste and continue stirring until all the paste has dissolved.

Some Sabraset dye colors dissolve more readily than others. The colors I find hardest to dissolve are sun yellow, magenta, violet, and turquoise. The yellow wants to stay in granules. Be persistent; continuous stirring will dissolve the granules. Magenta gets real gloppy and needs to be stirred a lot. It takes the longest of any color to dissolve. Be patient and keep stirring. Turquoise and violet tend to look tarry in the paste step, but the slow addition of boiling water, along with constant stirring, will gradually dissolve them.

Let the dyestock cool, then pour it into whatever jug or jar you plan to store it in. Finally, use the last 100 ml of (tepid) water to rinse any dye residue out of the mixing bucket; add the residue to the storage jug. Label the jug with the type of dye, the dye color, the concentration of solution, and the date it was made. Sabraset dyestocks stay fresh for at least six months if stored in a cool, dark, dry place.

Choosing and mixing colors of Sabraset dyes

You can buy thirteen different colors of Sabraset dyes, but I do not use them all. Here are the colors I use, with details about each.

There are two yellows available: *sun yellow* and *mustard yellow*. *Sun yellow* is a bright lemon yellow that makes bright mixtures. It's

SABRASET DYE COLORS AND CHARACTERISTICS

Dye number and color	Description of color characteristics
180 Sun Yellow	Bright lemon yellow
182 Mustard Yellow	Golden yellow, warmer, but not as bright as 180
380 Scarlet	Bright, orange red
383 Deep Red	Dull red, tends to be warm
385 Magenta	Dark blueish red, not good for bright color formulas
338 WF Acid Magenta	Bright fuschia, true reds
880 Violet	Bright intense violet, great for mixing strong colors
480 Turquoise	Blue-turquoise, great for mixing bright greens
483 Royal Blue	A true bright blue
485 Navy	Indigo-navy
680 Jet Black	A good black, can also be used for grays

especially good for mixing bright oranges and clear greens. *Mustard yellow* is a golden yellow. It makes more subtle, earthy mixtures.

There are three reds available: *scarlet, deep red,* and *magenta.* They are all important for mixing. *Scarlet* is bright, but tends toward orange and is not the strongest red in mixtures. Rich purples result when it is mixed with blue. *Deep red* is the dullest red. It tends toward orange. When mixed, it produces wonderful brick colors and rusts. *Magenta* is a dark blue-red that cannot be mixed to produce bright colors, but it does produce rich deep purples, wines, bordeaux, and browns.

Another red I use is not a Sabraset dye. The Sabraset range lacks a bright, fuchsia-type red. That color is available in a WashFast acid dye called WF *magenta 338.* This makes a good substitute because the size of the dye molecules is close to Sabraset and the process and conditions for using it are the same as for Sabraset. *Magenta 338* is very bright. It mixes with yellow into the brightest oranges; with other reds it produces a more "true" red. It also mixes well with turquoise to make a very bright range of red-violets.

Violet is a must-have color. It is very rich and possesses an intensity that cannot be achieved by mixing. Used in a blend, violet adds a unique luminescence. With *turquoise,* it can make an intense range of blue-violets. With *magenta 338,* it makes a great range of red-violets.

There are three blues available: *turquoise, royal blue,* and *navy. Turquoise* is really a blue-turquoise. It works well with yellow to mix bright, clear greens that cannot be obtained with the other blues. *Royal blue* is the "true blue". A very bright blue, it mixes well with all other colors. Greens that are mixed with *royal blue* are quiet, but very rich. *Navy* is like an indigo. When used instead of royal blue in a mixture, the colors are more subtle. I sometimes use *navy* to tone down very bright mixed colors.

The Sabraset *black* is a really good black. It gives a true jet black color and does not look "sickly" at lighter concentrations. A good range of grays can be dyed with this black.

The other Sabraset colors available are *brown, rust brown,* and *green. Brown* is a neutral brown that can be used to tone down other colors. I prefer using complements to tone down colors, so I don't use brown much. For the same reason, I rarely use *rust brown,* which is a reddish brown. I don't use *green* because I've been able to mix all the greens I've ever wanted.

Chemical assists used with Sabraset dyes

Four chemicals are used to complete the Sabraset dye process.

1. *Acetic acid* (56% strength) is used to adjust the dyebath's pH to between 4.5 and 5. Within this range, there is maximum dyebath exhaustion and minimum fiber damage. Acetic acid is available at chemical supply houses or from mail-order dye suppliers. You can also buy it at most photo-supply stores, but what they sell is 28% strength, so you have to use double the amount. When 56% strength acetic acid is used, it is used at 4% of WOF. Use this equation to figure how much acetic acid to put in the dyebath:

   WOF × 0.04 (4%) = amount of acetic acid to put in dyebath (ml). (Remember to use 0.08 [8%] of 28% strength acetic acid.)

   Measure the acid in milliliters, using a syringe or graduated cylinder. Be careful not to get any acid on your skin. Use plenty of water to rinse the container you measure acid in.

   As an alternative to acetic acid, you can use crystals of citric acid. The amount required is 4% of the WOF. Weigh out the crystals in grams, and dissolve them in the dyebath with plenty of stirring. Citric acid crystals are inexpensive and easy to use, but the colors you get may vary from those obtained with acetic acid.

2. *Albegal SET* helps produce more level or even distribution of the dye, so the fiber gets a uniform, not streaky color. It also helps with exhausting the dyebath (using up all the dye). Because the Albegal SET is very viscous, I usually dilute it to a 10% solution (one part albegal SET and nine parts water.) Use this equation to figure how much Albegal SET to put in the dyebath:

   WOF × 0.07 (7%) = amount of 10% Albegal SET solution to use (ml)

3. *Salt* (regular table salt works fine) is also used as a leveling agent in the dyebath. It helps the dye molecules find places to attach onto

USING THE EQUATIONS FOR SABRASET DYES

Example: How much of each chemical is needed to dye 227 grams (8 ounces) of fiber?

Acetic Acid (56% strength)
WOF × 4% = amount of acetic acid to use

227 grams × 0.04 = 9.1 ml of acetic acid to put in dyebath

Albegal SET
WOF × 7% = amount of albegal SET to use

227 grams × 0 .07 = 15.9 ml of albegal SET to add to the dyebath

Salt
WOF × 10% = amount of salt to use

227 grams × 0.10 = 22.7 grams of salt to add to the dyebath

Sodium Acetate
WOF × 1% = amount of sodium acetate to use

227 grams × 0.01 = 2.3 grams of sodium acetate to add to the dyebath

Water
WOF × 40 = amount of water to use for dyebath

227 grams × 40 = 9080 ml of water to use for dyebath

the fiber, regulating the speed and evenness of the dye distribution. It is used at 10% of WOF. Use this equation to figure how much salt to put in the dyebath:

WOF × 0.10 (10%) = amount of salt to add to the dyebath (grams)

4. *Sodium acetate* acts as a stabilizing buffer to fine-tune the pH level of the dyebath. It is used at 1% WOF. Sodium acetate is a powder that sometimes resists being dissolved—just keep stirring! Adding a small amount of hot water first helps. Use this equation to figure how much sodium acetate to put in the dyebath:

WOF × 0.01 (1%) = amount of sodium acetate to add to dyebath (grams)

Choosing depth of shade for Sabraset dyes

The depth of shade (DOS) describes the intensity and value of a dyed color, and is expressed as a ratio between the quantity of dye used and the weight of fiber being dyed (WOF). For example, DOS 1.0 means you multiply WOF times 1.0, and measure out that much dyestock; for example, 10 grams of fiber would require 10 ml of dyestock. You can choose whatever DOS you desire, depending how you want the color to look. For Sabraset dyes I normally work within the range of 0.1 (pale pastel) to 3.0 (very deep).

DOS RANGE OF SABRASET DYES

DOS	Number Description
0.1	Pale pastel
0.2	Medium pastel
0.5	Deep pastel
0.75	Light medium
1.0	Medium
1.5	Deep medium
2.0	Deep
2.5	Deeper
3.0	Very deep (Intense)

Figuring how much water to use with Sabraset dyes

Dyeing takes place most efficiently if a suitable amount of water is present in the dyepot. I use a larger proportion of water when dyeing fiber than when dyeing yarns. More water allows fiber to move freely without felting and dye as evenly as possible. For Sabraset dyes I use a ratio of forty parts water to one part fiber. Use this equation to figure the amount of water for a dyebath:

WOF × 40 = amount of water to put in the dyepot (ml)

Using dye formulas to figure how much of each dyestock is needed

Get out your calculator for this step. Two numbers are needed: the WOF (in grams) and the depth of shade (DOS). Multiply these numbers to figure the total amount of dyestock to put in the dyepot:

WOF × DOS = total amount of dyestock to use (ml)

Then figure how much of each separate color of dyestock is needed by using the dye formula (see chart on pages 82–83). Put the percentage of any color into the following equation:

(Total amount of dyestock needed) × (% of color A) = amount of color A dyestock to put in dyebath (ml)

Use this equation for each dye color in the formula. It's a good idea to calculate the amounts, then add them up to make sure they equal the expected total. Cross-check the numbers before you start measuring out the dyestocks.

FIGURING AMOUNTS OF DYESTOCK WHEN USING A DYE FORMULA

Example: To dye 227 grams of fiber at a DOS of 1.5 using a dye formula of 30% sun yellow, 50% scarlet, and 20% black.

To figure the total amount of dyestock to use:
WOF × DOS = total amount of dyestock needed

227 grams × 1.5 = 340.5 ml, total amount of dyestock needed

To figure the amount of each color of dyestock to put into dyebath:
Total amount of dyestock × percentage of each color = ml of that color's dyestock to use

340.5 ml × 0.30 (% of sun yellow) = 102.2 ml of sun yellow dyestock to use

340.5 ml × 0.50 (% of scarlet) = 170.3 ml scarlet dyestock to use

340.5 ml × 0.20 (% of black) = 68.0 ml black dyestock to use

To check your figuring, make sure the numbers add up to the total:
102.2 + 170.3 + 68.0 = 340.5 ml of dyestock (total amount needed

REMINDERS FOR SUCCESSFUL DYEING

The key aspect of hand-dyeing repeatable colors is consistency. You need to be consistent in weighing fiber and dyes, consistent in measuring dyestocks and chemicals, and consistent in procedure and timing. Also, pay attention to these points:

Use the right amount of water for each dyebath. Too much or too little water can make the process slow, inefficient, or ineffective.

Make sure the temperature of the dyebath is correct for the dye being used. Temperatures that are too hot or not hot enough can ruin the process.

Measure and use the chemical assists for each dye in the correct proportions and with appropriate timing. Without the assists, dyeing cannot take place or be completed.

Advice on using Sabraset dyes

The box on page 69 gives step-by-step directions for the Sabraset dye procedure and there's a worksheet for doing calculations on page 229. Here are some pointers that will help you get the best possible results.

First, weigh the fiber you plan to dye. All fiber must be scoured and dried before being weighed for dyeing; weighing fleece in the grease is inaccurate. (See box at right for washing fleece.) You do not know how much of the weight is dirt and grease and how much is fiber. Measure fiber to the nearest gram for the weight of fiber (WOF).

Fill a bucket or sink with very warm (about 110 to 130°F) tap water, stir in about five ml of Synthrapol (a wetting agent available from dye suppliers), then add the teased fiber. Let the fiber soak at least thirty minutes. The fiber can be soaking as you make calculations and measure out the chemical assists and dyestocks.

Pour the measured amount of room-temperature water into the dyepot, add the four chemical assists, and stir. Make sure everything has dissolved. Next, add the measured amount of each dyestock. Stir again. Last, add the wetted fiber.

Put the dyepot on the stove and turn on the heat. Raise the temperature to 180°F over the next half hour. The actual dyeing begins to take place after the dyebath reaches at least 150 to 155°F. Do not let the temperature go above 190°F, especially if using silk, which can lose its luster if exposed to temperatures over 185°F. The temperature is too high if you see the fiber "dome up" on the surface of the dyebath. If that happens, turn down the heat immediately!

Handle the wet fiber as gently as possible. Do not stir the dyepot because stirring tangles any kind of fiber and can cause the wool to felt. Instead, use two dowels to flip the fiber over. Flip the fiber once when the dyebath temperature reaches 180°F and again during the half-hour as the temperature is being held at 180°F.

After a total of one hour, check the pot to see if all the dye has been absorbed. One way is to

WASHING FLEECE

1. Sort fleece and remove vegetal matter, second cuts, or anything that is not of good quality. If portions vary in length or color, separate them now.
2. Fill a sink with very hot water (150°F). Grease on fleece melts at 110°F, so it is important that the water temperature be at least that hot, and hotter is better. Add approximately 3 tablespoons of Orvus for every pound of fleece. Dissolve the Orvus in the water before adding the fleece. If the fleece is very greasy, use more Orvus.
3. Pack the dirty fleece into the sink. It is OK to really pack the wool. It will help keep the temperature hot longer. Let the wool soak for about 10 to 15 minutes.
4. Pull out a small amount of the wool to see if it no longer feels sticky. If it does not feel squeaky clean, repeat the detergent soak. (To do this, set the wool aside, drain the sink, and refill it with hot water and detergent, then replace the wool and soak for another 10 to 15 minutes.)
5. In another 10 to 15 minutes, check again.
6. Rinse the fleece in hot, clean water until the rinse water runs clear.
7. For the last rinse, add a splash (about 30 to 50 ml) of vinegar to the water. (If you don't like the smell of vinegar, you can rinse once more to wash it away.)
8. Place the fleece in the washer and use the spin cycle to extract any excess moisture.
9. Spread on screen to dry.

STEP-BY-STEP PROCEDURE FOR USING SABRASET DYES

1. Weigh clean dry fiber to be dyed.
2. Soak clean weighed fiber in hot water and Synthrapol for at least 30 minutes.
3. Choose or make up a dye formula to use and decide on DOS.
4. Figure and measure amounts of each chemical assist: acetic acid, salt, Albegal SET, and sodium acetate.
5. Figure and measure amounts of each dyestock needed.
6. Figure the dye/water ratio, measure the appropriate amount of room-temperature water, and put it in dyepot.
7. Add the measured amounts of the chemical assists to the water and stir. Add measured amounts of the dyestocks to the water and stir. Be patient and keep stirring until everything is dissolved.
8. Add the wet, soaked fiber to the dyepot. Set the dyepot on the stove and turn on the heat. Heat the dyebath slowly over the next half hour, to a temperature of about 180°F.
9. Flip over the fiber. Maintain the dyebath temperature at 180 to 190°F for a second half hour. Flip the fiber again during that time.
10. Check the dyebath to see if the dye has been absorbed. If so, take dyepot off stove. If not, maintain the temperature at about 180°F for another half hour, flipping the fiber again during that time.
11. Check again to make sure the dye has absorbed, then take the dyepot off the stove. Let the dyepot cool to room temperature.
12. Lift fiber out of the dyepot and rinse it thoroughly in room-temperature water.
13. Use spin cycle of washer to remove excess moisture from the fiber, then spread the fiber out to dry.
14. Dispose of the dyebath.

look into the pot, but appearances can be deceiving. You may think there is lots of dye left, but you could be seeing just a reflection of the dyed fiber, not actual dye in the water. A better way to tell how much dye remains is to dip a cup into the pot, scoop up some liquid, and look closely as you pour it back. If the fluid looks somewhat transparent, chances are most of the dye has been absorbed. If the fluid appears to have lots of color left, then leave the dyepot on the stove at 180°F for another half hour. This extra half hour is sometimes necessary for dark colors, but rarely needed for pastel colors. (For comparison's sake, it's a good habit to dip out and pour back a sample of each dyebath when you first put it on the stove, so you'll know its darkness at the beginning of the process.)

When the dyebath looks exhausted (that's when all the dye has been absorbed), take the pot off the stove and let the whole thing cool down. This is an important part of the process because dye can still be absorbed as the dyebath cools.

When the fiber has reached room temperature, rinse it thoroughly in room-temperature water until the rinse water runs clear. This usually does not take long. Handle the fiber gently as you rinse it. It's okay to squeeze it, but don't rub it. Use the spin cycle of a washing machine to extract excess water from the fiber and speed up drying. Tease the fiber gently to loosen any compacted clumps. Then spread it out to air-dry on a screen or rack, or on a table or floor. Keep it out of direct sunlight. Drying may take hours or days, depending on the fiber and your climate. Be sure to wait until the fiber is thoroughly dry before putting it into a plastic bag or other airtight container.

Dispose of the dyebath. It should have very little dye left in it. Add a little soda ash to bring

Procedure for Sabraset dyes.

1. Weigh clean fiber to be dyed.

2. Soak fiber in warm water and Synthrapol.

3. Measure all chemicals, dyes, and water that will be in the dyepot.

4. Put everything into dyepot, stir, add fiber, place on stove and turn heat on.

5. Monitor temperature. Make sure it does not get too hot.

6. Check time and flip fiber with dowel rod.

7. Dip out a cup of dyebath to see if it is exhausted.

8. Let fiber cool down in dyebath.

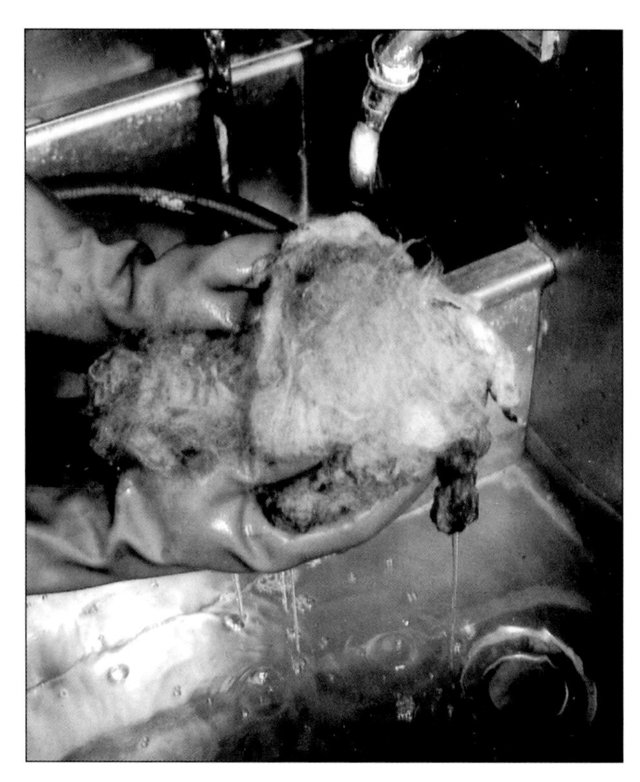

9. Rinse fiber in sink until water comes clear.

10. Tease fiber apart and spread it out to dry.

the solution close to neutral. It may bubble up when you do this, but that's okay—don't be alarmed. Pour the dyebath down the drain, followed with plenty of water.

USING SABRACRON F FIBER-REACTIVE DYES

Sabracron F dyes were designed for use on cellulose fibers. They can also be used on silk, but it takes more dye to dye silk the same color as cotton. Different fibers must be dyed separately for the colors to remain true because the dyes "strike" or attach to different fibers at different rates. They attach to cotton faster than they do to silk, so if you tried putting these two fibers in the same bath, they wouldn't turn out the same color.

Mixing the dyestock solutions

The procedure for mixing dyestock solutions with Sabracron F dyes is similar to mixing dyestocks with Sabraset dyes (see page 69), and safety precautions remain the same for working with all dye powders. Remember to wear a mask when you are working with dye powder.

Again, to prepare a 1% dyestock solution, mix one gram of dye powder with ninety-nine milliliters of water. Sabracron F dyes dissolve in water much more easily than Sabraset dyes. Warm tap water should be sufficient to dissolve the powder. First, weigh the dye powder and put into a container. Measure the appropriate amount of warm water. Slowly pour a little water onto the powder and stir to form a paste, then slowly pour all but the last one hundred milliliters into the container and stir continually until the paste has dissolved completely. Pour the dyestock into the storage container, rinse the mixing container with the last one hundred milliliters of water, and add that rinse water to the storage container. Label the container with the kind of dye, color, solution strength, and date. Store any unused dye-

SABRACRON F DYE COLORS AND CHARACTERISTICS

Dye number and color	Description of color characteristics
F-11 Sun Yellow	Bright yellow
F-14 Golden Yellow	Warmer yellow, not as bright in formulas
F-31 Flame Scarlet	Orange-red, acts like orange in formulas
F-33 True Red	Cool, almost true red
F-35 Fuchsia	Bright cool red
F-40 Turquoise	Bright, tends toward blue rather than green
F-42 Brilliant Blue	Bright royal blue, wonderful with fuchsia to mix bright purples
F-47 Deep Navy	Dark indigo-blue, tends toward dull
F-83 Royal Purple	Red-violet, mixes brighter colors than some of the blue/red formulas
F-61 Rich Black	Pretty good black, but doesn't give "jet black" on cotton
F-53 Earth Brown	Red-brown, used to mix some of the duller formulas

stock in a cool, dark, dry place. Sabracron F dyestocks will last up to two months.

Choosing and mixing colors of Sabracron F dyes

You can buy twenty-three colors of Sabracron F dyes. I use eleven in my dyeing.

For yellows, I use two dyes. *F-11 yellow* is a bright yellow that mixes well with turquoise for bright greens and with scarlet for bright oranges. *F-14 golden yellow* is a warmer shade that's a little more subtle and rich in mixtures, particularly browns.

For reds, I use three dyes. *F-31 scarlet* is an orange-red that acts more like orange in mixtures. When mixed with blue, *scarlet* gives a range of plums to rusty browns, instead of the purples you might expect. *F-33 red* is more of a true red, but on the cool side. It can be mixed with *scarlet* to obtain a nice range of corals. *F-35 fuchsia* is a bright cool red. It mixes well with *scarlet* to make a great red-red. It remains bright in mixtures. It is my favorite red to use for intense purples.

For blues, I use three dyes. *F-40 turquoise* is a bright color that tends toward blue. *F-42 brilliant blue* is a bright royal blue. It mixes well with fuchsia for clear purples. *F-47 navy* is more like an indigo and mixes dull colors. *Navy* works well for mixing very subtle browns.

Three other colors are sometimes helpful. I only use *F-83 purple,* a red-violet color, occasionally, since I can mix lots of great purples from reds and blues. *Purple* is helpful for mixing some violet hues. I use *F-61 black* to tone colors down. Compared to the jet blacks I can get on protein fibers (including silk) with Sabraset black dye, the colors I get on cellulose fibers with *F-61 black* are not as pure or dark. Another color I use occasionally is *F-53 earth brown.* It is a red brown that can serve as a base for some brown mixtures, or you can mix it with blues to obtain a range of subtle, neutral colors.

Chemical assists used with Sabracron F dyes

You need two chemical assists for Sabracron F dyes.

1. *Salt* (common table salt is fine) acts as the leveling agent; it helps the dye migrate from the dyebath to the fiber. The salt changes the electric charge on the fiber so the fiber can accept the dye. The more dye present in the dyebath, the more salt required. The amount of salt is based on the WOF (weight of fiber) and DOS (depth of shade), and ranges from 50 to 120%. Use this equation to figure how much salt to put in the dyebath:

   WOF × (percent number from chart, depends on DOS) = amount of salt needed (g)

2. *Soda ash* (also called *sodium carbonate*) ends the migration of the dye onto the fiber and completes the dye process by causing dye molecules to bond. The amount of soda ash to use is 10% of the WOF.

   WOF × 0.10 (10%) = amount of soda ash needed (g)

   The soda is not added at the beginning of the dye process. Wait until the dye has had time to attach to the fiber. To avoid any damage to the fiber, dissolve the soda ash in some hot water before adding it to the dyebath.

Choosing depth of shade for Sabracron F dyes

Typical DOS numbers for Sabracron F dyes range from 0.1 (pale) to 1.5 (medium) to 6.0 (deep intense), but actual colors vary according to the fiber being dyed. Silk requires more dye for dark values than does cotton. Another complication with Sabracron F is that the dye colors have different strengths. For example, fuchsia

DOS AND AMOUNT OF SALT FOR SABRACRON F DYES

DOS number	Amount of salt to use	Description
0.1	50% of WOF	Pale
0.2	50% of WOF	Pastel
0.5	50% of WOF	Medium pastel
0.75	60% of WOF	Deep pastel
1.0	60% of WOF	Light medium
1.5	80% of WOF	Medium
3.0	80% of WOF	Deep medium
4.0	100% of WOF	Medium intense
5.0	100% of WOF	Intense
6.0+	120% of WOF	Deep intense

USING THE EQUATIONS FOR SABRACRON F DYES

Example: How much of each chemical and dyestock is needed to dye 227 grams (8 ounces) of fiber at DOS 1.5?

Salt
WOF × 80% = amount of salt to add to the dyebath
227 grams × 0.80 = 181.6 grams of salt

Soda Ash (Sodium Carbonate)
WOF × 10% = amount of soda ash to dissolve, then add to the dyebath
227 grams × 0.10 = 22.7 grams of soda ash

Water for the Dyebath
WOF × 20 = ml of water to use for the dyebath
227 grams × 20 = 4540 ml of water

Amount of Dyestock Needed
WOF × DOS = total amount of dyestock to use
227 grams × 1.5 = 340.5 ml of dyestock to use

STEP-BY-STEP PROCEDURE FOR USING SABRACRON F DYES

1. Weigh clean dry fiber to be dyed.
2. Wet clean weighed fiber in hot water and Synthrapol for at least 30 minutes (soak silk; simmer cotton and other cellulose fibers).
3. Choose or make up a dye formula to use, and decide on DOS.
4. Figure and measure amounts of salt and soda ash.
5. Figure and measure amounts of each dyestock needed.
6. Figure the dye/water ratio, measure the appropriate amount of 110°F water and put it in a bucket or dyepot.
7. Add the measured amounts of salt to the water and stir. Add measured amounts of the dyestocks to the water and stir.
8. Add the wet, soaked fiber to the dyepot. Let it soak there, flipping or rotating it often to ensure good dye penetration.
9. Dissolve the soda ash in a little hot water. About 30 to 40 minutes after putting the fiber in the dyebath, lift it out, add the soda ash, stir well, and replace the fiber.
10. Leave the fiber in the dyebath for about one hour, flipping or turning it regularly. After one hour, remove the fiber, squeezing out excess moisture.
11. Rinse the fiber in several changes of lukewarm water. Now agitate the fiber in hot sudsy water for a few minutes, let it soak for a few minutes, then change the water. Repeat several times, continuing for about 30 minutes. Continue rinsing the fiber in hot water until it rinses clear.
12. Use spin cycle of washer to remove excess moisture from the fiber, then spread it out to dry.
13. Dispose of the dyebath.

takes a higher DOS number to obtain the same value as blue. Use the chart on page 77 for a starting point, and use your best judgment for adjusting the DOS number down or up.

Figuring how much water to use with Sabracron F dyes

The amount of water used is important with Sabracron F dyes. If too much water is present, the reaction will take too long or not happen at all. The ideal ratio is twenty parts water to one part fiber. This is only half as much water as you used with Sabraset dyes, so be sure to tease apart the fiber prior to dyeing to ensure even coverage. Moving fiber often during the dyeing is also helpful, and you don't have to worry about felting with cellulose fibers. Use this equation to figure the amount of water needed for a dyebath:

WOF × 20 = amount of water to put in the dyepot (ml)

Using dye formulas to figure how much of each dyestock is needed

The calculations for using Sabracron F dyes are the same as for using Sabraset dyes. Follow these steps:

Get out your calculator. Multiply the WOF (in grams) times the depth of shade (DOS) number chosen to figure the total amount of dyestock to put in the dyepot:

WOF × DOS = total amount of dyestock to use (ml)

Then figure how much of each separate color of dyestock is needed by using the dye formula (see chart on page 84). One at a time, put the percentage number for each color into the following equation:

(Total amount of dyestock needed) × (% of color A) = amount of color A dyestock to put in dyebath (ml)

Use this equation for each dye color in the formula. It's a good idea to calculate the amounts, then add them up to make sure they equal the expected total. Cross-check the numbers before you start measuring out the dyestocks.

Advice on using Sabracron F dyes

The box on page 75 gives step-by-step directions for the Sabracron F dye procedure and there's a worksheet for doing calculations on page 229. Here are some pointers that will help you get the best possible results.

First, weigh the fiber you plan to dye. Unlike wool fleece, most of the cellulose fiber and silk that you buy is very clean so you don't have to wash it before you weigh it. Measure the weight to the nearest gram for the weight of fiber (WOF) number.

To wet silk, fill a bucket or sink with very warm (about 110 to 130°F) tap water, stir in about five ml of Synthrapol, then add the silk and let it soak at least thirty minutes. Soaking in hot water is sufficient preparation for silk, but to maximize the dye penetration for cotton and other cellulose fibers, put the weighed fiber in a pot with one to two ml of Synthrapol per four liters of water, then heat and simmer for thirty minutes. Rinse the fiber and it is ready to be dyed.

While the fiber is soaking or simmering, make your calculations and figure out how much water, salt, soda ash, and dyestocks to use. Since you don't need to heat the dyebath for Sabracron F, you can do the dyeing in a plastic bucket or a regular dyepot. Measure out the required amount of warm water (about 110°F) and pour it into the dyepot. Add the measured amount of salt and stir until it is completely dissolved. Add the measured amounts of dyestocks and stir well.

Add the wetted fiber. Let it soak in the dyebath, flipping it regularly to ensure even dyeing. Meanwhile, dissolve the measured amount of soda ash in a little hot water. About thirty to forty minutes after you put the fiber in the dyebath, lift it out, add the dissolved soda ash, stir well, then replace the fiber. Leave the fiber in the dyebath for another hour, flipping or moving it regularly. At the end of the hour, lift the fiber gently from the dyepot and squeeze out as much of the moisture as possible.

Rinsing involves several steps. First, rinse the fiber in several changes of clear lukewarm water. Next, add a small spoonful of Orvus detergent to hot water and immerse the fiber. Gently squeeze or agitate the fiber for a few minutes, then let it soak for a few minutes, then change the water, adding more Orvus if a lot of dye is coming out. Repeat the agitating, soaking, and changing several times over a span of about a half hour. When less color is coming out, continue rinsing with hot water (no detergent) until the rinse water remains clear. If the fiber is not rinsed until clear, the dye will crock (rub) off at a later point in time. When rinsing is complete, use the spin cycle of the washer to extract extra moisture from the fiber, tease it loose, then lay it out to dry.

Dispose of the dyebath. It may look colored, but any dye left is bonded to the water so you can't use it to dye more fiber. Add some vinegar to bring the solution close to neutral. It will bubble up when you add the vinegar, but that's okay. Pour the dyebath down the drain, followed by plenty of water.

DYEING LUXURY FIBERS AND NATURALLY COLORED FIBERS

Dyeing luxury fibers is not any harder than dyeing wool if you use appropriate techniques for preparing and handling each fiber. Any luxury fiber can be dyed alone in a dyepot, or you can dye different fibers, including wool, at the same time. Different fibers accept dyes at different rates, so if you dye several fibers at a time, there

Procedure for Sabracron F dyes.

1. Weigh clean, dry fiber to be dyed.

2. Simmer cotton in water and Synthrapol for thirty minutes.

3. Measure dyes, salt, and water for dyebath.

4. Put measured ingredients into plastic bucket, stir, and add fiber.

5. Rotate fiber often to ensure even dyeing.

6. Check time, remove fiber, add the soda ash to dyebath, stir, return fiber to bucket.

7. Continue to flip and move fiber regularly for an hour.

8. Rinse fiber thoroughly until water remains clear.

9. Tease wet fiber apart and spread it to dry.

will be more color variation than if each fiber is dyed alone.

For good dye penetration and even results, you need to loosen or tease open any luxury fiber before you dye it. After dyeing, you must loosen and fluff the fiber again. Do this before it dries. It's much easier to pull apart dyed fibers while they are still damp. It's very frustrating, and damaging to the fibers, to try pulling them apart after they dry.

Alpaca and mohair

Alpaca and mohair can go into a dyepot with wool. These fibers easily separate from the wool after the dye process is complete. Mohair absorbs dye readily and has a luster that enhances the colors. I mostly dye scoured locks of kid mohair, which is easy to separate from wool in the dyepot. Mohair top also dyes well, if it has been pulled apart and teased thoroughly before immersion in the dyebath. Dyeing top gives more homogeneous results. Locks usually show some color variation, but that disappears when you card the mohair later. When dyed at the same time as wool, mohair dyes a little darker.

Natural white alpaca top is good for dyeing. It's nice and clean (alpaca fleece sometimes has a lot of hay in it), easy to tease apart, and it doesn't mat readily in the dyepot. When dyed at the same time as wool, alpaca ends up a little lighter. Alpaca typically has hairy fibers throughout that do not dye consistently. This gives an allover heather effect.

Angora and down fibers

I put luxury fibers such as angora, camel down, and cashmere into nylon net lingerie bags for dyeing. This keeps the fiber from drifting apart in the dyebath. Take the time to thoroughly tease open the fiber before placing it in the bag, and don't stuff the bag too full, or the fiber will not dye evenly. When I'm dyeing bags of luxury fiber and wool fleece in the same dyepot, I place the bags at the sides of the dyepot and the layered fiber in the middle. During dyeing, the fibers are moved and turned, but not stirred. That keeps matting to a minimum.

Angora dyes beautifully. I use either sheared German angora or plucked English angora. When dyed at the same time as wool, angora ends up about two shades lighter. Some angora has hairs that do not dye; this makes the color appear a little lighter than it would if all the fiber dyed evenly. Do not be alarmed if angora looks matted and sad when wet. After drying, the fiber fluffs up again.

Camel down dyes very deep and evenly. Because of its natural color, the dyed colors are not as bright as the same colors dyed on white fiber, but they are rich and beautiful. I use grade A dehaired camel down. Cashmere also dyes easily, but not as bright as white wool in the same dyebath. The final color depends on the original color of the cashmere. For both camel down and cashmere, the down fibers dye well, but any hair fibers do not.

Silk

I prefer to dye combed silk fibers, which you can buy in top or brick form. You can also dye silk noil or other forms of silk. Combed silk needs careful handling and is difficult to dye evenly. Tussah silk typically absorbs dye more readily than bombyx silk does.

For dyeing with Sabraset dyes, I prepare the silk by pulling off short lengths of the top or brick and spreading the fibers out to a thin film. Then I stack up alternate layers of wool and the well-loosened silk. The wool holds apart the layers of silk and lets the dye penetrate better. It is very important to soak the layered fiber in hot water with about four to eight ml of Synthrapol added. The silk is ready for the dyepot when it looks transparent in the water. To preserve the layered arrangement during dyeing, the layered fiber must be flipped over, not stirred. After rinsing, separate the silk from the wool while the fibers are still wet. While wet, the layers easily peel apart, but if you wait till they dry, they stick together.

To dye silk with Sabracron F dyes, the important thing is to tease the fiber. The dye won't penetrate wads or clumps well. You can put the teased fiber in a lingerie bag if you want to, but don't stuff the bag full.

Silk looks like old dishrags when it's wet. Don't be alarmed when you see this. The fiber will return to normal when it's dry.

Natural-colored fibers

Can you dye fibers that are not white to begin with? Of course you can! In fact, dyeing natural colors extends the color possibilities within a single dyepot. Fibers that are naturally white, beige, tan, camel, silver-gray, or dark gray can all be dyed in the same pot, producing a range of different but closely related colors.

There's one thing to remember: A dye color will not show up on a fiber if it's lighter than the original color of the fiber. For example, you can hardly see a pale yellow dye on a dark gray alpaca. The darker the natural color of the fiber, the higher the DOS must be to show up. Also, dye colors appear duller when dyed over natural colors. Gray fibers, in particular, tend to dull the color. Natural tans, camel, or moorit act almost like yellow, especially when they are dyed with blue.

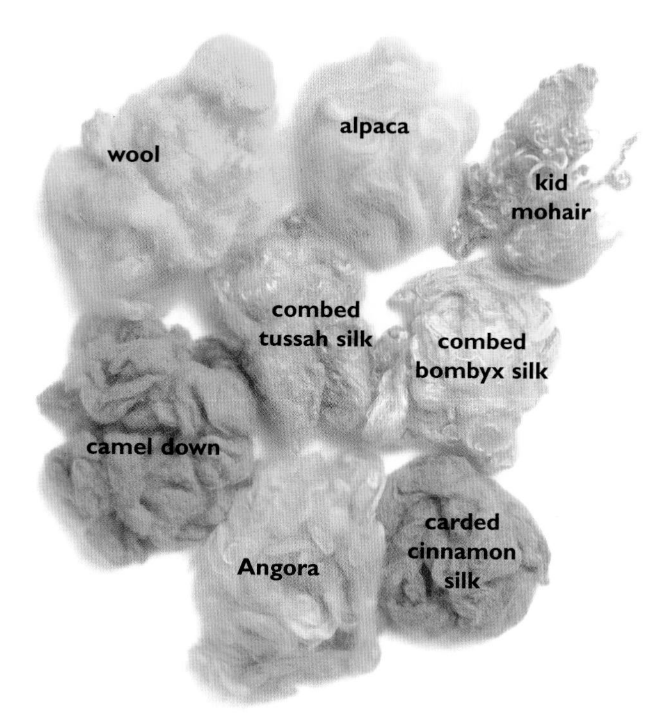

Assorted protein fibers dyed in the same dyebath.

DYE FORMULAS FOR SABRASET DYES

These formulas provide a good basic palette including a wide range of hues and intensities. These intensities can be varied by using higher or lower DOS.

No.	Color	DOS	Dye	Dye	Dye	Dye
1.	Intense Yellow	DOS 2	2% mustard yellow	98% sun yellow		
2.	Dull Yellow	DOS 1	98% sun yellow	2% violet		
3.	Dark Yellow	DOS 3	80% sun yellow	20% jet black		
4.	Yellow	DOS .5	45% mustard yellow	55% sun yellow		
5.	Yellow Orange	DOS 2	90% mustard yellow	10% sun yellow		
6.	Dull Yellow Orange	DOS 1	90% mustard yellow	10% violet		
7.	Dark Yellow Orange	DOS 3	75% mustard yellow	25% jet black		
8.	Yellow Orange	DOS .5	90% mustard yellow	7% deep red	3% turquoise	
9.	Orange	DOS 2	42% mustard yellow	45% sun yellow	13% 338 WF Acid Magenta	
10.	Dull Orange	DOS 1	35% mustard yellow 3% royal blue	40% sun yellow 2% turquoise	20% 338 WF Acid Magenta	
11.	Dark Orange	DOS 3	29% mustard yellow 16% jet black	31% sun yellow	24% 338 WF Acid Magenta	
12.	Orange	DOS .5	85% mustard yellow	15% deep red		
13.	Red Orange	DOS 2	20% mustard yellow 12% scarlet	50% sun yellow	18% 338 WF Acid Magenta	
14.	Dull Red Orange	DOS 1	14% mustard yellow 9% scarlet	37% sun yellow 12% turquoise	28% 338 WF Acid Magenta	
15.	Dark Red Orange	DOS 3	60% mustard yellow	10% deep red	10% magenta	20% jet black
16.	Red Orange	DOS .5	40% mustard yellow	20% sun yellow	30% deep red	10% magenta
17.	Intense Red	DOS 2	45% sun yellow	55% 338 WF Acid Magenta		
18.	Dull Red	DOS 1	42% sun yellow 5% turquoise	8% magenta	45% 338 WF Acid Magenta	
19.	Dark Red	DOS 3	8% sun yellow 20% jet black	12% deep red	60% 338 WF Acid Magenta	
20.	Red	DOS .5	10% sun yellow 30% scarlet	30% deep red	30% 338 WF Acid Magenta	
21.	Intense Cool Red	DOS 2	100% 338 WF Acid Magenta			
22.	Dull Cool Red	DOS 1	13% sun yellow 12% violet	50% magenta 5% jet black	20% 338 WF Acid Magenta	
23.	Dark Cool Red	DOS 3	30% magenta 10% jet black	5% violet	55% 338 WF Acid Magenta	
24.	Cool Red	DOS .5	10% sun yellow 5% violet	40% scarlet	45% 338 WF Acid Magenta	
25.	Red Violet	DOS 2	13% scarlet 53% violet	9% magenta	25% 338 WF Acid Magenta	
26.	Dull Red Violet	DOS 1 9% magenta	15% sun yellow 50% violet	13% scarlet	13% 338 WF Acid Magenta	

DYE FORMULAS FOR SABRASET DYES CONTINUED

These dye formulas can be varied by using higher or lower DOS.

27. Dark Red Violet	DOS 3	25% scarlet	10% magenta	50% violet	15% jet black
28. Red Violet	DOS .5	30% scarlet	20% magenta	50% violet	
29. Intense Violet	DOS 2	10% scarlet	5% magenta	80% violet	5% turquoise
30. Dull Violet	DOS 1	20% sun yellow 4% turquoise	8% scarlet	4% magenta	64% violet
31. Dark Violet	DOS 3	9% scarlet	5% magenta 10% jet black	71% violet	5% turquoise
32. Violet	DOS .5	90% violet	2% turquoise	8% 338 WF Acid Magenta	
33. Blue Violet	DOS 2	85% violet	5% royal blue	10% turquoise	
34. Dull Blue Violet	DOS 1	20% mustard yellow	68% violet	4% royal blue	8% turquoise
35. Dark Blue Violet	DOS 3	72% violet	9% navy	4% turquoise	15% jet black
36. Blue Violet	DOS .5	80% violet	20% royal blue		
37. Blue	DOS 2	10% violet	80% royal blue	10% turquoise	
38. Dull Blue	DOS 1 68% royal blue	14% sun yellow 7% turquoise	9% violet	2% 338 WF Acid Magenta	
39. Dark Blue	DOS 3	8% violet 15% jet black	34% royal blue	34% navy	9% turquoise
40. Blue	DOS .5	10% violet	60% royal blue	30% turquoise	
41. Blue Green	DOS 2	19% mustard yellow	4% violet	64% royal blue	13% turquoise
42. Dull Blue Green	DOS 1	14% sun yellow 68% turquoise	6% scarlet	4% violet	8% royal blue
43. Dark Blue Green	DOS 3	4% violet	8% royal blue	68% turquoise	20% jet black
44. Blue Green	DOS .5	20% royal blue	80% turquoise		
45. Green Blue	DOS 2	18% sun yellow	12% royal blue	70% turquoise	
46. Dull Green Blue	DOS 1	9% mustard yellow 60% turquoise	15% sun yellow	6% deep red	10% royal blue
47. Dark Green Blue	DOS 3	16% sun yellow	11% royal blue	63% turquoise	10% jet black
48. Green Blue	DOS .5	20% mustard yellow	20% royal blue	60% turquoise	
49. Green	DOS 2	70% sun yellow	30% turquoise		
50. Dull Green	DOS 1	43% sun yellow	15% deep red	32% royal blue	10% turquoise
51. Dark Green	DOS 3	56% sun yellow	8% navy	16% turquoise	20% jet black
52. Green	DOS .5	70% mustard yellow	30% turquoise		
53. Yellow Green	DOS 2	90% sun yellow	10% turquoise		
54. Dull Yellow Green	DOS 1	72% sun yellow 9% turquoise	8% 338 WF Acid Magenta		11% violet
55. Dark Yellow Green	DOS 3	70% sun yellow	10% turquoise	20% jet black	
56. Yellow Green	DOS .5	90% mustard yellow	5% royal blue	5% navy	

DYE FORMULAS FOR SABRACRON F DYES

This is a basic palette including a wide range of hues.
The intensities can be varied by using a higher or lower DOS.

Color	DOS	Dye 1	Dye 2	Dye 3	Dye 4
1. Lemon Yellow	DOS 3	100% sun yellow			
2. Buttercup Yellow	DOS 3	50% sun yellow	50% gold yellow		
3. Cornsilk	DOS 3	98% sun yellow	2% fuchsia		
4. Golden Yellow Orange	DOS 3	80% gold yellow	20% flame scarlet		
5. Subdued Yellow Orange	DOS 3	40% sun yellow	40% gold yellow	10% flame scarlet	10% royal purple
6. Bright Yellow Orange	DOS 3	85% sun yellow	15% true red		
7. Bright Orange	DOS 3	50% sun yellow	50% flame scarlet		
8. Salmon	DOS 3	65% gold yellow	35% true red		
9. Cantaloupe	DOS 3	35% sun yellow	40% gold yellow	25% fuchsia	
10. Shrimp	DOS 3	85% flame scarlet	15% true red		
11. Intense Red Orange	DOS 3	35% sun yellow	25% gold yellow	40% fuchsia	
12. Medium Red Orange	DOS 3	5% sun yellow	90% flame scarlet	5% fuchsia	
13. Warm Red	DOS 3	25% fuchsia	75% flame scarlet		
14. Red	DOS 3	30% fuchsia	60% true red	10% scarlet	
15. Cool Red	DOS 3	85% fuchsia	15% true red		
16. Red Violet	DOS 3	15% true red	10% fuchsia	75% royal purple	
17. Intense Red Violet	DOS 3	75% fuchsia	25% brilliant blue 42		
18. Rich Red Violet	DOS 3	25% true red	10% brilliant blue 42	65% royal purple	
19. Grape	DOS 3	65% fuchsia	35% deep navy		
20. Bright Violet	DOS 3	20% fuchsia	5% true red	75% brilliant blue 42	
21. Violet	DOS 3	10% true red	60% royal purple	30% brilliant blue 42	
22. Cornflower	DOS 3	25% fuchsia	75% brilliant blue 42		
23. Intense Lavender	DOS 3	25% royal purple	65% brilliant blue 42	10% deep navy	
24. Blue Violet	DOS 3	25% fuchsia	10% royal purple	65% deep navy	
25. Cool Blue	DOS 3	70% brilliant blue 42	15% turquoise	15% royal purple	
26. Intense Blue	DOS 3	15% fuchsia	70% brilliant blue 42	15% deep navy	
27. Blue Azure	DOS 3	75% brilliant blue 42	25% turquoise		
28. Deep Blue Green	DOS 3	25% gold yellow	50% brilliant blue 42	25% deep navy	
29. Intense Blue Green	DOS 3	15% gold yellow	35% brilliant blue 42	50% turquoise	
30. Deep Sea	DOS 3	20% sun yellow	80% brilliant blue 42		
31. Deep Green	DOS 3	80% sun yellow	20% deep navy		
32. Intense Green	DOS 3	45% gold yellow	30% brilliant blue 42	25% turquoise	
33. Green	DOS 3	40% sun yellow	30% gold yellow	30% brilliant blue 42	
34. Young Green	DOS 3	85% sun yellow	15% brilliant blue 42		
35. Deep Yellow Green	DOS 3	40% sun yellow	35% gold yellow	25% deep navy	
36. Yellow Green	DOS 3	75% gold yellow	15% turquoise	10% brilliant blue 42	

chapter 3 chapter chapter

Painting rovings for multicolored yarns

—3—

Painting rovings for multicolored yarns

There's more than one way to dye fiber. Chapter 2 explains how to dye fibers by immersing them in a dyebath. This chapter explains how to paint dye onto fibers. Painting uses the same dyes as in Chapter 2, but in a different way.

THE BASICS OF PAINTING

To make painted rovings, you apply short stripes of different colors to commercially prepared rovings instead of dyeing the whole roving one solid color. Compared to immersion dyeing, painting has three advantages. First, it preserves the alignment of already prepared fibers. Many luxury fiber blends, as well as wool, come in "ready to spin" form. Painting the fibers is less disruptive than immersion-dyeing them. Second, painting is an easy and efficient way to design multicolored yarns for small projects. You dye only what you need for each project. Third, yarns spun from painted rovings have a more subtle appearance than multicolored yarns made by other techniques. Painting produces small, intense dots of colors because the fibers can be painted in areas much shorter than the staple length. You can't achieve this "pointillist" effect—small, distinct dots of color—with any other coloring technique.

After painted rovings are dyed and dry, pull them apart lengthwise into thin strips. You can spin strips from a single roving, or combine strips from two or more different rovings and spin them together to make complex and fascinating yarns.

The differences between painting and immersion dyeing

I use the same dyes and dye formulas for painting and for immersion dyeing. What changes is the way the dyestocks are prepared and applied to the fibers. When you are painting rovings:

The dye is put directly onto the fibers. In immersion dyeing, something "happens" in the dyepot while you wait and watch. In painting fibers, you deliberately place the dye where you want it, using brushes.

About twice as much dye is required for the WOF being dyed. This accounts for some waste and inefficiency but gives you a little "fudge factor" to work with, too.

No leveling agent is used. In immersion dyeing, some chemical assists in the dyepot regulate the evenness of the dye on the fiber. In painting, *you* regulate the leveling by doing your best to apply the dye evenly.

Regulating depth of shade (DOS) is different. In immersion dyeing, DOS is determined by the ratio between the amount of dye and the amount of fiber. In painting, the intensity of the dyed colors is determined by the concentration of the solution you paint with. The higher the concentration, the more intense the color.

The dye is set or cured in a separate step after you finish painting.

Japanese stencil brushes. These are ideal for painting rovings.

Equipment and facility requirements

The equipment used for painting is similar to that needed for immersion dyeing, with these additional requirements:

Coffee filters for testing dye colors. Get the white paper kind used in coffee machines.

Japanese stencil brushes. These are round, flat-bottomed brushes that come in sizes ranging from one-quarter-inch to two-inch diameter. Look for brushes that are made specifically for fiberwork. The stencil brushes meant for painting hard surfaces do not work quite as well.

Old towels for blotting up excess dye.

Paper towels for cleaning brushes and blotting.

Plastic cups to hold dyes. Short, squat nine-ounce cups work great. They hold enough dye for a painting job, and hardly ever tip over.

Plastic wrap to protect your work surface and wrap the rovings. Don't use the kind designed for microwaves—it gets too mushy. Other kinds work fine. Restaurant-supply places carry wide plastic wrap for large jobs.

Rack that fits inside your dyepot to support the rovings above an inch or so of water. This can be a vegetable steam rack, a cake rack, or anything else you can rig up.

Straight stick. This can be an old ruler, part of a yardstick, or a paint stirrer.

Tape measure for measuring color repeats on the rovings. Use a flat tape measure, not the roll-up kind.

The facilities for painting are similar to those for immersion dyeing. You'll need a heat source for steaming dyed fibers, an outlet for running water, a place to measure and mix dyes and chemicals, and a table or surface to paint fibers on. Preferably, the work surface should be at least two yards long, at whatever height is comfortable for you (this depends on whether you'd rather sit or stand as you work). Good lighting is always a plus. Finally, you need a rack or clothesline for hanging rovings to dry.

Choosing rovings to paint

Almost any commercially-made roving, top, or sliver can be painted, but some kinds hold together better than others. A roving that is densely compacted stays together through the steps of wetting, painting, rinsing, and stripping. Don't worry that it will be too dense to spin. Stripping opens up any dense configuration and makes the fiber very pleasant to spin. By contrast, loose rovings that are pleasant to spin "as is" are harder to handle for painting.

Compact rovings of most breeds of wool work fine for painting. Washable wool dyes beautifully, but tends to feel slimy when wet, and the top acts slippery. That's no surprise because the process that makes the wool machine-washable removes the scales that normally hold wool fibers together.

Alpaca and mohair behave fine in roving while dry, but must be handled gently when wet because the fibers tend to drift apart. Support the wet roving from underneath. Don't let the wet roving hang loose, or it will slip apart and end up in pieces. Treat any luxury fiber blend with care. Wet a small piece of the roving to see if it holds together before you start painting a whole batch.

Cotton preparations drift apart easily because of cotton's short staple length, but you can work with cotton if you tie both ends of a bundle of roving or braid lengths of roving together.

Pencil rovings or other very thin rovings are difficult to control when wet and impossible to strip, so I don't recommend them for painting.

Choosing values to paint. The top yarn uses a narrow range of values (most subtle). The middle uses only very dark and very light values (results in a "barber pole" effect). The bottom has light, medium, and dark values (appears most complex).

Choosing and combining colors to paint

All the color theories presented in Chapter 1 apply to painting rovings, and you may want to refer back to that chapter as you think about making the following choices.

Choosing values

From a distance, value is the first characteristic your eye perceives, so think carefully about the range of values you want to include in a yarn. The closer the values, the quieter or more subtle the final yarn will appear. The wider the range of values, the wilder or more dramatic the yarn appears. Wide differences in value tend to make the yarn look like a barber pole. To minimize "barber-poling", add some middle values.

Choosing hues

This is where all the color theory from Chapter 1 comes in handy. In particular, the *color harmonies* (see pages 40–45) work very well for designing painted rovings. Choosing a harmony limits the number of hue families. This is an easy way to focus yourself and not get overwhelmed by too many choices. Choosing closely related or analogous colors results in a more subtle yarn, but if your colors are too close together, the differences don't show up and the final yarn appears dull and muddy. Yarns based on complements are more exciting. Overall, the farther the chosen colors are from each other on the color wheel, the livelier the yarn.

It is hard to be too bold when choosing colors for painted rovings. Always use colors that are lighter and brighter than the desired finished yarn. Each roving you paint may not be appealing, but remember, each roving is *not* a finished yarn. Although you may not like certain colors side by side in the roving stage, when that roving is split and combined with

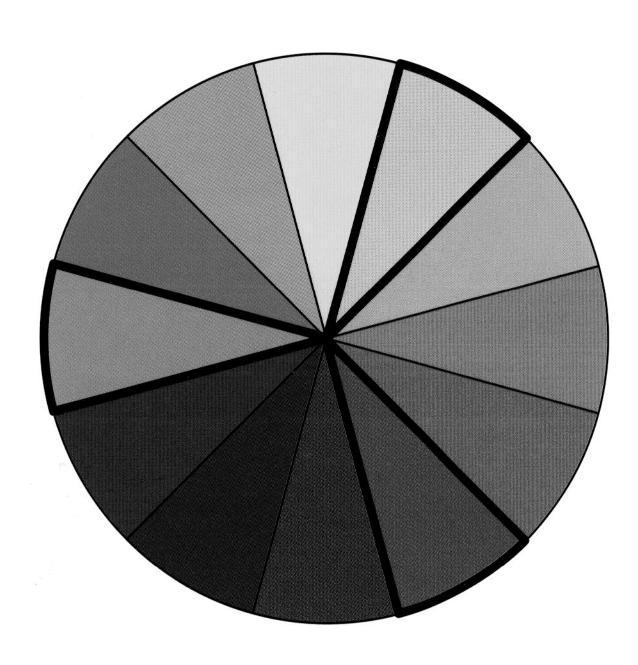

Using a color wheel to design painted rovings. A triad of yellow-orange, red-violet, and blue-green is used to choose the twelve colors used in the yarn at right.

Two ways to use a color harmony. The top skein and swatch were spun from the top roving which includes all twelve colors. The bottom skein and swatch were spun from the other three rovings (same twelve colors, four in each roving). Colors remain brighter when placed in several rovings, then spun together.

other rovings, it may add just the right touch to the final yarn.

Choosing saturation

The brightness or dullness of the colors you paint on a roving makes a difference in the appearance of the yarn. Brighter colors "pop out" more than dull colors. This phenomenon is accentuated when bright colors are placed next to dull colors.

How many colors to use

The sky is the limit on this. The final yarn tends to have a barber-pole or striped effect if fewer than six colors are used, especially if there is also a wide range of values. The yarns I design include between ten and forty colors, with the average around twelve to twenty-four. I choose certain hue families, then increase the total number of colors by picking several saturations and values from each family. This makes a rich, interesting yarn. Using lots of colors also reduces the perception of barber poling. When your eye is distracted by the number of colors and their interactions, it does not focus so much on the value contrasts.

How much of each color to use

The amount of each color you use affects the appearance of the yarn. For example, you might decide you want to have one hue dominate the yarn. Instead of using a large amount of a single color, however, the yarn will look much more special and one-of-a-kind if you choose several related colors from that hue family. For example, if you want a yarn that is predominantly green, you could choose twelve colors to combine, such as eight shades of green—kelly green, forest green, dull medium green,

Making a hue family dominant. The bottom left roving uses blue, mint green, kelly green, and lime; the one above it uses olive, forest, cornflower, and dull medium green; the roving at top left uses gray green, blue lavender, rust, and khaki. The roving at right combines the other three.

gray-green, lime green, bright mint green, olive green, and khaki—and four other colors: royal blue, cornflower, light blue-lavender, and rusty brown. When colors are used together this way, the yarn gives the overall impression of green, but it's a fascinating green, not just a simple green.

I usually use equal amounts of each selected color for a roving. This makes it a lot easier to figure how much of each dyestock I need. If I want one hue family to dominate the yarn, I choose at least half the colors from that family.

When warm and cool colors are used in the same yarn, it takes a larger quantity of cool colors to appear equal to the quantity of warm. Warm colors are more aggressive and will dominate a color combination faster, especially if the saturations of the warm colors are brighter.

How long should each stripe be?

The longer the stripe you paint on a roving, the longer that color appears in the yarn. The longer a color appears in the yarn, the more striped the finished fabric appears. For example, if you paint a four-inch red stripe on a roving, then strip the roving into twenty-four strips and spin the strips into a singles yarn, you might end up with one-foot red stripes in the yarn. If the stripe on the roving is one-inch long, it will appear in the yarn for only three inches, not one foot. A three-inch length of color in a yarn may make four to six stitches in knitting, whereas a one-foot stripe shows up much longer in knitting. Of course, all this depends on how thin you spin the yarn. The thinner you spin, the more important it is to paint short stripes. For example, a one-inch stripe on a roving could end up as a three-inch stripe in a 1,000 yd/lb yarn, or a nine-inch stripe in a 3,000 yd/lb yarn.

My rule of thumb is to paint stripes no longer than three inches. Making stripes longer than that defeats my purpose. I want to paint stripes shorter than the staple length of the fibers being

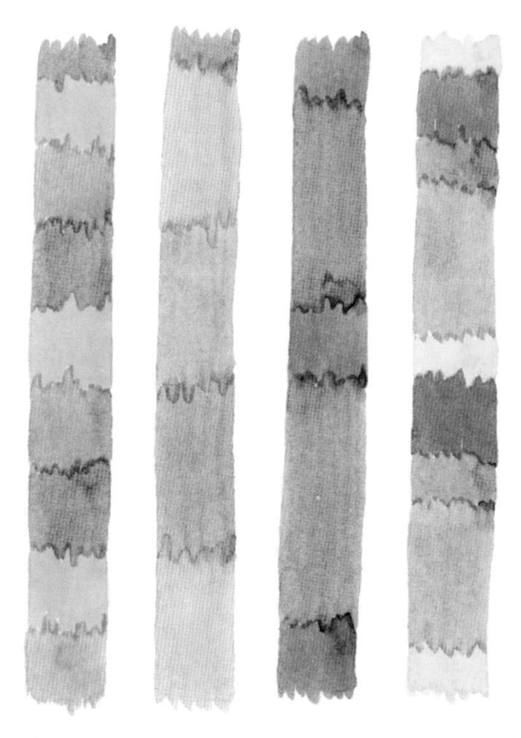

Examples of stripe sequences to paint onto rovings. Left to right: one inch of each color; two inches of each color; alternating one-inch and three-inch stripes; One-half-inch, two-inch, one-half-inch, one-inch repeat.

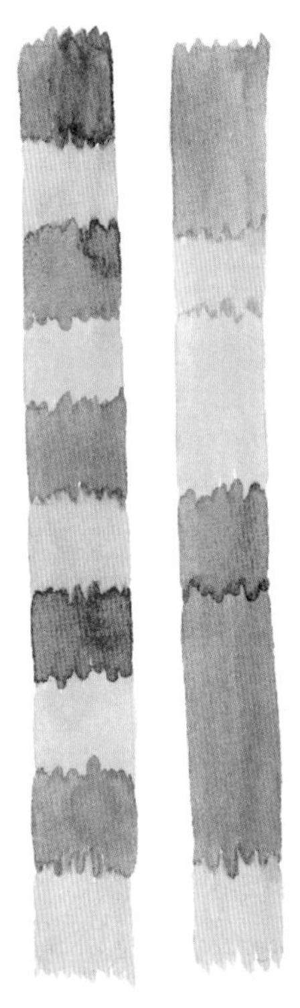

Lengths of color repeats on rovings. Left roving has a four-inch repeat, one inch each of four colors; the right roving has a seven-inch repeat with the sequence of one inch, three inches, one inch, two inches of the same four colors.

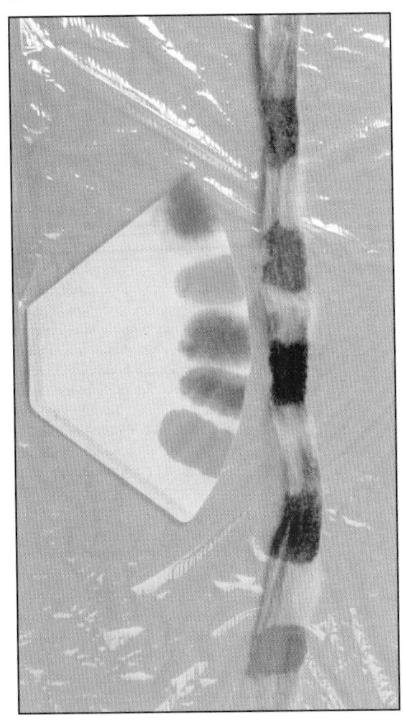

Make samples. Test dye formulas on coffee filters first, then make a sample roving. The roving can be cut up later and put into a dye notebook.

painted. This gives the most exciting results, and for me, the more complex yarns. (For simple color effects, I use other preparation methods, which are faster.)

The stripes on a roving don't all need to be the same length. Varying the stripe length is a good way to make colors become dominant or act as accents. Painting short stripes of varied lengths makes the most unique yarns.

How long should the repeat be?

Stripes of different colors are arranged in a regular sequence that you repeat along the length of the roving. This design element—the length of the repeat—affects the appearance of the yarn. The longer the repeat on the roving, the longer it takes for the colors to repeat in the yarn. It helps if you have a project in mind when you paint your rovings. If you are planning to knit a vest in the round, for example, you may want a long repeat, but for knitting a hat in the round, the length of the repeat will be shorter, so color changes will appear more often. Knitting something back and forth may call for a different repeat length.

When designing several rovings for a yarn, use different repeat lengths. That way, when strips of the rovings are placed side by side for spinning, the colors will interact in ever changing ways, creating a more complex yarn.

Testing and fine-tuning your choices

Once you're made design choices, figured dye formulas, and mixed some dyes, it's time to test the colors to see if they give the desired effect. First test dye colors by painting them on white coffee filters. This will give you a general idea of what the colors look like. Then fine-tune the dye formulas, adding drops of this or that, and test again.

When you're pleased with how the colors look on the coffee filters, move to fibers. Soak a portion of a roving, squeeze out as much water as possible, and paint a test swatch of each color onto the fiber, leaving one-half-inch strips of bare fiber between colors. Look at the colors on the fiber and decide how you want to arrange them. Later, you can cut the roving between colors and put the separate color samples in your dye notebook, along with their formulas. When you've decided how you want to arrange the colors and how long the individual stripes and overall repeats should be, make notes or a sketch that you can refer to when you start to do the actual painting.

PAINTING PROTEIN-FIBER ROVINGS WITH SABRASET DYES

1. *Measure and weigh rovings to be painted.* The amount of dye to use is based on the weight of fiber (WOF) to be painted. I limit the length of each roving to no longer than six feet or the weight to no more than one ounce, whichever comes first. Anything longer than six feet is hard to manage in the painting and stripping steps. Standardizing the length of all the rovings simplifies the rest of the procedure.
2. *Soak weighed rovings.* Dissolve one-half teaspoon of Synthrapol per pound of roving in a bucket of hot water. Submerge and soak the fibers for at least thirty minutes or until the fibers are completely wet. Silk needs to soak for a couple of hours.
3. *Choose dye formulas and depth of shade, and calculate the amount of each dyestock to use.* Decide how many colors you want to paint on the roving, and what depth of shade (DOS) you want for each color. Group the colors according to DOS. Remember that painting uses twice as much dye as immersion dyeing for the same WOF. Now you have to do calculations for each DOS and each color.

   a. For each DOS, use this equation:

   (WOF × DOS × 2) = (total number of colors) = (amount of dye required for each color used at that DOS (ml)

   b. Then, for each color that you want to mix, figure how much of each separate color of dyestock is needed by using the dye formula. For any color, put the percentage number (from the dye formula) into the following equation:

   (Amount of dye needed for each color) × (% of dyestock A) = (amount of dyestock A to measure out (ml)
4. *Measure and mix the dyestocks.* For most painting projects I mix the dyes in short nine-ounce plastic cocktail cups. I mix all the dye colors for the roving at the same time. I start out with the first dyestock color on the dye record sheet and put the measured amount of that dyestock color in each cup that needs it. Then I move on to the next dyestock color and add it to each cup as needed, continuing until each cup holds all the required colors of dyestock.
5. *Regulate the depth of shade (DOS).* If you have chosen more than one DOS, the cups of dye won't all be filled to the same level. They will all have the same *concentration* of dye, but different *amounts* of dye. Before painting, you need to reverse this situation by filling all the cups to the same level. Then they'll all have the same *amount of dye*, but they'll be at *different* concentrations. Taking this step regulates the DOS that ends up on the roving.

   The liquid you add is a solution of one part acetic acid and ninety-nine parts water. I call it "chemical water"; it keeps the pH the same in all the dye cups.

   Here's how to proceed. Since the range of DOS used with these dyes is between .1 and 3, DOS 3 is the most intense a color will be. That is the point of reference for the total volume of liquid needed in each cup—the volume of dye used for a color at a DOS of 3.

   WOF × 6 = Total volume of liquid needed in dye cup at DOS 3 (ml)

Calculations for painting with Sabraset dyestocks.

Four colors for painting 28.4 grams (1 ounce) of roving

Color A at DOS 1:	100% scarlet
Color B at DOS 1:	50% yellow, 50% magenta
Color C at DOS 0.5:	25% magenta, 75% blue
Color D at DOS 3:	40% violet, 60% magenta

AMOUNT OF DYESTOCK NEEDED FOR EACH DOS USED ON THE ROVING

(WOF × DOS × 2) ÷ (total number of colors) = amount of dyestock required for each color or cup used at that DOS (ml)

(28 grams × 1 × 2) ÷ 4 = 14 ml dyestock needed for each color at DOS 1

(28 grams × 0.5 × 2) ÷ 4 = 7 ml dyestock needed for each color at DOS 0.5

(28 grams × 3 × 2) ÷ 4 = 42 ml dyestock needed for each color at DOS 3

AMOUNT OF DYESTOCK TO USE FOR EACH COLOR

Multiply the total amount of dyestock needed for each color (this depends on DOS, as you've already figured) times the percent for each dyestock in that dye formula.

Color A at DOS 1—100% scarlet
14 ml × 1.0 (100%) = 14 ml of scarlet dyestock

Color B at DOS 1—50% yellow, 50% magenta
14 ml × 0.50 = 7 ml of yellow dyestock
14 ml × 0.50 = 7 ml of magenta dyestock

Color C at DOS 0.5—25% magenta, 75% blue
7 ml × 0.25 = 1.7 ml of magenta dyestock
7 ml × 0.75 = 5.2 ml of blue dyestock

Color D at DOS 3—40% violet, 60% magenta
42 ml × 0.40 = 16.8 ml of violet dyestock
42 ml × 0.60 = 25.2 ml of magenta dyestock

ADDING "CHEMICAL WATER" TO REGULATE THE DOS

WOF × 6 ÷ number of colors = Total volume of liquid needed in dye cup

28 grams × 6 ÷ 4 = 42 ml liquid needed in each cup

Total volume of liquid – amount of dyestock = volume of chemical water to add to cup

Color A. 42 ml – 14 ml = 28 ml chemical water to add

Color B. 42 ml – 14 ml = 28 ml chemical water to add

Color C. 42 ml – 7 ml = 35 ml chemical water to add

Color D. 42 ml – 42 ml = 0 ml chemical water to add

AMOUNTS OF DYE ASSISTS TO ADD TO EACH CUP

(WOF × 4%) ÷ number of cups = amount of acetic acid to add to each cup

(28 grams × 0.04) ÷ 4 = .3 ml (rounded up) acetic acid to add to each cup

(WOF × 1%) ÷ number of cups = amount of sodium acetate to add to each cup

(28 grams × 0.01) ÷ 4 = .07 grams of sodium acetate to add to each cup

Regulating the DOS of dye for painting. Volume of liquid is the same in all three cups. The cup on the left is DOS 0.1; middle DOS 1.5; right DOS 3. The red represents the dyestock in the cup, the gray the amount of chemical water used.

If you're using any colors at DOS 3, you don't have to add any chemical water to those cups. For all the other cups, here is how to figure how much chemical water to add:

(Total volume of liquid needed) – (amount of dye in cup) = (amount of chemical water to put in that cup (ml)

Make the calculations, measure the required amount of chemical water, pour into dye cup, and stir. Double-check by making sure the cups are filled to the same level when you are done.

6. *Calculate the required amounts of acetic acid and sodium acetate, and add them to the dye cups.* Acetic acid and sodium acetate are the two chemical assists needed for painting with Sabraset dyes. They serve the same functions in painting as they do in immersion dyeing and they're added at the same proportions. Use these equations to calculate how much you need:

WOF × .04 = Total amount of acetic acid needed for whole roving (ml)

WOF × .01 = Total amount of sodium acetate needed (g)

Dividing the total amount of acetic acid needed by the number of colors determines how much to add to each cup. Measure the acetic acid in milliliters.

Weigh the total amount of sodium acetate powder needed and put it in an empty cup. Multiply the number of colors times two, measure that many milliliters of very hot water, add it to the sodium acetate, and stir until it is completely dissolved. Now add two milliliters of the solution to each dye cup. (Adding dissolved sodium acetate to the cups is easier and more accurate than trying to weigh the small portion of powder needed for each cup.)

Step-by-Step painting with Sabraset dyes.

1. Ready to paint. Plastic wrap is down, roving has been spread out, tape measure is in place, and straight stick is on the roving ready for the first stripe to be painted.

7. *Lay out the rovings.* Tear off a piece of plastic wrap a little longer than the length of the rovings being painted and spread it on the table. Carefully lift the rovings out of the soaking bucket (support them from underneath) and squeeze out as much water as possible. The rovings should not be drippy or squishy. If too much moisture is present, the dyes may "run" or wick down the rovings.

One at a time, lay a roving on the plastic wrap. Firmly hold one end of the roving with one hand. Place the other hand about ten inches away, and use it to put that ten-inch portion of roving under a little tension and fan the fibers open. Proceed down the length of the roving, repeating the tensioning and fanning-out steps. This helps eliminate any dense spots so the dye can penetrate evenly throughout. Do a careful job. If the fibers are nice and straight before painting, it's easier to strip the roving later.

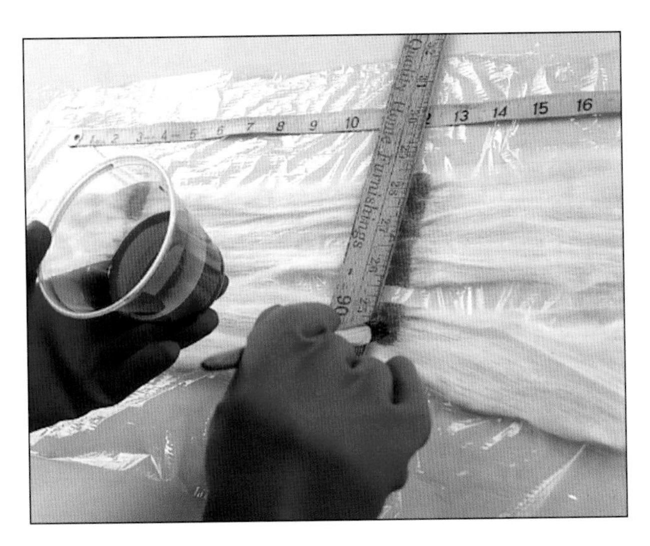

2. First color is being painted. Note: Do not apply pressure to the straight edge; colors will run underneath the stick. The straight edge is used to keep lines even. Move the brush firmly in an up-and-down staccato motion.

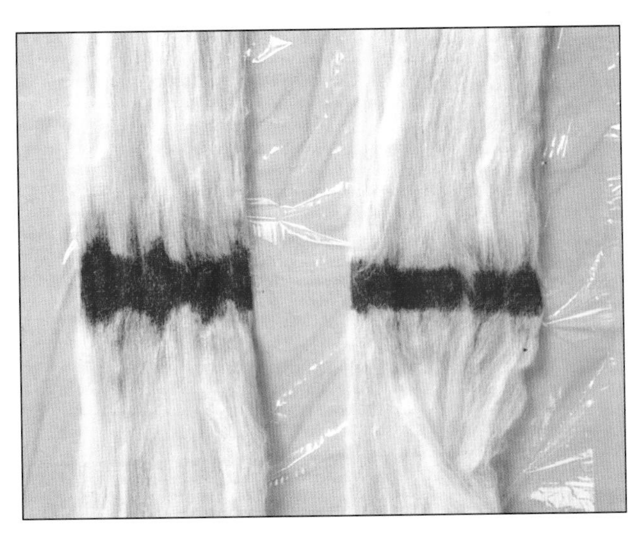

3. Painting dos and don'ts. In the sample at left, the brush was held on fibers too long and not overlapped enough. The roving on the right looks like it is supposed to.

Lay a flat tape measure parallel to the roving on the table. This will be a guide for placing the stripes.

Get out your notes or sketch of how the colors will be arranged and how long the stripes and repeats should be, so you can refer to this plan as you do the actual painting. It helps tremendously to have a plan of the stripe sequence, length of each color, and length of the repeats before you start to paint.

8. *Paint the rovings.* With the straight stick, cup of dye color A, a stencil brush, and the painting plan, you're ready to begin. Starting at one end of the roving, hold the straight stick across the top of the fiber. You'll use the stick as a guide to help keep the stripes straight. Paint the first stripe of color A. Use the tape measure to find the beginning of the next repeat, put the straight stick there, and paint the next stripe of color A. Continue until you have painted all the color A stripes. With a clean brush, paint all the color B stripes. The stick is not needed for B and subsequent colors; it is just required to keep the initial stripes straight.

There's a knack to using the brush effectively. Dip it one-half inch deep into the dye, then press it against the side of the cup to squeeze out any excess. Having too much dye in the brush makes the dyes run on the roving and muddies the colors.

Paint with a firm, staccato up and down motion. This pushes the dye into the roving at the precise location you choose. Stroking or rubbing a roving with the brush mats the fiber and makes the dye wick lengthwise, disturbing the stripe sequence. Each time you press the brush against the roving, it makes a dot of dye. These dots must overlap to ensure that the stripe forms a straight line. If they don't overlap enough, the row of dots will look like the profile of a snowman, not a straight line.

How much dye is enough, and how much is too much? Ideally, a small fuzzy "halo" of fibers should appear on top of the roving after it has been painted. If the roving looks soaked and there are puddles of dye on the plastic wrap, you've used too much. Quickly use a cloth or paper towel to sop up the excess before the colors run together, get muddy, and blur the stripes. If the roving looks motley and dry, add a little more dye.

4.Turn roving over to paint the other side. Notice the white spots that need to be painted yet.

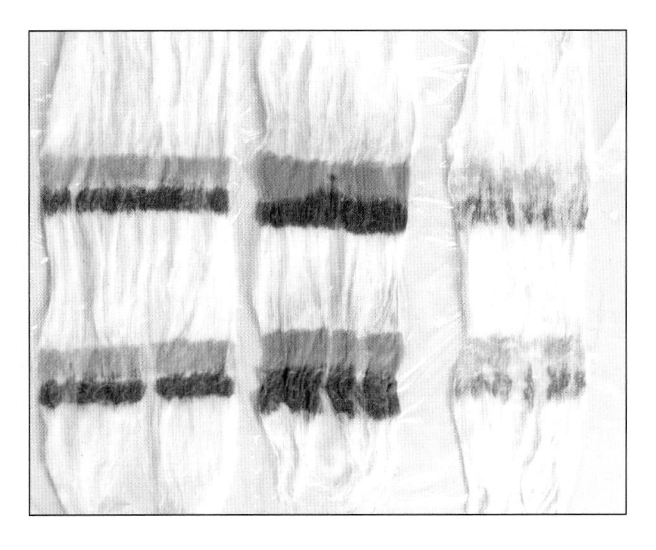

5. More dos and don'ts.The roving on the left is "just right".The middle one has too much dye—the colors are running and the surface looks soaked.The one at right does not have enough dye.

If you don't use enough dye, the result is lighter overall colors and a spottiness that makes the colors appear duller in the yarn.

9. *Touch up the other side of the rovings.* No matter how carefully the top side is painted, there are always some spots left unpainted on the bottom, so you need to turn over the rovings and touch up the bare spots. I flip rovings end to end, using my left hand to peel the roving off the plastic wrap and my right hand to support it.

   Smooth the flipped roving, if needed. Examine it closely. Check for the "halo" effect. If the roving looks soaked and squishes when you press it with your finger, there is too much dye. White spots and a dry look throughout indicate too little dye. The roving is just right if the "halo" is present and the colors seem saturated, but not soaked, throughout each stripe.

   If there's excess dye, mop it up. If there's a suitable amount of dye and just a few white spots, use your rubber-gloved finger to press on the roving and move the dye where it is needed. If this is unsuccessful, use the brush and add just a little more dye. The goal is to end up with solid dye coverage and crisp lines between colors. If the stripes are hazy or indistinct now, the colors will be even muddier and less distinct in the yarn.

10. *Cure and steam the rovings.* Let the painted rovings sit and rest in the open air. This step enables the dye to soak into the fibers properly. For wool and most protein fibers, sitting for thirty minutes is enough. The rovings are ready to steam when the dye has been absorbed. To check, use your rubber-gloved hand and press on the roving. If the glove comes up fairly clean, but wet, the rovings are ready to steam. If a lot of dye comes up on your glove, let the rovings sit longer. When you think the rovings are ready to steam, gently blot up any excess dye and moisture with an old towel. Do not blot hard, because too much pressure will cause the colors to lighten up more than they should. Just tap the towel lightly with your finger tips.

    Silk and silk-blend rovings need more time than wool. Let them sit overnight, if possible—this makes the colors more intense. However, when silk sits out all night, the rovings dry out, so spritz them with water before steaming them.

    Steaming the roving at 180°F for at least twenty minutes "sets" the dyes permanently

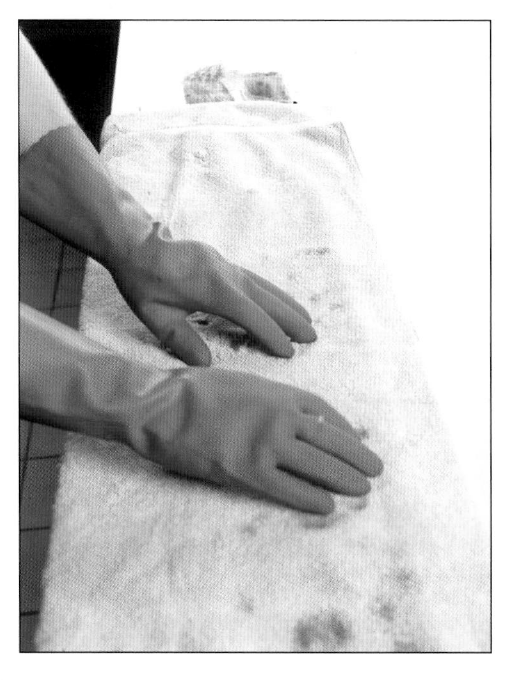

6. After the roving has cured, blot up excess dye *gently* with a towel. If you blot too hard, the roving will be much lighter than anticipated.

7. Fold the plastic wrap over the roving, then roll the roving into a coil to steam.

8. Rovings in dyepot used for steaming. The rovings are placed in the pot on a canning kettle base with cake cooling racks on top. Anything that elevates the rovings above the bottom of the dyepot will work.

9. After steaming, remove plastic and rinse the rovings until the water comes clear. Remember to support the rovings from underneath, so they do not drift apart.

10. Squeeze out any excess moisture and hang the roving to dry.

on the fibers. This substitutes for heating the dyebath in immersion dyeing. Steaming brings the dye and fiber to the required temperature without ruining the painted stripes.

Fold the plastic wrap around the rovings and roll them up. Put about one inch of water in the bottom of a dyepot, set your rack in place, then lay the wrapped rovings on the rack. Put the lid on the pot and turn on the heat. When the water boils and fills the pot with steam, start to time the twenty minutes. It's better to steam for longer than twenty minutes than not long enough. If you don't steam the rovings long enough, the dyes will rinse out. When the time is up, turn off the heat and let the rovings cool in the pot.

11. *Rinse and dry the rovings.* When the rovings have cooled enough to handle with ease, take them from the pot, carefully remove the plastic wrap, and rinse the rovings in warm water. Continue rinsing the rovings until the rinse water is clear. This should not take anymore than a few rinses. If dye continues to run after a few rinses, it means you used more dye than the fibers could absorb, or you didn't steam the rovings long enough. When the rinsing is complete, hang the fibers to dry.

STEP-BY STEP DIRECTIONS FOR PAINTING PROTEIN-FIBER ROVINGS WITH SABRASET DYES

1. Measure and weigh rovings to be painted. Divide into lengths shorter than six feet.
2. Soak weighed rovings in hot water with Synthrapol added.
3. Choose dye formulas and depth of shade. Calculate the amount of each dyestock to use.
4. Measure and mix the dyestocks. Put each color in its own cup.
5. Regulate the DOS by adding "chemical water" to the cups as needed.
6. Calculate the required amounts of acetic acid and sodium acetate and add them to the dye cups.
7. Lay out the rovings.
8. Paint the top side of the rovings according to your plan.
9. Flip over the rovings and touch up the other side.
10. Cure and steam the rovings.
11. Rinse and dry the rovings.

PAINTING COTTON ROVINGS WITH SABRACRON F DYES

The design elements and color choices for painted rovings are the same no matter what dyes you use or what fibers you paint. There are several differences, though, in how the dyes work on the fibers and how the rovings themselves react. You can use Sabracron F dyes to paint any kind of cellulose-fiber roving, but I'll use cotton as an example here.

Painting on cotton poses some unique problems. First, waxy compounds on the surface of cotton fibers make it hard for water and dye to penetrate and wet the fiber. Second, a mass of cotton fiber compresses when wet and resists dye penetration. After dyeing, cotton remains compressed and matted, which can make dyed cotton hard to spin. Third, because of the short staple length, cotton rovings tend to drift or pull apart when wet. This causes problems when you're wetting and handling them and during the extensive rinsing required for fiber-reactive dyes. Finally, the time span for using Sabracron F dyes after soda ash has been added is about one hour, which is not necessarily enough time to complete painting. Solutions to these problems are explained in the step-by-step directions.

Another problem with painting cotton should be addressed at the design stage. Colors wick further along cotton rovings than on protein-fiber rovings. On cotton, expect a color to wick as far as an inch in both directions. Wicking causes more blending of stripe colors with cotton than with protein fibers, so plan for it carefully as you choose which colors to place side by side. Remember how color theory applies to mixing dyes—complementary colors mix to form muddy hues. Analogous colors blend into closely related colors. On cotton rovings, two inches seems to be the minimum stripe length to ensure clear, bright unmuddied colors. Strong contrast of hue and value is necessary for different colors to show up in the final yarn. Cotton is spun thin, so high contrast is needed for the small dots of color to be distinctly visible.

STEP-BY STEP DIRECTIONS FOR PAINTING COTTON ROVINGS WITH SABRACRON F DYES

1. Weigh rovings to be painted and divide into about three-foot lengths.
2. Simmer and "charge" the weighed rovings in water with Synthrapol and soda ash added.
3. Prepare 2% dyestocks, choose dye formulas, and do the calculations and measurements.
4. Regulate the depth of shade, adding the required amounts of plain water.
5. Lay out the rovings.
6. Paint the rovings. Be careful to keep the colors separate.
7. Touch up the other side of the rovings.
8. Cure the rovings by steaming or batching.
9. Rinse the rovings thoroughly and hang them to dry.

Step-by-step directions for painting cotton rovings

1. *Weigh rovings to be painted.* Weigh the rovings to determine WOF. Break the roving into pieces no longer than three feet. Because the staple length of cotton is short and the roving drifts apart easily, especially when wet, three-foot pieces are easier to handle than longer pieces. Make all rovings to be painted at one time the same length; this simplifies the whole procedure.

   To keep the rovings from drifting apart when wet, tie bundles together at each end and once in the middle, or make loose three-strand braids. Either approach will keep the rovings intact and manageable, but braiding results in less distinct stripes.

2. *Wet and "charge" the weighed rovings.* Wetting cotton rovings is more difficult than wetting protein fibers because of the surface waxes on the fibers. Cotton also tends to float. But dyeing will not take place unless the rovings are completely wetted, so you need to follow a special process to hold the cotton down. Instead of simply soaking the rovings, simmer them in a solution of hot water with a little Synthrapol plus some soda ash. This not only wets the cotton but "charges" it with soda ash, which is needed for the dye to react with the fiber. Charging the fiber also prevents the problem of having the dyes react with soda ash in the dye cup. If the soda ash is on the fibers instead, the reaction cannot take place until it comes in contact with dye. This gives you unlimited time to do your painting.

   The ratio of water to soda ash to WOF is important. To make sure the full amount of soda ash is absorbed by the fibers, use a 20:1 ratio of water to WOF. For soda ash, use 10% WOF. Use these equations to figure how much water and soda ash to put in the pot:

WOF × 20 = amount of water (ml)

WOF × 0.10 (10%) = amount of soda ash (g)

Add a little Synthrapol, too. Place the tied or braided cotton rovings in the pot, and put a rack or screen on top of them to hold them under water. Heat to simmering (not boiling) and simmer for about one hour. By keeping the temperature under boiling, the fibers do not get as woozled by the movement of the water, and the rovings remain intact. After an hour, turn off the heat and let the rovings cool in the pot before you paint them.

3. *Prepare 2% dyestocks, choose dye formulas, and do the calculations and measurements.* When painting cotton, it takes a higher concentration of dye to achieve intense colors than for immersion dyeing, so instead of using 1% dyestock solutions, start with 2% solutions. That means you combine two parts of dye powder with ninety-eight parts of water. Do the mixing and dissolving as usual.

   Use these 2% dyestocks to mix your colors, following the same dye formulas as for immersion dyeing. To prepare your dye cups, first decide which colors you want to combine on the roving, and what depth of shade (DOS) you want for each color. Now do calculations for each DOS and each color.

   a. For each DOS, use this equation:

(WOF × DOS) ÷ (total number of colors at that DOS) = amount of dye required for each color used at that DOS (ml)

   b. Then, for each color that you want to mix, figure how much of each separate color of dyestock is needed by using the dye formula. Put the percentage number for any color into the following equation:

(Amount of dye needed) × (% of color A) = amount of color A dyestock to measure out (ml)

   Do all the calculations, then measure the required amount of each dyestock for each cup and mix well. No other chemicals need be added to the dye cups because the soda ash is on the fiber and salt is not necessary.

4. *Regulate the depth of shade.* If you've chosen more than one DOS, the cups of dye won't all be filled to the same level. They will all have the same *concentration* of dye, but different *amounts* of dye. Before you can paint, you need to reverse this situation. You'll add enough plain water (not the "chemical water" used with Sabraset dyes) to fill all the cups to the same level. Then they'll all have the same *amount* of dye, but they'll be at different *concentrations*. Taking this step regulates the DOS that ends up on the roving.

   Here's how to proceed. Since the range of DOS used with these dyes is between .1 and 6, DOS 6 is the most intense a color will be. That is the point of reference for the total volume of liquid needed in each cup—the volume of dye used for a color at a DOS of 6.

WOF × 6 = Total volume of liquid needed in dye cup at DOS 6 (ml)

   If you're using any colors at DOS 6, you don't have to add any water to those cups. For all the other cups, figure out how much water to add:

(Total volume of liquid needed) – (amount of dye in cup) = (amount of water to put in that cup [ml])

   Make the calculations, measure the required amounts of water, pour into dye cups, and stir. Double-check by making sure the cups are filled to the same level when you are done.

5. *Lay out the rovings.* Spread out plastic wrap the length of the rovings. Squeeze out the charged, cooled rovings as thoroughly as possible, then blot them gently in a towel. Dyes wick on cotton more than on protein fibers, so it is important to extract as much moisture as possible before painting begins. Lay the squeezed rovings on the plastic wrap. You don't have to spread them as thinly as protein fiber, but if they are braided, separate the strands so there is as little overlap as possible in order to maximize dye penetration.

   Place a tape measure along the rovings to gauge stripe length. Have a stripe order and length of repeat in mind.

6. *Paint the rovings.* The actual painting motion is the same staccato, up and down movement used on protein fibers. Again, start with color A, use the straight edge to make straight lines, and using the tape measure as a guide, apply color A to its position in every repeat.

   Because colors tend to wick along cotton rovings, it's very important not to have too much dye in the brush. Also, use a brush that's much smaller than the desired stripe length. For example, if you want a two-inch stripe on the roving, use a one-half-inch brush and know that the colors will run an inch in each direction. Leave a little space between stripes to anticipate the movement of the dyes. Another way to work around the wicking problem is to paint the wider stripes first, leaving spaces between, let the colors wick, then go back with very thin brushes and paint narrow stripes in the spaces that are left. Colors are a little more distinct if you paint the stripes this way.

7. *Touch up the other side of the rovings.* Carefully flip the rovings over and examine the other side. There are always some light spots, and the stripes will need to be sharpened up. If the stripes do not look clear now, they will not be clear when dried. This is even more true with cottons than with protein fibers.

   Cottons do not show the fiber "halo" that protein fibers do. If the rovings squish under your gloved hand, there is too much dye, so blot it up with a towel. If the rovings look dry and/or there are white spots, repaint the stripes with more dye, but be careful not to overdo or the colors will blur.

Wicking. Dye wicks more on cellulose fibers, so be sure to use smaller brushes and leave sufficient room (about one inch) between stripes for the dye to migrate.

8. *Cure the rovings.* When the painting is complete, cover the rovings with extra plastic wrap and let them sit for an hour or so. There are two methods for setting the dye: steaming and batching.

   Steaming cotton rovings is similar to steaming protein-fiber rovings, but the time is increased to approximately thirty minutes. Wrap the rovings in plastic wrap, place them on the rack, and don't start counting the time until the pot has filled with steam. Steaming is quick, but the rovings end up a little stiff under this method of setting the dye.

The second method for setting the dye, called *batching,* is simply letting the dyed rovings, covered with plastic wrap, sit for twenty-four to forty-eight hours after the painting is complete. During this time the dye, fibers, and chemicals "do their thing" and become permanently fixed. This is possible because fiber-reactive dyes can react at room temperature; they don't require heat. The longer the batching time, the more intense the colors can become.

9. *Rinse the rovings.* Rinsing is a very important step with fiber-reactive dyes whether the rovings have been steamed or batched. It is impossible for all the dye applied to the fibers to react and be absorbed, so you have to rinse away as much excess as possible. Rinsing the rovings thoroughly now means you won't have to rinse the yarn so much after it is spun.

   Unwrap the rovings and place them in a warm-water rinse. Continue rinsing and changing water until the water runs clear. As you work, support the rovings from underneath because they are fragile when wet and may pull apart. Next, place the rovings in a hot-water and detergent bath to soak for about thirty minutes. Agitate occasionally by gently squeezing the rovings. Continue rinsing with hot water, changing water frequently until the water remains clear. Carefully blot the rovings in a towel, unbraid or untie them, and hang them up to dry.

SPLITTING AND COMBINING PAINTED ROVINGS

Before spinning, you need to divide a painted roving into thin strips of fiber by pulling it apart lengthwise. Splitting a roving into strips serves three purposes. First, rovings get matted during the painting and rinsing stages. Splitting them loosens the fibers and makes them easier to draft and spin. Second, splitting the rovings to an easily spinnable size helps preserve the order of the colors you've painted. Third, by putting two or more different strips together, you can incorporate more colors into the final yarn.

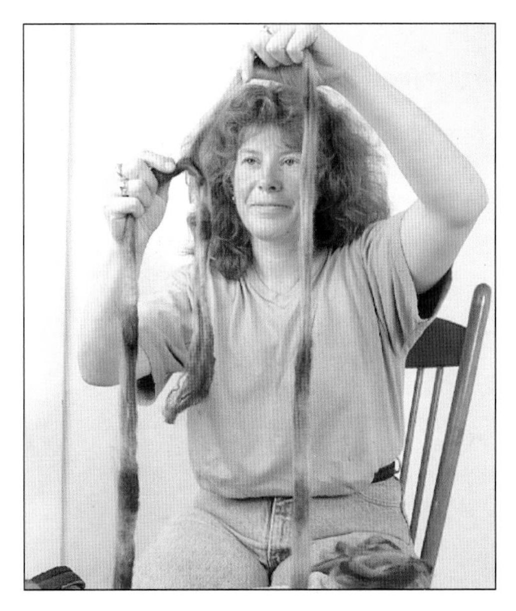

Splitting rovings into strips that are ready for spinning. Begin by splitting the roving in two, then progress thinner and thinner. Start at one end and begin splitting. Move your hands and support the roving as it is being split so it does not drift apart.

How to split a roving

Begin by splitting the whole roving into two strips. Then split each strip in half. Continue splitting the fiber into thinner and thinner strips. Support the roving as you split it, so it doesn't slip apart. As you make thinner and thinner strips, the procedure becomes more delicate. Take your time. Start at one end, split a little ways, slide your hands down to the next section of the roving, split a little farther, and continue until you reach the other end. When you've finished doing the splitting, wind the strips loosely into soft coils or "nests", or lay them out on a table, ready for the next step.

How many strips should you make? It depends on the kind of fiber, the particular roving, and the kind of yarn you want to spin.

Making thick or thin strips. The ball on the far right is the intact roving. The top fiber, swatch, and skein are from the roving split into thick strips and spun; the bottom samples are from the roving split into thin strips and spun.

Some rovings can easily be split into forty or more strips that still hold together. Others can only be split twelve times before the strips begin to drift apart. You've reached the limit if the strips start falling apart. The strips must stay intact for the spinning process. Also, if you split too many times and make the strips too thin, the clarity of colors disappears and the effect becomes muddy.

To a point, the thicker the strips, the bolder the colors in the spun yarn. But the size of the fiber supply must be proportionate to the size of the final yarn. The thicker you plan to spin the yarn, the thicker your strips can be. The thinner the yarn, the thinner the strips. The fibers have been split enough when a group of strips can be spun to the desired size of yarn without a lot of drafting. Another indication that the roving has been split enough is when the fibers in the strips are loose enough that you can draft them easily.

Combining strips of rovings

When you spin a single strip of painted roving, the stripe sequence is very obvious in the finished yarn. Unless the painted stripes are very short and the roving has been split into very thin strips, yarn spun from single rovings looks striped in the finished product.

Usually the result is better if you bundle two or more strips together and spin them at the same time. Using more strips means you can put more colors into a yarn. For example, if you combine four strips, each painted with four colors, that adds up to sixteen colors in the yarn. With more colors spun side by side, the multiple interactions of color and value make for an interesting yarn, and the barber-pole effect of alternating light and dark values is much less obvious.

Including strips from more than one painted roving in a yarn increases the design possibilities greatly. By varying the colors, the lengths of

Using multiple rovings in one yarn. From right to left: only the purple/orange roving is used; a purple roving is added; a green roving is added to the other two; a gold roving is added to the other three. Fabric appears more complex as rovings are added.

the stripes and repeats, and the number of rovings that you bundle together, you quickly multiply the number of color combinations in the final yarn.

How many strips can you combine?

The number of strips you can combine for a yarn depends on the size of the yarn to be spun and the size of the strips of roving. The finer the yarn to be spun, the smaller the bundle of strips may be. The bundle of strips has to be proportional to the finished yarn. You shouldn't have to do much drafting when spinning from the bundle of strips. That is how the color arrangement stays in order and the colors remain bright.

The thinner the individual strips, the more can be incorporated into a single bundle, up to a point. There are too many strips if you can't control the bundle as you spin and draft simultaneously from all of them. The strips should draft together to incorporate all of the colors into the yarn. If they don't draft together, the order of the painted colors will be disturbed, the colors will get muddy, and the yarn won't turn out as you anticipated.

I usually put four strips together. Rarely do I use more than six strips at once.

Color and design considerations

The design possibilities for spinning yarns from painted rovings are almost endless and depend on the size of the strips, their stripe sequences, the colors and values chosen, and the number of strips put together. Changing just one of these elements can drastically change the yarn. A wonderful, pleasing yarn can *always* result. If the first combination you try doesn't turn out as you desired, change one or two strips and give it another go.

A few guidelines can help you choose which rovings to put together, or how to paint a group of rovings, to create specific effects in the final yarn. These guidelines are based on the color relationships described in Chapter 1. (Please

DESIGNING PAINTED ROVINGS FOR A SPECIFIC YARN

Planning for a specific project or yarn is not overwhelming if you proceed one step at a time. Each decision helps you to make the next decision until the whole project is planned out. Follow these steps:

1. Decide how much finished yarn you need (think generously).
2. Choose the color palette or color harmony.
3. Decide on the total number of colors.
4. Decide on the appropriate fiber(s).
5. Choose the dye; design or choose the dye formulas.
6. Decide on the number of different rovings for the yarn. Calculate the total amount of yarn needed for the project and divide evenly for the amount in each roving. Figure generously for waste. You can always use leftovers for another project or experiment.
7. Design the stripe sequence for each roving.
8. Follow painting procedure as covered in this chapter.

Using a color harmony. A four-roving yarn using a double split complementary color harmony. From the top: turquoise, red-violet, and yellow-orange; yellow-orange and orange; red-violet, red and blue-green; red-violet, red-orange, and yellow-orange.

refer back to that chapter whenever you need inspiration or guidance for making your color decisions.)

The range and contrast of *values* is the first thing you notice in a yarn. For subtle yarns, choose rovings that have a narrow range of values. For livelier yarns, choose rovings that represent a wider range of values. Use the *value scale* on page 16 to get ideas for value design possibilities.

If you want one *hue* family to dominate a yarn, at least half the total colors on the roving strips must include that family. The colors can be any variation of the family. Yarns with a dominant hue tend to be quiet. Yarns appear more complex if several hue families are included. Using a wide range of hue families and values will reinforce the variations in the rovings you combine. Quiet yarns are more likely if you use both close values and close hues, but the quietness of a yarn is relative. The accent colors can make a big difference in the final appearance of the yarn.

Color harmonies are helpful when choosing rovings to bundle together for a yarn. For example, a yarn based on the double split complementary harmony could include four rovings painted in this way: (1) turquoise, red-violet, and yellow-orange, (2) yellow-orange and orange, (3) red-violet, red, and blue-green, (4) red-violet, red, orange and yellow-orange. Although each roving would have distinctly different colors, when bundled together for one yarn, they would produce a color harmony, as shown above.

Look at the length of the stripe sequence of the rovings being bundled. The *repeat length* of each roving should be different, if possible, to maximize the number of color interactions.

The *size of the strips* affects the appearance of the yarn. The thicker the strip, the clearer the colors, but thicker strips also increase the length

Varying repeat lengths. Combine rovings with different repeat lengths for more complex and interesting yarn. The top roving has a fifteen-inch repeat, the middle a four-inch repeat, and the bottom a seven-inch repeat. The skein and swatch show the results.

of each color stripe in the yarn because there is more fiber of one color to draft and spin before the next color comes up. This can give the final piece a striped appearance. Split the rovings as thin as possible to make shorter stripes of color in the yarn. This gives a more muted effect in the final product, an overall impression of color dots rather than color stripes.

Texture can be varied by adding strips of different fibers in one bundle. The different fibers appear as dots of texture or luster, and show up especially well after you have washed the yarn. Combine fibers of similar staple length—that makes it easiest to draft them together and control them as you spin.

Preparing bundles of rovings for spinning

After the splitting is done and the design decisions made, take one strand of each strip for the bundle, and lay them side by side on a table or workbench. Starting at one end, loosely wind the strips into a ball. As one strip ends, overlap it with a new strip. Continue winding and overlapping strips until all the fiber is wound onto the ball. Depending how many one-ounce rovings you start with, your ball will probably weigh two, three, or four ounces—enough to fill a bobbin or make a skein. If you've painted enough rovings for a big project—a sweater, for example—prepare several balls, making each one the same way. Spinning goes much faster and smoother if you finish all the preparation before you sit down at your wheel.

SPINNING YARN FROM PAINTED ROVINGS

The key to spinning painted rovings is the splitting technique. If the splitting has been done well and the strips are thin enough, the rovings should draft easily. If the strips are still matted, split them again.

Roving strips are slippery, especially before predrafting. Predraft the bundle by pulling the fiber gently but deliberately between your hands. Pull a short distance—less than half the average staple length—then move your hands

Combining rovings. This yarn uses several wool rovings and one silk roving. The luster of the silk shows up against the texture of the wool.

and pull again. Work back and forth along the roving until it is two to four times thicker than the yarn you plan to spin. Predrafting serves the function of holding the strips of roving together, letting the colors draft evenly into the yarn, and making the fiber easier to spin.

Any drafting technique can be used for the actual spinning. If the rovings have been predrafted sufficiently, you can spin with a long draw if you choose. Take your time, though, and if you ever lose control of the color sequence, stop, regroup, and continue spinning. I tend to use a cross between worsted spinning and long draw. I pull out some colors and continue drafting fibers back and letting twist in until I need to reestablish control of the colors. Then I pinch off the twist, adjust the fiber, and resume drafting.

SELF-STUDY EXERCISES

The exercises for this chapter come in two parts. First you paint a series of rovings. As you do this, you'll learn the painting technique and how to use color harmonies for design. Then, as you learn different ways to bundle and spin the rovings you've painted, you'll get ideas about how to combine colors, textures, and repeats, and you'll make sample skeins that you can use for reference when designing future rovings and yarns.

Part I. Painting a series of rovings

For series 1 through 6, use commercial white-wool roving divided into one-ounce lengths. Paint one length of roving for each of the colors or series of colors listed. The exact dye formula choice is up to you. The stripe sequence is also up to you.

Series 1—*Monochromatic colors.* Choose four colors to paint on each roving. Do twelve rovings, one for each of the following hue families: Yellow, yellow-orange, orange, red-orange, red, red-violet, violet, blue-violet, blue, blue-green, green, yellow-green.

Series 2—*Analogous colors.* Choose four colors to paint on each roving. Do fifteen rovings, one for each of the following ranges:

- yellow to red-orange
- yellow-orange to red
- orange to red-violet
- red-orange to violet
- red to blue-violet
- red-violet to blue
- violet to blue-green
- blue-violet to green
- blue-green to yellow
- blue to yellow-green
- violet to blue
- blue to green
- green to yellow-orange
- yellow-green to orange
- orange to red

Series 3—*Complementary colors.* Using five colors for each roving, do six rovings in all, one for each of the following pairs:

- yellow and violet
- yellow-orange and blue-violet
- orange and blue
- red-orange and blue-green
- red and green
- red-violet and yellow-green

Series 4—*Split complementary colors.* Using four colors for each roving, do twelve rovings in all, one for each set of split complements:

- yellow, blue-violet, and red-violet
- yellow-orange, blue, and violet
- orange, blue-green, and blue-violet
- red-orange, green, and blue
- red, blue-green, and yellow-green
- red-violet, green, and yellow
- violet, yellow-green, and yellow-orange
- blue-violet, yellow, and orange
- blue, yellow-orange, and red-orange
- blue-green, orange, and red
- green, red-orange, and red-violet
- yellow-green, violet, and red

Series 5—*Triad of colors.* Using six colors for each roving, do four rovings in all, one for each of these triads:

- Yellow, red, and blue
- Yellow-orange, red-violet, and blue-green
- Green, orange, and violet
- Yellow-green, red-orange, and blue-violet

Series 6—*Warm and cool colors.* Using four colors for each roving, paint two rovings with warm colors only and two rovings with cool colors only.

Series 7—*Painting colors on natural-colored wool rovings.* Choose any color combination and paint it on both a white roving and a gray or tan roving to see how the natural fiber color affects the final colors. Do at least two rovings, or as many as you like. Try warm and cool colors, bright and dull colors, light and dark colors. Compare the effects on white fiber and gray or tan fiber.

Series 8—*Painting luxury-fiber rovings.* Use any color combination and paint tops of bombyx silk, tussah silk, alpaca, mohair, blends, etc. The number of rovings is up to you.

Part 2. Splitting and combining rovings

After the rovings are painted and dried, they are ready to be split into strips, bundled, and spun. Here is a series of suggestions for how to choose and use the rovings you have painted. When a color is suggested, it doesn't have to be the *only* color on the roving, but it should be the *dominant* color.

1. *Strip thickness.* Choose a roving. Split it into strips of various thicknesses and spin the strips separately so you can feel how they draft and spin. Notice how the length of the color repeat in the yarn is affected by the thickness of the strip.
2. *High contrast.* Choose two rovings with a high contrast in value or hue. Split them into similar-size strips, bundle two strips together, and spin. Watch to see that both rovings are drafting evenly. This should be easy to see because of the high contrast.
3. *Color effects.* Combine strips of two rovings that have colors in common, but are not the same. Observe how colors recede and pop out in the yarn.
4. *Try three strips.* After you are comfortable spinning a two-strip bundle, try spinning three strips at once. Right now the color choices are not as important as concentrating on controlling the spinning technique.
5. *Three rovings with a common hue.* Choose three rovings that have at least one hue family in common. The other colors on the rovings do not matter. Split the rovings, bundle three strips together, and spin.
6. *Triad.* Choose three rovings that represent a triad, such as primarily red, primarily yellow, and primarily blue. Split, bundle, and spin.
7. *Value contrast.* Choose four rovings with colors that contrast in value. Split, bundle, and spin. Practice controlling and drafting from four strips at once. The yarn will look "active".

   Now choose four rovings that are similar in value. Split, bundle, and spin. The yarn will look more subdued.
8. *Cool and warm colors.* Choose three different rovings that are all warm, and one that includes cool colors. See which colors pop out and which colors recede.

   Now choose three different rovings that are all cool, and one that includes warm colors. Examine the color interactions to see which colors are dominant and which colors recede.
9. *Complementary colors.* Choose two complementary rovings. Look to see if the colors intensify each other. If not, try spinning a different size of yarn or choose a different value or saturation of one of the rovings.

   Now choose two rovings in an analogous range and one that includes some of the complements. This will show how complements can act as accents.
10. *Add natural or solid colors.* Choose one or two painted rovings and add a strip of either a natural or dyed solid-color roving. Try using a roving that is similar in value to the painted rovings, one that has a value significantly lighter than the painted ones, then one that is significantly darker than the painted ones.
11. *Add continuity.* For a series of yarns, include strips from one roving in all the skeins but vary all the other strips. This gives all the skeins a common element.
12. *Make progressions.* For a series of yarns, make subtle color or value progressions by changing one roving at a time.
13. *Try a random combination.* Choose three or four rovings at random and spin them together. Sometimes unlikely combinations give wonderful results.

Now you are ready to play. Try things you don't think will work. Try things that seem safe. Try combinations that look impossible. Use colors you do not like with those you do like. The possibilities are endless!

chapter 4

Blending colors and fibers with a drum carder

–4–

Blending colors and fibers with a drum carder

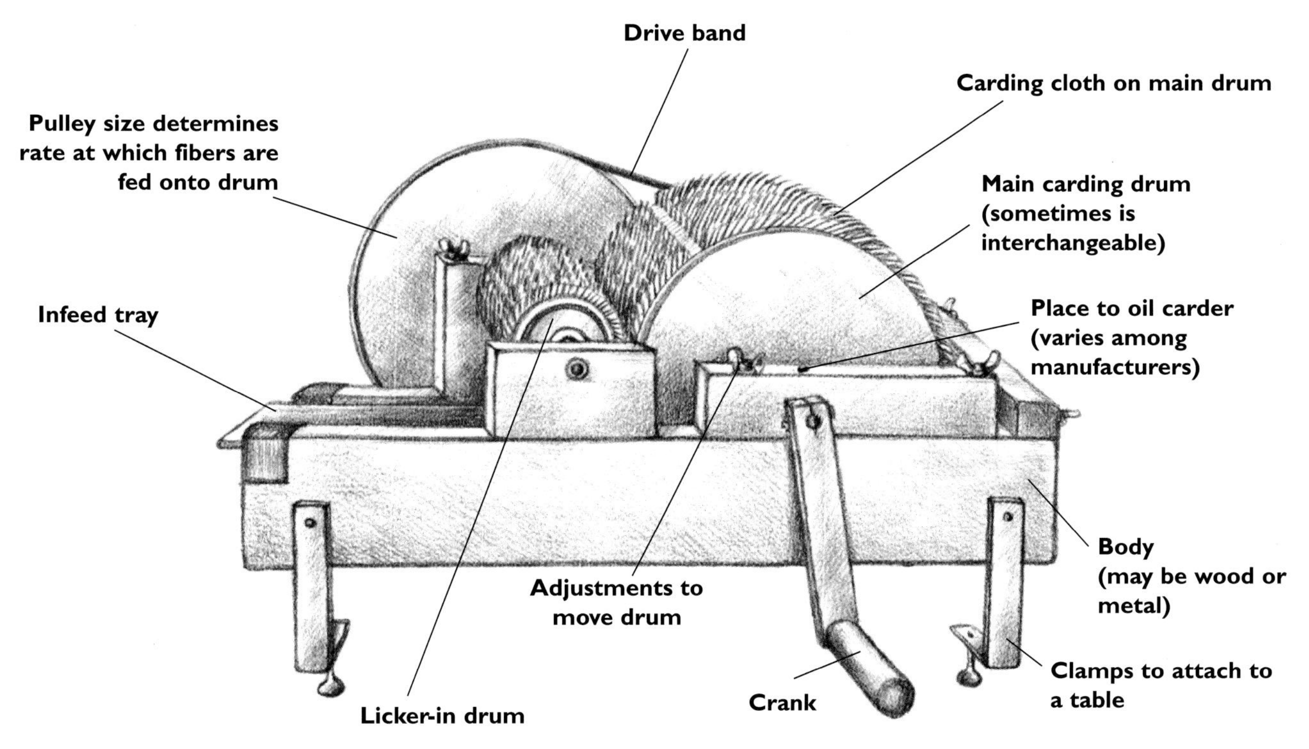

Drum carder with parts labeled.

Blending colors and/or fibers with a drum carder is a versatile and satisfying method of fiber preparation. The batts you make are delightful to spin, and you end up with beautiful yarns. Yarns spun from thoroughly blended colors and fibers look uniform from a distance, but on closer inspection they have a rich and heathered appearance that is achieved only by combining several colors and/or fibers at the carding stage.

Blending means you don't have to worry too much about producing even colors as you dye because the carding eliminates any unevenness. Also, blending means you can start with a limited palette of dyed fibers yet still produce a wide range of yarn colors. Finally, blending is a way to combine the qualities of different fibers, such as the loft of wool with the luster of silk.

Thorough blending begins with basic carding. First you have to card each color of dyed fleece (or other fiber) separately. You can't blend successfully unless the initial carding of each color is well done. Equipment plays an important part in carding and blending, and you need to use it properly. Without the appropriate tools and techniques, you'll be frustrated by the process and disappointed with your results, so this chapter starts with the basics of choosing and using a drum carder. Spend time mastering the basics, then you'll be ready to explore the exciting world of blending colors and fibers.

CHOOSING A DRUM CARDER

Although you can blend colors and fibers with hand cards, I prefer to use a drum carder. Drum carding is more efficient and thorough, and it's easier to consistently produce repeatable results with a drum carder than with hand cards. Using an appropriate drum carder and careful carding techniques, you can make carded fiber preparations at home that are equal to or better than commercially carded fibers.

If you're shopping for a drum carder, you'll find several models to choose from. They vary considerably, and a carder that may work very well for one application can be inappropriate for another. Think carefully about your carding requirements and goals to make the best choice. You may decide to buy more than one carder. That is not extravagant. You will spend as much time, if not more, on fiber preparation as on spinning. A good carder is well worth the investment. It should be as important to you as your spinning wheel.

For the kind of blending described in this chapter, I've found that these carder features and qualities are most important:

A sturdy body. The body of the carder should be constructed of solid wood. A heavy main drum will actually assist in the carding action by keeping the drum rolling. It acts like a fly wheel. The drum carder should weigh enough to stay put as you card. It helps if there's a way to clamp the carder to your work table.

Appropriate carding cloth. It is *very* important to have carding cloth that is compatible with the fibers being carded. Hand cards use a variety of carding cloths. So do industry carding machines. It is impossible to card all kinds of fibers with a single type of carding cloth. Knowing the range of fibers you work with most will help you decide what kind of carding cloth you need. The things to consider when looking at carding cloth are:

The diameter of the wire used for the teeth. Thicker teeth, made from heavy-gauge wire, are suitable for carding coarser fibers. Heavy-gauge wire does not bend easily, so the carder can take more abuse (such as overloading the drum or trying to card matted fibers) without damaging the teeth. But thick teeth leave spaces or furrows in the batt. Thinner teeth, made from fine-gauge wire, work well for carding fine fibers and make smooth-surfaced batts, but you need to treat a carder with thin teeth gently.

The spacing of the teeth in the cloth. The wider the teeth are spaced on the carding cloth, the coarser the fibers can be. The closer the spacing, the finer the fibers. Close-spaced teeth produce a finely carded, smooth-surfaced batt. Usually the spacing is related to the size of the teeth: wide spacing goes with thick teeth and close spacing goes with thin teeth. A more versatile combination, which works on a wide variety of fibers, is thin teeth at medium spacing.

The length of the teeth. This determines how much fiber you can card into one batt. The longer the teeth, the thicker and heavier a batt can be. Short teeth can produce only a thin, lightweight batt.

Interchangeable drums. Because one kind of carding cloth will not serve all your needs, it's helpful to buy more than one drum for your carder. By changing the drum, you can have more than kind of one carding cloth without the expense of another whole drum carder.

Licker-in cloth. The cloth on the licker-in or small drum should be compatible with the cloth on the large drum. The licker-in teeth should only be long enough to transfer fibers from the infeed tray to the large drum. If they're too long, they accumulate excess fiber.

A reasonable infeed rate. The infeed rate is the speed at which the licker-in feeds fibers onto the large drum. This is very important to the quality of the batt. If the rate is too fast, the fibers get gulped onto the large drum, resulting in an uneven, inadequately carded batt.

A slower rate results in a smoother, better carded batt.

The type of drive band. The drive band should be sturdy and easy to put on and take off the carder. It should also be readily replaceable when worn out. I prefer the smooth stretchy nylon drive bands to chain-drive bands. You have to grease chain-drive bands, and dirty grease can get on the fibers. If fibers get caught in the chain, it's hard to get them out. (Never let your fingers, hair, or clothing get caught in the chain!) With a chain drive, it's harder to adjust the drum spacing. Some people think a chain drive is a good idea because smooth-drive bands can slip, but slippage is a sign that you're trying to card too much fiber at once. Slowly feeding small amounts of fiber gives much better results, makes it easier to crank the carder, and prevents slippage.

Adjustability of the drums. From time to time, a drum carder needs to be adjusted so that the two drums are parallel and close, but not touching. Some carders are easily adjusted with no additional tools, while others require four hands, extra tools, and a large amount of determination. When evaluating a carder, ask: How easy is it to make the appropriate adjustments? Do I need additional tools?

Ease of cranking. It should be very easy to turn the crank while carding fibers. There is no reason that cranking the drum should be difficult.

An option to cranking is a motor drive. They're not available for all kinds of carders, and not inexpensive, but a motor drive does have advantages: it turns the drums at a consistent speed, it lets you use both hands on the fiber, and it can produce good-quality batts with one less pass.

Size of the infeed tray. The tray should be large enough to provide space for arranging the teased fibers as you feed them in.

Ease of cleaning and oiling. A drum carder should be easy to disassemble for periodic cleaning and easy to reassemble afterwards. No matter how careful you are, some fibers will get caught on the crank or in odd spots, and you'll have to get them out. Oiling a drum carder should be just as easy as oiling a spinning wheel.

Related equipment

A doffer stick. You'll need a sturdy tool to remove the batt from the carding teeth. Some people use knitting needles, crochet hooks, ice picks, or sharpened sticks, but these tend to be too flimsy. A doffer stick is specially designed for this job. It should be sturdy enough to lift fibers off, long enough to reach across the drum, and sharp enough to catch all the fibers.

A fetling brush. This is a brush designed to clean the carding cloth of a drum carder. It's most effective if the teeth are as long as the teeth of the cloth being cleaned. You can substitute a dog or cat brush or flick carder, but these tend to be less effective because their teeth usually aren't long enough to reach the base of the carding cloth.

A burnishing tool. This is a hand-held wooden card with long flexible teeth that, when held against the large drum during carding, acts like a supplemental drum in a commercial carding operation. Using a burnishing tool can eliminate one pass through the carder and speed up the total carding process. It also helps keep the carding cloth teeth clean and sharp. Finally, by slightly compressing the batt, it helps you doff the batt (remove it from the drum) more cleanly.

Tweezers. These come in handy to fish out fibers caught on the axles or in odd spots.

Oil. Use a lightweight motor or sewing machine oil on moving parts, according to the manufacturer's instructions.

Adjustment tools. The specific tools will vary with the kind of drum carder you have. I keep pliers and a set of allen wrenches handy.

USING A DRUM CARDER

Many spinners misunderstand what drum carders are designed for and can do. A drum carder cannot perform miracles. A drum carder cannot make wonderful fibers out of junk, it is not designed to remove vegetal matter from fibers, it won't remove short fibers or second cuts, and it cannot do a thorough job in one pass. It *can* arrange fibers in a generally parallel direction, distribute them evenly, and make them easier and more pleasant to spin. A drum carder can process a larger amount of fibers in a shorter time than hand cards. But it does take some time and commitment to become proficient at using a drum carder, just as it takes time to learn to use hand cards or spin.

Here is the basic step-by-step procedure for effective drum carding.

1. *Wash the fiber.* All fiber should be as clean and grease-free as possible for carding. Wool fleece must be thoroughly washed. Greasy wool is hard to card because the fibers tend to stick together. They don't slip past each other freely. Worse yet, any grease in the fiber gets deposited on the carding cloth and teeth, where it attracts dirt which then gets deposited onto fibers in the next batt.
2. *Tease the fiber.* Fiber must be opened up before you feed it into a drum carder. Putting compacted fiber into a drum carder strains the tool and gives poor results. You can tease the fiber by hand, flick locks with a flicker, or use a picker. Using a picker speeds up the process when you have a lot of fiber to card. In any case, be sure to remove any matts, second cuts, or vegetal matter before you start carding.
3. *Properly adjust the drum carder.* If possible, clamp the carder to the table. Oil the moving parts so they rotate smoothly. Remove any fibers caught on the axle.

   Make sure the drums are parallel and almost but not quite touching. They should be so close that you can just insert a business card between them—nothing more. Also, make sure the drums are parallel. If not, batts will be over-carded on one side and under-carded on the other.

   If a carding tooth is bent, straighten it by removing the lead from a mechanical pencil, inserting the empty pencil on the bent tooth, and bending the tooth back to its original position. This does not take long and it improves the quality of the batt.
4. *Make sure the drums are free of fiber.* Clean the carding cloth on both the licker-in and large drum. Start with the licker-in. Hold

Basic carding procedure.

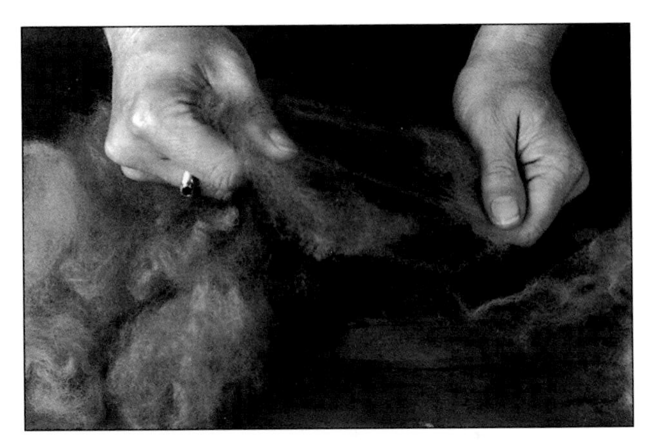

1. Fiber must be teased sufficiently before being carded. Fiber can be teased by hand, with a flicker, or with a picker. Be sure to remove any matts, vegetal matter, or second cuts.

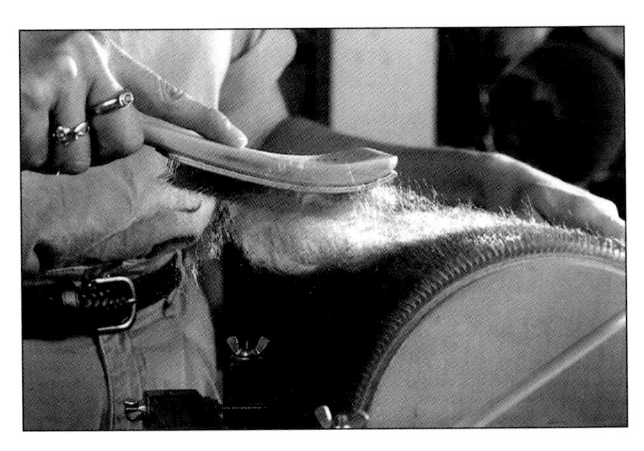

2. Clean both the licker-in drum and main drum with a fetling brush before introducing new fibers or colors to the carder.

3. Slowly feed fiber onto the drum carder. You should be able to see the infeed tray through the fibers as they enter the carder. If not, you are feeding too much at a time. Remember, not to use more than one-half ounce per batt.

4. Turn the crank slowly as the fiber is being fed onto the drum. The crank should be easy to turn. Cranking at a steady, slow speed ensures a smooth, even batt.

the fetling brush against the licker-in with the brush handle pointing toward the right and crank the drum as usual. Move the fetling brush across the drum until the licker-in is clean. Next, hold the fetling brush gently against the larger drum with the brush handle pointing toward the right and crank in the opposite direction. Peel the fibers off the fetling brush, and continue until the drum is completely clean. To get those last stubborn fibers off the drum, use tweezers or pat the fetling brush against the drum in a quick series of motions.

5. *Feeding fiber onto the carder.* The key to feeding fiber onto a drum carder is to add just a *small* amount of well-teased fiber at a time. You should be able to see the infeed tray through the teased fiber. Feed the fibers onto the drum slowly and consistently. Don't try to card too much fiber at once. Approximately one-half ounce is a good amount for one batt. It takes a lot more effort to adequately card large thick batts than to card thin ones. In the long run, making smaller batts is easier, more efficient, and gives better results.
6. *Turn the crank slowly.* While feeding teased fiber onto the drum, turn the crank slowly but steadily. If it's hard to turn the crank, one of several things could be wrong. Most likely you are feeding too many fibers in too fast, or matted fibers are caught in the carding cloth, or fibers are wrapped around the axle. Check to correct the problem and continue to crank slowly until all the fibers have been fed onto the drum. If you have a burnishing tool, use it to help smooth the batt.
7. *Remove or doff batt from drum.* On the large drum, there should be a small strip called a

5. Using a burnishing tool is optional. A burnishing tool makes a denser batt with a little smoother surface; it comes in handy when blending stubborn fibers. Hold the burnishing tool lightly against the main drum with your left hand while cranking with your right hand.

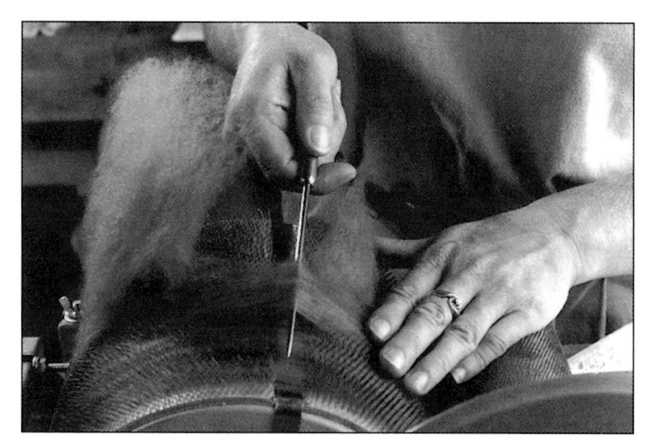

6. Separate the ends of the batt on the drum with a doffer stick by inserting it at the doffer groove.

7. Take the opened fiber and gently peel the batt from the drum until it reaches the back beam. Use the beam for tension as you continue pulling. While the batt is being pulled off, control the main drum by placing your hip next to the crank.

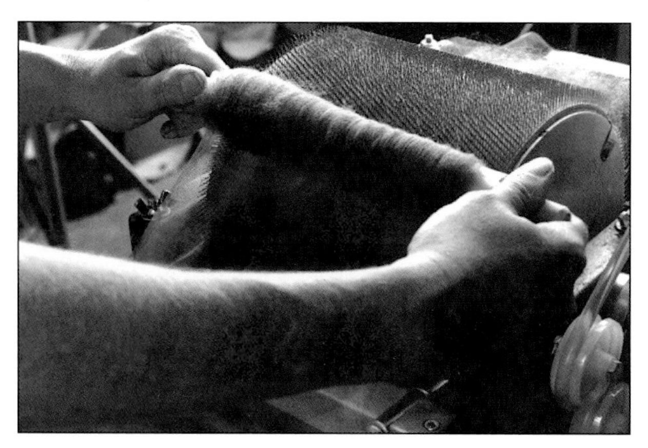

8. Another way to remove the batt is to use a dowel rod with a piece of heavy plastic attached. Roll the batt around the rod; the plastic supports the batt. This works when the batt is very thin and needs some encouragement to be cleanly removed.

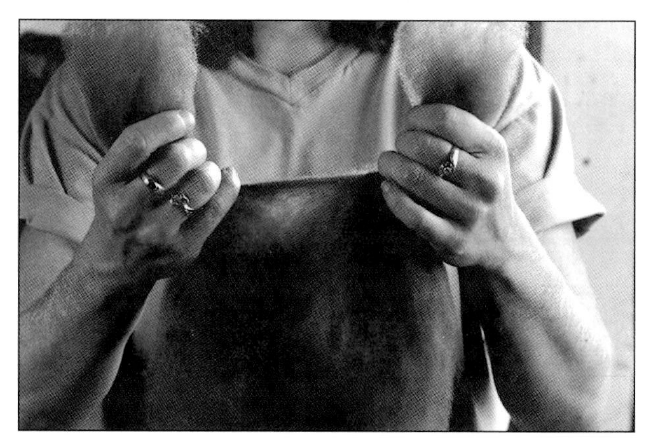

9. Once through the carder is not enough. To prepare the batt for a second pass, split it in half lengthwise.

doffer groove that is free of carding cloth. Turn the drum until the doffer groove is visible. At the groove, insert the tip of the doffer stick a few inches under one side of the batt, then raise gently to pull the fibers apart and separate the ends of the batt. Continue across the drum until the fibers have all been separated. *Never* cut a batt to remove it from the drum.

After you've separated the fibers across the width of the batt, grip the part of the batt to the right of the doffer groove and peel the batt to the right, pulling it down gently over the back beam. As you pull, the drum will turn in the direction opposite from carding. With the small amount of tension imposed by pulling the batt over the back beam, the batt should peel cleanly off the drum. If it does not, the carding teeth may have rough spots that catch the fibers, or teeth may be bent.

Another approach to doffing batt is to use a dowel with a length of plastic attached to it. After separating the batt, take the dowel to the right of the drum and wind the end of the batt around it. Continue rolling until the batt is fully removed.

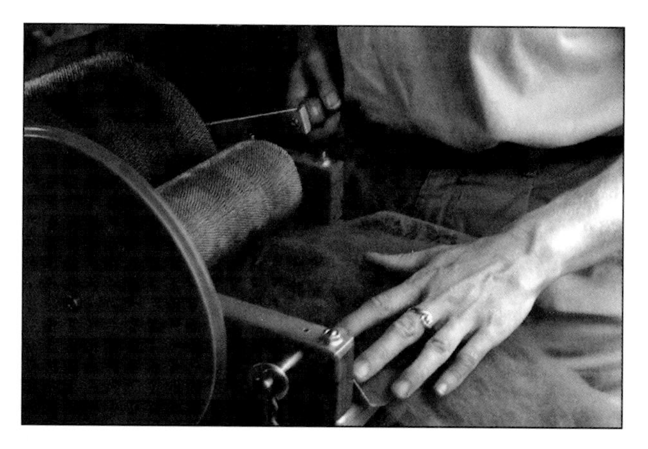

10. Spread one half-batt evenly across the infeed tray and slowly crank. If the batt wants to "gulp" in, stop and thin out the fiber some more; if you don't do this, there will be thick and thin spots in the batt.

11. To evaluate when the batt is "done", hold it up to the light and look at its texture and the distribution of the fiber. If it looks easily spinnable, it's done.

COMMON CARDING PROBLEMS

Fiber won't feed through.

- You're feeding in too much fiber, too fast
- The fiber needs more teasing.

There are lumps and dense spots in the batts.

- You're feeding in too much fiber, too fast
- The fiber needs more teasing
- The licker-in is pulling fiber in too fast
- The fiber was not evenly distributed on the infeed tray
- The drums are not parallel.

The crank is hard to turn.

- You're feeding in too much fiber, too fast
- The fiber needs more teasing
- Fibers are wedged around the axle
- The crank needs oiling.

Fiber accumulates on the licker-in drum.

- You're holding back on the fiber on the infeed tray
- The drum is full and cannot hold any more fiber
- The fiber being carded is too short for the carding cloth
- The space between the drums needs to be adjusted.

8. *Divide the batt and recard it.* One pass through a drum carder is not enough to thoroughly prepare fiber. At least one more pass is necessary, and it may take several to do the job right. Tear the batt lengthwise. Gently spread each half-batt thin enough to fill the entire width of the drum, and slowly feed them back onto the drum carder. Remove as before. If you have a burnishing tool, use it to enhance the carding process and improve the top surface of the batt. Continue dividing and recarding the batt until you are satisfied. To evaluate your results, examine the batt closely (try holding it up to the light), looking for any thin, thick, or tangled spots. The fiber should be uniformly distributed and smooth. If it's not, continue carding.

CARDING TO BLEND COLORS

Thoroughly blending color in carding is different than blending colors of paint. No matter how many times fibers are carded, the same number of colors are present when you are done, even though they visually blend to form what appears to be a new color. That principle is called a *pointillist effect* and is achieved through *optical mixing*. Optical mixing is the visual blending of small dots of colors so that, when seen from a distance, they give the impression of a new color (see page 25–26). The blended color tends to be an average of the hues and values of the parent colors, depending on the quantity of each employed.

Blending colors by carding is a good way to broaden the range of your yarns without dyeing more fiber. Colors produced by blending are richer than their solid counterparts.

How a color can be altered

Before you begin blending, decide what color you want to end up with and identify the colors you have to start with. You'll save time, materials, and frustration if you think through the process of blending before you start feeding fibers onto the carder.

As you learned in Chapter 1, you can describe any color in terms of its hue, value, and saturation or intensity. Use those terms now to describe your desired color. That will help you decide how to create it by blending.

There are six ways to affect a color through blending: you can make the hue warmer or cooler; you can make the value lighter or darker; you can make the saturation brighter or duller. Sometimes two or more effects will occur simultaneously. Use the color wheel to choose colors for blending. Locate both the colors you are starting with and the color you want to end up with. Think about the six possible color effects and decide which will transform the original color to the desired color.

Changing the hue

This will make the original color look more like one of the colors beside it on the color wheel. The new color will be either warmer or cooler than the original. To *warm* a color by blending, choose an analogous color warmer than the original. This color should fall between the original and orange on the color wheel. To *cool* a color by blending, choose an analogous color cooler than the original, one that falls between the original and blue on the color wheel. For example, if you start with green, you can cool it by blending with blue, or warm it by blending with yellow. Blending occurs more easily if the colors you start with are close in value. Also, the closer the hues are on the color wheel, the easier it is to blend them (see page 121).

Changing the value

This produces a blend that appears lighter or darker than the original. First determine the value of the original by comparing it to a gray scale. It may be lighter or darker than you think. If you want to *lighten* the color, blend it with white, light gray, or any color that is lighter in value. To *darken* a color, add black, dark gray, or any darker color. Changing the value usually dulls the saturation (see page 122).

Changing the saturation

This results in blended colors that are brighter or duller than the original. The purer the color, the brighter, more intense, or saturated it is. The more colors that you blend together, the duller the final color becomes.

To make a color *brighter,* choose a color from the same hue family, but one that's more intense than the original. Brightening may be impossible if the original color is already the brightest one available.

Making a color *duller* is easy. There are several ways to do it, and each gives different results. Adding a small amount of the color's complement gives a rich, interesting, but duller version of the original color. Adding some gray of the same value as the original color makes a blended color that is duller, but not any darker or lighter. Adding black makes the color duller *and* darker. Adding white makes the color duller *and* lighter (see page 123).

Applying the color harmonies to blending colors

The color harmonies described in Chapter 1 (see pages 40–45) are helpful when you're choosing colors for blending. Remember also

Changing the hue. The green fiber shown at left was blended with blue fiber to create a cooler green. The same green was blended with the yellow fiber to create a warmer green.

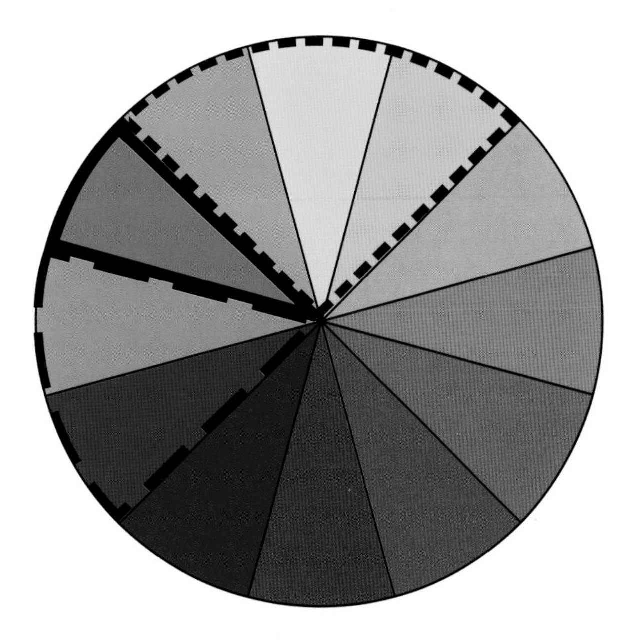

The color wheel shows where to choose colors that will make the green either warmer or cooler. The solid line shows the original color, the short dotted line shows the warmer colors, and the long dotted line shows the cooler colors.

Changing the value. The green fiber shown at right was blended with dark purple to create a darker green, and with light lavender to create a lighter green.

Same photograph as above but in black and white shows that the blends truly are lighter and darker in value than the original green.

Changing the saturation. The green fiber shown at right was blended with gray to create a duller green. A livelier green was blended with the same green to create a brighter green.

from Chapter 1 that every color has an undertone; to make bright blends, start with the colors whose undertones are closest to the desired color.

Choosing colors for *monochromatic* or *analogous* color harmonies is easy because the colors have to come from a small wedge of the color wheel. When the values are close, it is very easy for the resulting blend to appear as a solid color. Choosing compatible saturations and values is important. These blended yarns will look brighter, but not as interesting as some of the other color harmony blends. More than four to six colors get lost in a blend.

Blending *complementary* colors is the fastest way to make neutrals. From a distance, neutral blends can appear dull, but up close, they are rich, lively, and complex. For the most interesting blends, choose various saturations of the complements, but be sure to include some very bright ones to keep the blend lively. Six colors are enough to blend; using more doesn't add any character to the yarn.

If you want the richness of the complementary blends but a little brighter overall color, the *split complementary* harmony can do the trick. It takes a little more carding to dull this blend than it does a pair of complements. Six colors work easily in this blend without losing the complexity. To draw from more color families, use the *double split complementary* harmony, and choose five to ten colors. This makes a pleasing and intriguing blend.

The *triad* and *double triad* harmonies produce exciting blends. They are most successful when one hue family is dominant. It is easy to overcard this combination; if you do, you'll lose the brightness of the blend and it will look like mud. Choose four to eight colors, no more, for these blends.

The *tetrad* harmony is two sets of complementary colors. It has the potential to be very exciting, but can become dull real fast. Do not overcard! Choose very bright colors to begin with, so that the blend will remain lively. Four to eight colors is the limit here (see page 125).

Universal blending concepts

No matter which or how many colors you are blending, some principles apply to any blending process. Your blends will be more successful and predictable if you observe these guidelines.

Card each color separately first. Before you start any blending, card each color individually. This accomplishes two things. First, each carded batt evenly distributes each color across the width of the drum and keeps inconsistencies of color distribution to a minimum. Second, because the fibers are open and already prepared, you don't have to make many passes to blend the colors together. This reduces the risk of overblending.

Do not overcard the blend. It is easy to get so excited about a blend that you continue to card until the distinct colors disappear. There is a fine line between a blend where the original colors are distinctly present and a blend that has lost the individual colors and appears dull. When the colors have been carded separately first, it takes less carding than you think to obtain an even, but exciting blend.

Value is very important. Colors that are close in value are easier to blend than colors that have very different values. It takes more carding to thoroughly blend colors of contrasting value, and any inconsistency in the blending is more obvious than when the values are similar. The final appearance of a blend that combines only very light and very dark values is bold and has a heathered or frosted appearance. From a distance, close-value blends look like solid colors.

Choose colors lighter and brighter than your goal. To obtain clear, bright blending, start with colors that are much lighter and brighter than the intended finished yarn. Several things happen in the blending and spinning processes that make the final yarn darker and duller than the original fibers.

Brightness is easily lost. The more colors in a blend, the less saturated the final color. Bright blends are possible only when you start with saturated, analogous colors. Blends that include complementary colors will be duller.

Browns and neutrals are easily produced. There are many possibilities for blending browns and desaturated colors by combining proportions of all three primary colors. One or another color can be dominant in the blend, if you choose.

Blending colors with a drum carder

Once colors have been carded separately, they are ready for the blending process. Split the batts into halves or smaller pieces, depending how many colors you want to combine.

Arrange the partial batts in the order they will be fed onto the drum carder. How to decide? If values are drastically different, alternate dark with light. If hue families are drastically different, alternate them. Place the most contrasting colors next to one another.

Slowly feed each color onto the drum carder, one at a time. Be sure to thin out the batts so they feed on smoothly. Repeat feeding on batts until all the colors are on the drum, but limit the total weight of the blended batt to one-half to three-quarters ounce. Remove the layered batt.

For the second pass, rip the batt in half lengthwise, spread out both half-batts and feed them through again. Remove this batt and decide if it is blended enough. If not, continue the stripping and refeeding steps until the batt is blended as thoroughly as you want. One or two passes through the carder after the initial layering is usually sufficient to consistently blend most colors, but not lose them. Six passes will result in a very homogenous blend.

Making repeatable blends

If you want to prepare a single batch of blended batts, you can just choose your colors and start carding. But if you want to prepare enough fiber for a project and have all your batts turn out the same, you need to pay attention to what you're doing. Thorough color blending can be approached in one of two ways. In the recipe approach, you weigh the colors and figure percentages. This approach is very repeatable and predictable. In the painterly approach, you "eyeball" how much of each

Analogous blend. Four colors from blue to violet hue families were blended together to make a new color. There is some value difference so the blend is not too boring.

Complementary blend. Six colors from two hue families blended. The result is much duller than the original colors, but not neutral. The overall effect is much more complex than a solid color would be.

Split complementary blend. Six colors from three hue families were blended. The same amount of carding was done as for the complementary blend, but the final effect is brighter.

Triad blend. Seven colors from three hue families were blended. One of the hues must be dominant so the blend is not too muddy. The colors were blended so that distinct colors are still present in the final blend.

Blending colors. Blend already-carded fiber. Slowly feed one color at a time onto the drum carder. Remove batt, split in half, and repeat until the desired results are reached.

Closeup of color-blended batts. All colors were fed onto the drum carder in layers. From bottom to top: batt put through drum carder two times; same batt carded four times; batt carded six times.

color to use. This approach is more intuitive and not as repeatable, but it is more flexible.

Recipe color blending

In this approach, the amount of each color in the blend is expressed as a percentage of the whole weight of the blend. You need accurate scales for weighing the fiber in grams. Although this is called recipe blending, the trick is that you have to make up your own recipes—there is no place you can look them up. If you want to try this approach, begin your own carding notebook. All you need are plastic slide holders (the kind designed for holding twenty slides, punched to fit a 3-ring binder). You can save a tuft of each blend you prepare, write which colors you started with and what proportions you used on a slip of paper or sticky label, and store the tuft and label in one slot of the holder.

To start, blend equal amounts of two colors and keep track of the results. Once you have a point of reference, you can change the proportions of the colors to extend the possibilities. All kinds of color relationships can be utilized in the recipes. For example, start with a complementary combination of red and green, and try blending 50% red and 50% green, 25% red and 75% green, and 75% red and 25% green. Or choose four colors. Try blending 25% of each, then make four 40:20:20:20 blends, trying each color as the dominant 40%, and see how that affects the mix (see page 127).

How do you decide on proportions? The more dominant you want a color to be in a blend, the higher the percentage to use. It takes some practice to learn how to predict this, but that's where the notebook comes in handy. Groups of colors can also act as dominant colors for a blend. For example, if you want a yarn that is dominantly red, you could use 20% each of a warm red, a cool red, and a dark red. That means a total of 60% of the blend comes from the red hue family.

The advantages of recipes are that they're repeatable and predictable. The disadvantages are that it takes time to figure out which recipe to use, then weigh out each color of fiber. Also, if you decide to fine-tune the blend when you're partway through the carding process, it's

Recipe color blending. Red and green fibers were blended in different proportions. The bottom skein is 75% red, 25% green, the center is 50% of each, and the top skein is 25% red and 75% green.

Recipe blending. This example uses four colors: green, orange, lilac, and light green. Far right shows yarn/swatch made with 25% each of the colors. The other samples use a ratio of 40/20/20/20, changing which color is 40%. From the top left moving clockwise, the dominant colors are: green, light green, lilac, and orange.

Painterly blending. The goal was to match the color on the left. First I carded red violet, then dulled it with two yellows. The color needed to be bluer, so I added a bluer violet, then added a second blue violet. To lighten, I added lavender then white until the value was right. Note that the colors look a little different because we're comparing paper to fiber.

hard to figure out and keep track of how that decision changes the percentages.

Painterly blending

This is the approach I usually use. It requires less record-keeping. I do keep track of the colors included in a blend, but don't always weigh or figure out the percentages. This approach is not as repeatable as using recipes, but with some practice your "eyeballing" can become fairly consistent. Describe the amounts of each color you use as handfuls or pinches or locks—whatever makes sense to you. Although it does not involve meticulous records, painterly blending is certainly not haphazard.

Start by describing the color you want to end up with. Then choose a base color to begin with. Card that base color thoroughly, as described in basic carding. Every color you subsequently blend with it must also be carded separately first. I usually have a range of colors that are carded and ready to use for blending purposes.

The blending is done by feeding layers of color onto the drum carder. I usually start with the base color and add one or two colors in the first layering. When I take the batt off the drum, I look at it and evaluate how it compares to the color I anticipate. If it's right on target, I split it, card it again, and am happy.

But of course the color doesn't always turn out right on the first pass. If not, study the batt and analyze what needs to be different. If you know what to change, you can go back to the color wheel and figure out how to get the results you want. It may take two or three tries before the color is just what you had in mind. Once you've added the last color, the blending may be almost done, or you may want to make a few more passes.

The key to successful painterly blending is to proceed conservatively and only add a little of a color at a time. It is easy to get impatient, try to change the color too much, and go overboard. Once you are past where you want to be, it is hard to go back to where you were.!

The advantage of this approach is flexibility. It's fun to "play" with colors and see what happens. Just because we are "adults" doesn't mean we can't play! Also, working this way lets you keep fine-tuning the blend until you have exactly the color you desire. However, painterly blending is not as predictable as using recipes, and you can waste time and fiber. Also, it's easy to overcard the blends and end up with dull, muddy colors.

I can't give you any more rules or theories. At this point, you are ready to card! There is no substitute for hands-on work with fibers and a drum carder. Yes, it will take practice. There are no short cuts. For some specific directions on where to start, use the self-study exercises at the end of the chapter.

CARDING TO BLEND FIBERS

Some of the most popular and successful blends combine wool and luxury fibers. Blending luxury fibers with wool is not meant to replace using pure luxury fibers for special projects. Nothing can replace the feel of an all-luxury-fiber piece. But in many situations, blending fibers is practical and desirable.

Blending makes efficient use of your time, money, and materials. Blending can make expensive fibers go farther without losing too much of that luxurious feel. By making the luxury fibers go farther, blending brings down the cost of a project. And blending can save time if it makes the fiber easier to work with and spin.

Blending can improve a yarn's performance. Adding wool to a blend can lend strength and practicality to a fragile luxury fiber. If you choose appropriately, blending can highlight each fiber's best features and minimize its shortcomings.

Blending can change a yarn's appearance and feel. Any of a fiber's properties, such as hand, drape, luster, loft, or resilience, can be altered with blending. By blending, you can create special effects that you can't get from a single fiber.

FIBER BLENDING TIPS

- Carefully choose your wool. Consider its softness and staple length. Have an end purpose in mind. Your blend cannot be any better than the fibers being blended.
- For easier spinning and smoother yarns, choose wool that is comparable in fiber diameter and staple length to the luxury fibers being blended.
- For successful blending, always card less than the drum will hold. The size of the batt should be in proportion to the fineness of the fibers.
- As little as 25% luxury fiber can alter the appearance and hand of a yarn.
- Use at least 20 to 25% wool for its characteristics to show in a blend.
- Use at least 50% silk for its luster to show.
- Use at least 25 to 33% mohair for its luster to show.

Fiber properties

As with any other multi-step process, there are several questions to answer before you begin blending fibers. Focus on why you are blending and what qualities you want to end up with. By putting in some thought up-front, you can avoid surprises and expensive mistakes later. Ask yourself:

- Why do I want to blend fibers?
- What qualities do I want to see in the finished yarn?
- What fibers can give me the appearance I am looking for?
- What will the finished yarn be used for? What blend is suitable for that purpose?
- How thoroughly should the fibers be blended?

A wide variety of natural fibers is available to spinners today. In order to prepare successful blends, you need to review the pros and cons of any fiber that you're considering. Here are the important properties of wool and other popular protein fibers that you may want to blend with wool.

Wool

I use wool as the base in most of my blends because it's easy to work with, relatively inexpensive, and readily available. Wool comes in many natural colors, including pure white, creamy white, many shades of silver and gray, a few shades of brown, dark brown, and black.

The many breeds of sheep offer a wide range of wool qualities. Wools are graded primarily by fiber diameter, but variations in fiber length and crimp are also considered. In *fine wools,* fiber diameter ranges between fifteen and thirty microns. Fine wools are the softest, warmest, most elastic; they are also the least abrasion-resistant, weakest, and lowest in luster. In *medium wools,* fiber diameter ranges between thirty and forty microns. These wools are less soft, less warm, and less elastic than fine wools, but they have better abrasion resistance and more strength and luster. In *coarse or long wools,* fiber diameter is greater than forty microns. These wools are least soft, least warm, and least elastic, but they are very strong and abrasion-resistant and can be lustrous. Fine wools make comfortable clothing, while medium and coarse wools make sturdy outerwear but can feel itchy and uncomfortable next to your skin.

Wool's strengths include resilience—the ability to bounce back to its original shape after being stretched or compressed. Wool is very elastic and wrinkle-resistant. It is also absorbent and warm. A wool garment can absorb up to 30% of its weight in moisture and still feel dry. Wool's tendency to shrink and felt can be an advantage or a drawback, depending on the situation. Blends of wool and another fiber may or may not shrink and felt as readily as pure wool does; it varies from case to case, depending on the particular fibers and the proportions blended. Wool is quite susceptible to insect damage, but other protein fibers are, too.

Alpaca and llama

Alpaca fiber comes from alpacas, which are similar to but smaller than llamas. The fiber ranges between twenty-four and twenty-nine microns in diameter. Because the fibers are straight, not crimped, alpaca does not have the resilience or elasticity of wool. A pure alpaca yarn feels dense and heavy compared to a pure wool yarn. In a blend, however, alpaca adds softness and warmth to wool. Alpaca can shrink or felt a little, but much less than wool does. Llama fiber is similar to alpaca, but typically somewhat coarser. Both alpaca and llama come in many natural colors, including white, black, and many shades of brown, gray, and red.

Angora

Angora is the fur from angora rabbits. The fibers are very fine, typically between twelve and fifteen microns in diameter, and feel very soft. Angora fibers are straight and slippery, so the fiber ends work their way out of a yarn and form a fuzzy halo above the surface of the fabric. It doesn't take much angora in a blend for this characteristic fuzziness to appear. Angora doesn't shrink much, but it felts easily. A garment made from pure angora is too warm for most occasions, so adding wool adds breathability. Wool also supplies the elasticity that angora lacks. Angora is expensive, so blending makes it more economical to use. Finally, spinning an angora/wool blend is easier than spinning pure angora. Angora comes in pure white and various shades of brown and silver-gray.

Camel down

Camel down is the fine, soft fiber from the undercoat of a camel, with all the longer, coarser outer hairs removed. The down fiber diameter ranges between sixteen and twenty-three microns, so camel down feels very fine and soft. Because the fibers are usually just one to three inches long, camel down can be a little more challenging than wool to spin. Wool/camel down blends are easier to spin, and make nice textured yarns. Camel down doesn't shrink or felt readily and typically comes in "camel" color.

Mohair

Mohair fiber comes from angora goats, which are usually sheared twice a year because the hair grows quite quickly—about an inch per month. The fiber diameter increases as the animal matures, from about twenty microns for baby animals to more than forty microns for adults. The finest mohair comes from the first shearing of a kid goat. With each successive shearing, the fibers get slightly coarser and less soft, until the goat reaches about two-and-a-half years, when the fiber stops thickening. Because of this transition, four grades of mohair are available to spinners—spring kid, fall kid, yearling, and adult. When you're choosing mohair for a blend, be sure to choose a suitable grade.

Mohair fibers are strong, abrasion-resistant, and wrinkle-resistant, but mohair is not as elastic as wool. Mohair doesn't shrink much, but it can felt. Depending how it's spun, a mohair yarn can be very dense and heavy or light and fuzzy. A wool/mohair blend is easier to spin than pure mohair. Because mohair dyes beautifully and is lustrous, it adds brightness and sparkle to a blend. Mohair is typically bright white, but a few breeders are producing brown or gray "colored" mohair.

Protein fibers dyed in same dyebath. Fibers from top, left column: angora, camel down, kid mohair, cashgora; middle column: Corriedale wool, Merino wool, Lincoln wool, adult mohair; right column: alpaca, bombyx silk top, tussah silk top, silk noils, cashmere.

Cashgora

Cashgora comes from goats, but not from any particular breed. The only requirement is that the goat produce a double coat—an outercoat of coarse hairy fibers and an undercoat of much finer down fibers. The down fibers measure between eighteen and twenty-two microns in diameter, which means cashgora is slightly coarser than cashmere, but finer than kid mohair. The fiber staple length of three to four inches also lies between cashmere and mohair.

Cashgora is incredibly soft and warm. It is lustrous and can add sheen to a blend. The fibers are slippery and smooth, with no crimp, so by itself cashgora tends to make a dense, heavy, inelastic yarn. Adding wool makes it easier to spin and produces a lovely blend. Cashgora is typically pure white and dyes well.

Cashmere

Cashmere is the downy undercoat of a cashmere goat. Because such goats only produce a small amount of cashmere every year, this is one of the more expensive fibers. The fibers themselves are very fine, about fifteen to seventeen microns in diameter, and the staple length ranges from one to three inches. Cashmere's most outstanding properties are its softness and warmth, qualities which enhance a blend. It comes in white and various light browns and grays.

Silk

Silk comes from the cocoons of silkworms. There are different kinds of silkworms and different ways the fiber can be prepared. For blending, my favorite forms of silk are combed tops of bombyx or tussah silk. Bombyx silk is pure white, with a fiber diameter ranging between ten and fourteen microns. Tussah silk is honey-colored, with a fiber diameter from twenty-six to thirty microns. In both cases, the average fiber length in a combed top is usually quite uniform, but it can be anywhere between four and eight inches, depending on the particular batch of top you purchase.

Both bombyx and tussah silk are strong, drapable, warmer than the same weight of wool, resistant to pilling and felting, inelastic and liable to stretch, and absorbent. Silk is lustrous and looks beautiful when dyed, but can be faded or weakened by prolonged exposure to bright light. In blends, silk adds luster, softness, and strength. Tussah silk is easier to handle, dye, and blend with wool than bombyx silk is.

Silk noils are the short bits and waste leftover from processing silk cocoons and preparing combed tops. The fibers in a batch of silk noils are usually about an inch long, which means they appear less lustrous than combed silk. The main use for noils is adding a wonderful "nubby" texture to a blended preparation.

How to blend fibers by carding

It is essential to have the right equipment when you're blending luxury fibers with wool on a drum carder. A fine-toothed drum and an infeed fade that feeds fibers onto the large drum very slowly will produce the best results. To end up with evenly blended batts, you have to be consistent in measuring out the fibers, feeding fibers onto the drum, and turning the crank. Listening to music or using a metronome can help you crank at a slow, steady speed. Follow these steps for successful blending:

1. *Card each color of wool separately at least twice.* The wool batts should be thoroughly carded before the luxury fiber is introduced.
2. *Split each carded wool batt in half crosswise.* Take one-half of the wool batt and spread it out until it is twice as wide as the drum carder. At the same time, elongate the batt a little, too. What you are after is a thin, film of wool that resembles cheesecloth.
3. *Tease open whatever fiber you want to blend with the wool.* Loosen any matts or compacted areas.
4. *Add the desired amount of teased fiber.* Spread it evenly across the wool batt. As in color blending, you can blend fibers by weighing the amounts of each fiber and figuring percentages, or you can "eyeball" the amounts. Make a sample batt to see what proportion of each fiber you should use in order to create a blend with the qualities you want.
5. *Fold the batt like a burrito, tucking the luxury fiber inside the wool.* This "fools" the drum carder into acting as if there is only one fiber present, and prevents the luxury fiber from getting stuck on the licker-in drum. The folded batt should be approximately the same width as the drum carder. After folding the batt, gently elongate it, so

Blending fibers.

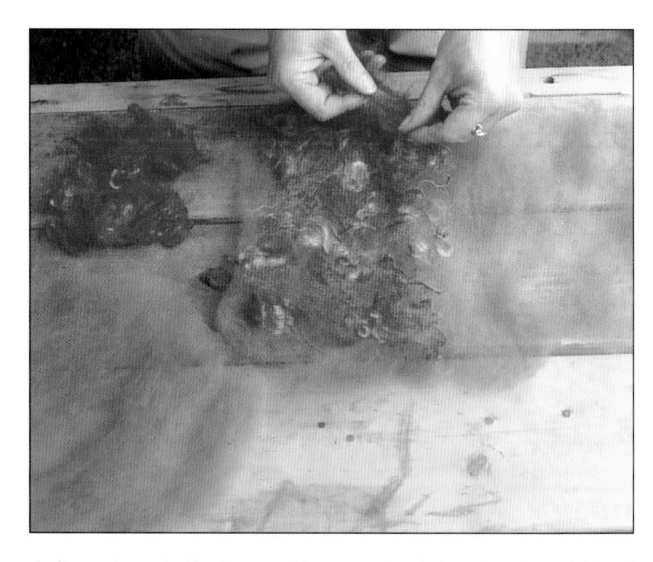

1. Spread out half of a wool batt so that it is twice the width of the drum. Place teased luxury fiber onto half of this wool and fold the wool around the luxury fiber. Elongate the folded batt so the fibers will feed smoothly onto the drum.

the fibers won't feed onto the carder so fast. Make sure the luxury fibers are evenly distributed inside the folded batt; otherwise, it will take more passes to achieve even blending.

6. *Feed the folded batt onto the drum.* Crank slowly but steadily. If the fibers are trying to feed in too fast, stop cranking and elongate the batt a little more. Do not hold back on the batt as you crank, or it will catch onto the licker-in drum. Just let go of the fiber and let it feed through.

   If there's a hole or thin spot in the wool batt, the luxury fiber can leak out and catch on the licker-in. If that happens, stop cranking, adjust the wool to patch the hole, then continue carding.
7. *Repeat steps 4 to 6 with the other half of the batt and more teased fiber.* If the drum already looks fairly full from the first half-batt, remove it and make two blended batts instead of one. It takes less time to thoroughly card two thin batts than one thick batt.
8. *Remove the batt from the carder.* It will look layered, uneven, and somewhat streaky at this point. That's okay. You're not done yet.
9. *Tear the blended batt in half lengthwise and recard.* Spread out each half to the width of the carder. Slowly feed each half back onto the carder again. If you're preparing a larger batch of fiber (enough for a project), follow steps 3 to 8 and make several batts, then randomly use different halves of different batts to even out the overall blending for the project.
10. *Repeat steps 8 and 9 until the batt is blended to your satisfaction.* This may take a few passes or many, depending on how thoroughly you want to blend the fibers. It's your decision.
11. *Pull each batt into a roving.* To do this, pull the batt lengthwise (in the same direction the fibers are aligned). Make several passes back and forth. If you plan to spin a thin yarn, pull the batt into a thin roving. For a thicker yarn, make a thicker roving. When the pulling is complete, roll the roving loosely into a ball. Carded fiber blends store well for long periods of time this way. (Sometimes batts feel stale if they are not spun shortly after being carded.)

2. Place the elongated batt on the infeed tray and slowly feed the fiber onto the drum. Do not hold back on the fiber, or it will end up on the licker-in drum.

3. When finished feeding the fiber onto the drum, remove batt. First time through, the batt will look splotchy and streaky. Don't worry; more carding will solve that.

4. Split the batt in half lengthwise, elongate both half batts, and slowly feed onto the drum carder again. Do not hold back the fiber. If you feel tension, stop and spread the fiber out more.

5. Roll the batt up lengthwise and gently pull the fiber into a roving. You will need to go back and forth several times to obtain roving that is small enough to control as you spin. Wind the fiber into balls for easy storage.

PUTTING COLOR AND TEXTURE TOGETHER

You know how to blend colors, you know how to blend fibers, and you know how to dye fibers. Now is the time to put it all together. Blending color and fibers can happen simultaneously. You can change the color of the batt at the same time you are blending a luxury fiber with wool. It just means there's one more choice to make: texture.

Here's an example (shown opposite). Start with a bright blue wool. You want to make the color duller and lighter at the same time. You also want the blend to have some luster.

Where to start? The desired color has been defined and the end result determined. To make the blue duller, choose its complement, which is orange. Orange is lighter than the blue, so it will lighten the value at the same time. To add luster, you can use combed silk or mohair, or some of each. Look for an orange silk and an orange mohair. The oranges need not be the same.

First, card the blue wool thoroughly. Split the batt widthwise in two. On one half spread out the teased orange silk. Fold and elongate that batt, feed it onto the drum carder, then remove it. On the other half, spread the teased orange mohair, then fold, elongate, card, and remove that batt. Split the two batts in half, then spread and elongate all the portions. Feed one of the silk-wool half-batts onto the drum carder, then one of the mohair/wool half-batts. Remove and repeat with the other half-batts. Look at the blend, then repeat. Keep splitting batts and recarding until the blend is what you want. See, blending isn't hard. Just take it one step at a time!

SELF-STUDY EXERCISES

Basic carding

1. Weigh out one-half ounce of clean wool, tease it, and card a batt on the drum carder. Count the number of passes through the carder to see how many it takes until the batt is thoroughly carded. This will depend on the fiber, the teasing, and the carder used.

   From here on through the end of the exercises, if you weigh the fibers and keep track of formulas, you will end up with a notebook full of recipes! All the exercises can be approached as series of color studies, not just single experiments.

Blending color and texture. A blue wool is used as the base. The bottom skein is the blue wool carded with orange kid mohair. The center skein shows the same blue carded with orange tussah silk. The top skein is a blend of all three fibers.

Color blending

For these exercises, choose one color of wool and card five half-ounce batts of that color. When thoroughly carded, split each batt in two widthwise. One half-batt will be used for each exercise. For the other colors to blend with these half-batts in each exercise, choose one-quarter ounce of the color, card it thoroughly by itself, split the batt in half, and use only half for blending. Use the half-batts of other colors in any of the later exercises.

2. *Make a color warmer.* Choose an analogous color warmer than the original.
3. *Make a color cooler.* Choose an analogous color cooler than the original.
4. *Make a color lighter.* Choose any color that is lighter in value than the original.
5. *Make a color darker.* Choose any color that is darker in value than the original.
6. *Make a color brighter.* Choose a color in the same hue family that is brighter than the original color.
7. *Make a color duller.* Choose a color that is complementary to the original color.
8. *Make a color duller.* Choose a gray that is the same value as the original color.
9. *Make a color duller.* Add black to the original color.
10. *Make a color duller.* Add white to the original color.
11. *Blend close values.* Choose any two colors that are close in value and blend them. Watch carefully to stop carding before they blend too much.
12. *Blend different values.* Choose from the same two color families as exercise 11, but use two colors that have very different values.
13. *Blend all three primary colors.* Choose a yellow, a red, and a blue. Card one batt using equal amounts of each color. Then do batts with each color being dominant.

Color harmony blending

Reminder: For best results, thoroughly card all colors separately before beginning to blend.

14. *Monochromatic.* Choose equal amounts

(25% of each) of four colors, all from the same hue family, but with varying saturations and values.

15. *Analogous.* Choose equal amounts (25% of each) of four colors within an analogous range on the color wheel. Be careful not to blend too much.
16. *Complementary.* Choose two colors each from a complementary pair of color families. Use some saturated colors. For the first blend, use equal amounts (25% each) of all colors. Then blend different batts using the proportions 50:30:10:10. Give each color a chance to be dominant. See how many combinations are possible.
17. *Split complementary.* Choose two colors from each of the three color families and blend several batts in different proportions. The first batt would be equal parts (16.6% each) of all colors. Then give each color a chance to be dominant.
18. *Triad.* Choose six colors with different values and saturations from a triad *other than* red, yellow, and blue. Try making different batts, each with one color dominant. Take your time. It is easy to overcard.
19. *Tetrad.* Choose four *very* saturated colors from each of the four color families. This combination works best if one of the colors is dominant. Be careful not to overcard!

Painterly approach to blending

20. Choose a color chip or something whose color you want to match. Choose a base color of wool, then choose color(s) for blending that will duplicate the desired color. Mastering this kind of blending takes some practice, but it gets easier with repetition. Try it again and again!

Fiber blending

21. Start by carding at least five half-ounce batts of fine wool (Merino, fine Corriedale, etc). The color is not important (yet). Split the wool batts in half widthwise. Try blending wool with each of the following fibers: alpaca, angora, camel down, cashgora, cashmere, mohair, combed bombyx silk, combed tussah silk, silk noils. If you like, repeat this exercise, using different proportions of wool and each other fiber.

Color and texture blending

Start with assortments of carded and dyed wools and dyed luxury fibers, and choose what you want for each exercise.

22. *Warmer color.* Choose a wool and a dyed luxury fiber to make a blend that is warmer and fuzzier. (You could also try warmer and more lustrous, then warmer and softer.)
23. *Cooler color.* Choose a wool and a dyed luxury fiber to make a blend that is cooler and more lustrous.
24. *Lighter color.* Choose a wool and a luxury fiber to make a blend that is lighter-colored and softer.
25. *Darker color.* Choose a wool and a luxury fiber to make a blend that is darker-colored and any texture you choose.
26. *Brighter color.* Choose a wool and a luxury fiber to make a blend that is brighter. (Hint: luster enhances brightness.)
27. *Duller color.* Choose a wool and any luxury fiber to make the wool look duller.
28. *Painterly approach.* Choose a color to duplicate. Also decide on a texture you want to acheive. Then blend one or more luxury fibers with wool to obtain the desired result. Add small amounts of one fiber at a time until you reach your goal.

chapter **chapter** 5 chapter

Drum carding for multicolored yarns

—5—

Drum carding for multicolored yarns

Unlike yarns spun from thoroughly blended batts, the yarns you will spin from batts described in this chapter have multiple colors that are distinctly visible even from a distance. Making these multicolored yarns is a several-step process. First, you dye clean fibers in a range of colors and card each color separately. Then you take portions of different batts and feed them onto the drum carder a final time, arranging the colors in specific ways in order to make predictable, multicolored effects. Finally, you make a stack of up to five multicolored batts that you will combine in a single yarn, putting in as many colors as possible yet keeping them separate and distinct. Either roll this stack of batts or split it into a continuous strip, then gently pull into pencil-size roving to spin.

Why go to all this trouble when you could just "rainbow" dye? Because you want to design and make yarns that cannot be purchased. The yarns produced using techniques in this chapter tend to be complex, with colors that are clear, not muddy; finished products made from these yarns will not be splotchy. By creating the fiber, you have full control over the appearance of the final piece. Paying attention to the colors you choose and the way you arrange them in the batt lets you create unique but repeatable yarns.

MAKING MULTICOLORED WOOL BATTS

While the thoroughly blended batts described in Chapter 4 have the appearance of a single color from a distance, multicolored batts maintain a distinctly multicolored appearance. Waiting until the last step to put the colors together is the key to keeping them distinct.

Carding each color separately is the first step in the multicolor process. Basic carding guidelines are the same. Make batts no larger than one-half ounce. You can use either solid-color batts or thoroughly blended batts that give the appearance of one color. Either way, the batts must be thoroughly carded *before* you begin striping and layering, or the stack will not pull easily and the colors will not remain where they belong.

I don't feed colors randomly into a batt because that usually gives muddy results. Instead, I arrange colors in three ways: long stripes, short stripes, and thin layers. These three ways are easy to record, easy to repeat, and easy to perform with a drum carder. Each technique has a different purpose. They can be used singly or in combination, depending on how many colors you want to put into a yarn and what effects you want to create.

One batt is not enough to hold as many colors as I want in a yarn and still maintain their clarity. Putting too many colors into a single batt muddies. I prefer to use fewer than nine colors per batt, then stack two or more batts to get more colors in the yarn. Using multiple batts minimizes the amount of contact between colors, which maintains their clarity and makes a brighter yarn.

The batts in a stack don't all have to be the same weight, and they shouldn't be too large. It's better to stack many thin batts than a few big ones. Depending on the carding cloth on your drum carder, you can card about three-quarters to one ounce of wool into a single batt.

Maintaining clarity. To keep colors bright in the final yarn, separate colors into more than one batt. Both sets of samples use the same nine colors. The top samples used two batts to arrange colors. The bottom samples used the same colors in one batt, making them muddier and more blended.

(This is more than you can process in the initial carding, but it's okay for color arrangement.) Using a burnishing tool will enable you to fit more fiber onto the drum without sacrificing color control. When you cannot see the carding teeth on the main drum, or when fibers end up on the licker-in, the drum is full and will hold no more.

Long stripes

These stripes of color run the entire length of the batt. In a yarn, long-stripe colors appear regularly, coming and going, depending how evenly and slowly the stack has been pulled into roving. Variables in making long stripes include:

- The width of the stripes in the batt. The wider the stripe, the more the color appears in the yarn.
- The thickness or depth of each stripe in the batt. The thicker the stripe, the more the color appears in the yarn.
- The number of stripes across the batt. The more stripes, the less distinct each color. For a standard-size drum carder, I find that it is difficult to feed on and hard to see more than six stripes across the width of the batt. Two to four colors works well.
- The contrast in value and hue between adjacent stripes. The greater the contrast, the bolder the yarn.
- The amount of overlap between stripes. The more they overlap, the more the colors will be mixed and dulled.

How to make long stripes in a batt

Each color should be fed onto the drum singly. For each color, pull off a portion of a carded batt and elongate it. Feed this elongated fiber onto a specific area of the carder as you slowly turn the crank. Feed on all the color for that stripe. If you have problems with the fibers getting gulped onto the drum, stop and elongate them more. Remember, you should be able to see the infeed tray through the fiber supply as you are feeding the fibers onto the drum. It is important to make an even, smooth batt.

Elongate a portion of the next color batt and feed that onto the drum. Adjacent colors can be feathered into one another to make the color transitions a little more subtle. This will also help with the stability of the batt. Repeat this procedure until all the colors have been fed onto the drum. The entire width of the drum should be evenly covered. If one stripe is thicker than another, add more fiber to even it out. Finally, remove the batt from the carder.

Making long stripes.

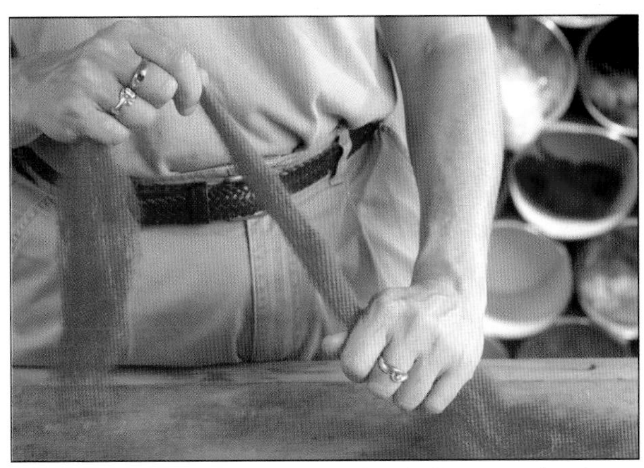

1. Elongate already-carded single colors before returning the fiber to the carder. Elongation will create a more even distribution of fiber in the final batt.

2. Feed elongated fiber onto the drum one color at a time. Colors can overlap.

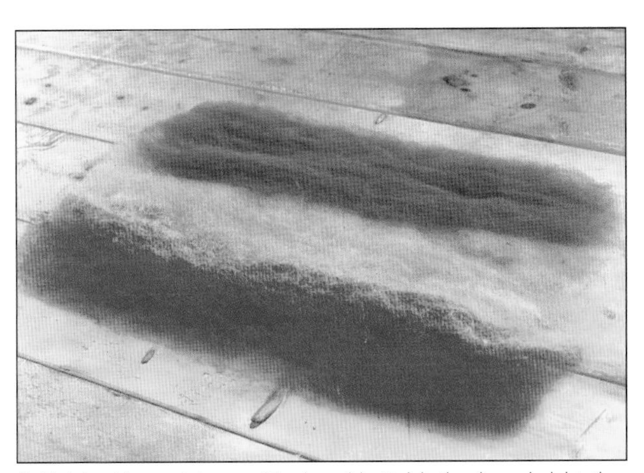

3. Finished long-stripe multicolored batt. Notice how bright the colors remain.

Short-stripe effects.

A multicolored batt that uses two colors alternately in short stripes. The swatch shows how the short stripes appear in a fabric as alternating colored areas.

A multicolored batt that uses a color progression in short stripes. The colors go from red at one end to blue at the other. The fabric shows that progression.

Short stripes

These stripes travel across the width of the batt and change along its length. In the yarn, the colors of the short stripes appear for a while, then disappear when the next stripe appears. For example, if the short-stripe colors alternate, you'll see color A for a while, then color B for a while, then back to color A and so on throughout the length of the skein spun from that batt. Color progressions are another way to use short stripes in a yarn. For example, you could arrange a series of stripes that runs from red to red-violet to violet to blue-violet to blue. From a batt like that you could spin a skein of yarn that changes from one hue family to another.

In the yarn, short-stripe colors are bold. Of all the multicolored carding techniques, short-stripe colors are most obvious in the yarn. This is a good place to put colors you want to use as accents. Variables in making short stripes include:

- The length of each short stripe. The stripe cannot be any shorter than the staple length of the wool being used; in fact, it will be a little longer.
- The number of short stripes in the length of the batt. This is determined by the staple length of the wool, the size of the big drum on your carder, and the extent to which adjacent short stripes overlap.
- The thickness of each short stripe. The thicker the stripe, the bolder the color in the yarn.
- The contrast in value and hue between adjacent colors. The more contrast, the bolder the yarn.

How to make short stripes in a batt

Position the big drum so the doffing groove (the strip where there are no teeth) is on top, and keep the carder from turning by stopping the handle with your hip. Pull off a small portion of carded fiber in the first color. With the drum carder still, place the fiber directly onto the main drum, starting just right of the doffing groove, and overlapping the groove with the first stripe. To do this, catch the fibers onto the carding cloth with your left hand. Use the palm of your right hand to press down on the fibers, and at the same time, gently tug with your left hand to leave a staple length of fibers caught in the teeth of the drum. Repeat, loading fibers across the width of the drum. Slowly crank the carder a couple of times to secure the fibers of the first stripe onto the drum.

Don't load on too much fiber at once. If you do, the short stripe will drift around the drum and form a longer stripe instead. The stripe should end up only slightly longer than the staple length of the fiber. If the fibers are migrating too far, either you're loading too many fibers or you're not adequately anchoring them with your right hand. The fibers need to be embedded into the carding cloth to stay where you place them.

Load one color at a time onto the drum, crank, then load the next color and crank. Overlap the stripes a little to make the batt stronger. If you want to make short stripes thicker, add the colors in two or three layers instead of putting too much fiber on each stripe at once. Continue until the drum is full, then remove the batt.

Batts that include short stripes are not very stable and sometimes fall apart. To stabilize a batt, you can feed a thin layer of fiber onto the drum before you start making short stripes, and feed on another thin layer afterwards. The thin layers act like sandwich bread, holding the short stripes together.

Thin layers

These are small amounts of fiber that are spread across the entire width and length of the batt. The color of a thin layer is visible throughout the final yarn and gives a subtle background color to the skein. The colors in thin layers get blended much more than in

Making short stripes.

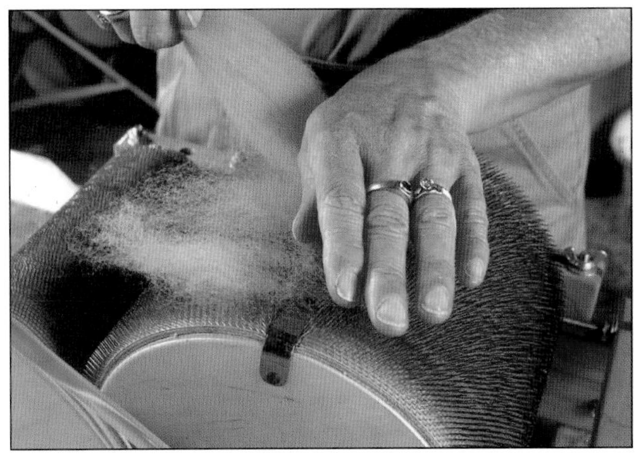

1. I apply the first short-stripe color onto the drum, holding the drum still with my hip. Push fiber into the drum with the right hand, and pull excess fiber away with the left.

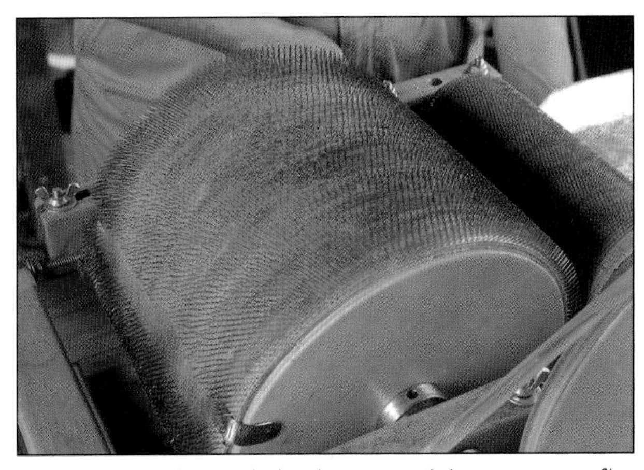

2. After each color, crank the drum several times to secure fiber.

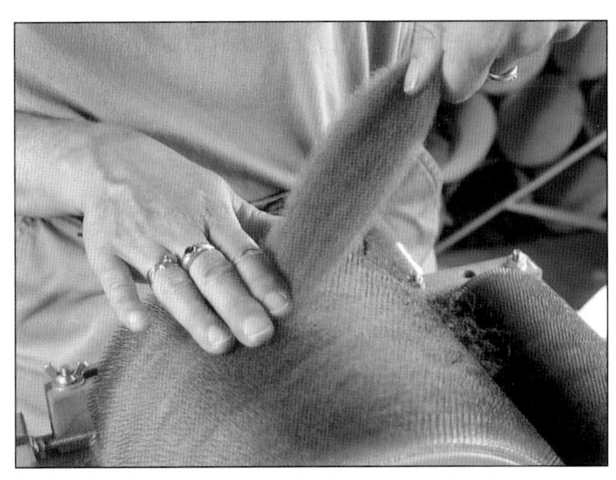

3. Overlap the colors and apply the second color the same way as the first. After each color, crank the drum several times to secure fiber.

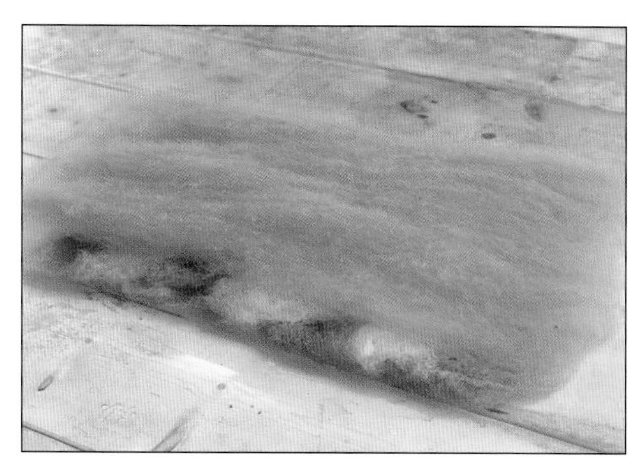

4. Short-stripe batt as it comes off the carder. The thin layers of green on bottom and top hold the short stripes together.

two-stripe techniques and do not appear as boldly in the yarn. A thin layer is a good place to put the colors that you want to include in a yarn but don't want to see clearly. Thin layers can dramatically tone down a very bright color. Variables in making thin layers include:

- The thickness of each thin layer. The thicker the layer, the more clearly the color will show up in the final yarn. Very thin gauze-like layers will show only a hint of their color in the final yarn.
- The number of thin layers in the batt. The more thin layers, the more the colors will blend. Remember that layering is the first step in making thoroughly blended batts. It is easy to get too subtle and lose the clarity of colors.

How to make thin layers in a batt

Choose a small amount of a carded wool batt. Spread out and elongate the carded fiber and place it on the infeed tray. Slowly crank the drum and feed the fiber onto the drum as evenly as possible. Evenness is very important. If the fiber doesn't feed onto the drum evenly, try one or all of the following:

- Loosen the fiber more before feeding it onto the drum.
- Feed the fiber onto the carder more slowly.
- Crank more slowly so the fiber doesn't get gulped in so fast.
- Continue feeding the fiber onto the drum until the layer is as thick as you want it. Repeat with other colors until the drum is full, then remove the batt.

Making thin layers. Feeding the first color on the drum for a thin layer. Before putting it on the drum, elongate the already carded batt to ensure a smooth, even final batt.

A thin-layered batt. The thicker the thin layers are, the bolder the colors will appear in the yarn.

STACKING, ROLLING, AND PULLING WOOL BATTS

You can't spin directly from a stack of batts because you'd lose control. So this stack of beautifully carded fibers must somehow be transformed into a spinnable roving. One method that works well is to roll the stack like a jelly roll, then slowly pull the roll into pencil-size roving. Here's the procedure, one step at a time.

1. *Stack the batts evenly atop one another.* I put up to five batts, or about two and one-half ounces of wool, in one stack. When you're learning, use a smaller stack. If the stack is too tall or heavy, it's hard to control and very difficult to pull into roving.

   Think about how to arrange batts in the stack. The bottom batt needs to have a smooth surface. Place either a thin-layer or long-stripe batt on the bottom because it becomes the outside of the roll. Short-stripe batts are not as strong and need to be in the middle or top of the stack. For more contrast in the yarn, place contrasting colors against each other in the stack. To minimize contrast, place related colors against each other in the stack.
2. *Put a dowel on top of the stacked batts.* Use a quarter-inch dowel that's a little longer than the batts. Place it lengthwise on the stack, about one-third of the way across the top batt. If the dowel is placed too close to the edge, the stack will get rolled too tightly. (Using a dowel thicker than one-quarter inch can also make the roll too tight.)
3. *Fold the stack of batts loosely around the dowel.* Then form the stack into a loose roll, typically five to nine inches in diameter.
4. *Pull the dowel out of the roll of batts.* Be sure the open edge of the roll is laid against the table—this helps keep it under control. The dowel should slide out easily. (If it doesn't, the stack is probably rolled too tight. Gently undo it and roll it again, but more loosely this time.)

PULLING TIPS

The purpose of pulling a stack of batts into roving is to preserve the color order of the stack and at the same time make the fiber supply thin enough to control as you spin. The pulling motion must be slow and deliberate, consistently easing the fibers apart. The goal of pulling is to end up with a thin roving that consists of ribbons of changing colors. If you pull too far too soon, there will be irregular areas of color and the yarn will turn out striped.

- Pulling is not hard, but you cannot rush it. There are no shortcuts! Keep one hand anchored against the table while you are pulling. This keeps you from pulling too much, keeps you more in control, and keeps you from pulling the roving into two pieces.
- Relate the pulling to the staple length of the wool. The distance between your hands has to be *more* than the staple length. If pulling is hard, move your hands farther apart. For the first couple of passes along the length of the roving, each pull will be considerably *less* than the staple length. In subsequent passes, you can pull a little farther each time, but always less than a staple length.
- The larger the roll, the farther apart your hands need to be. If your hands are too close together, it's impossible to pull the roll into a thin roving. Instead, you'll pull it in two.
- If the surface of the roll looks woozled or not smooth, you are not holding the roll tight enough. Your hands are moving across the surface of the fibers instead of the fibers moving between your hands. A weak grip may also make the batts slip apart. Then you will have a yarn very different from the one you planned.

5. *Place one hand at each end of the roll.* It is important to grip the roll firmly. Include all the batts. Don't let any of the fibers move inside your grip. All of the fiber movement in the following steps should take place *between* your hands, not inside your grip.

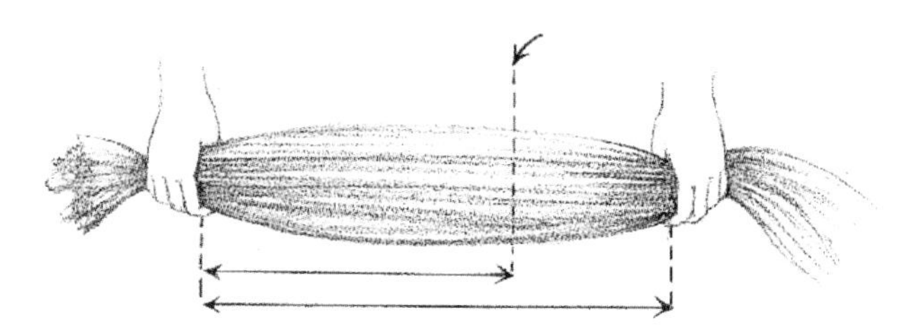

For the first pull of the stack, place hands approximately eighteen inches apart and pull until fibers begin to move, then stop. Move the left hand to where the fiber moved. Hands should remain fifteen to eighteen inches apart in this step. Diameter of the roll is seven to nine inches. (Steps 6–8.)

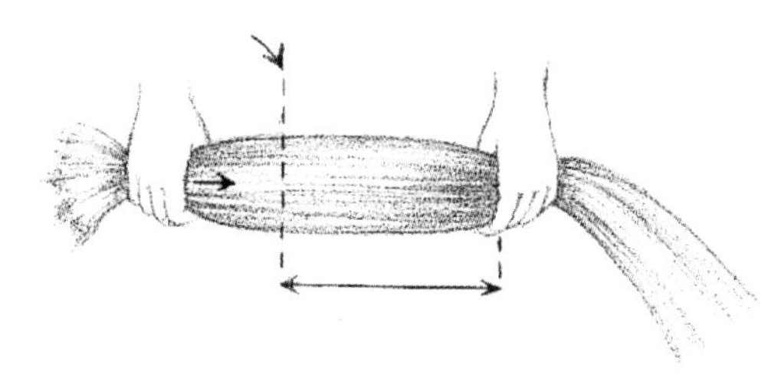

Hands are no closer than ten inches when the diameter of the roll is five to seven inches. Continue to move one hand to where the fiber is moving and overlap the hand postions along the roll. (Step 9.)

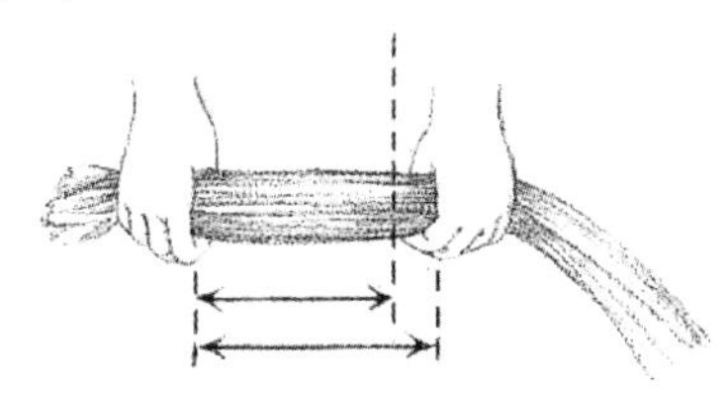

Roll is now three to five inches in diameter. Place hands eight to ten inches apart and work along the roving. Each pull should be shorter than the staple length. (Step 10.)

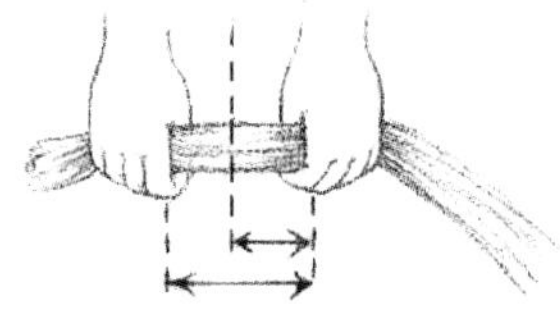

Diameter is now three inches or less. Hands can be five to seven inches apart for the pulling. (Step 11.)

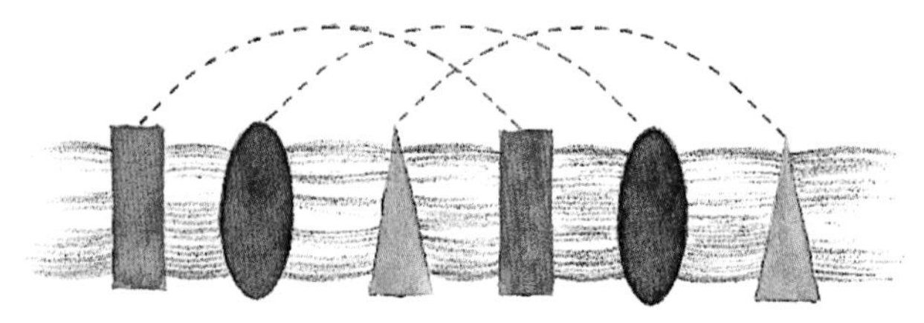

Overlap the hand positions along the roving as the pulling takes place. The distance between hands is reduced as the roll of batts gets thinner.

6. *Begin to pull* gently *with both hands.* Keep one hand anchored on the table. As soon as you see the fibers on the surface of the roll move, STOP! There will not be much movement at this stage. You'll have to pull rather hard, but pull only a very short distance. At this stage, you are only easing the fibers apart a little, in preparation for further pulling.
7. *Move only the hand that is closest to the fiber movement.* This movement will be close to one end of the roll. It doesn't matter which end—just observe where the fibers are moving. Move the hand from that end of the roll to where you observed the fiber movement. Keep the other hand at the far end of the roll. Hold the roll firmly with both hands. Remember, the fiber movement should happen *between* your hands, not inside your grip.

   Holding the roll firmly, pull a little more. Stop as soon as you see fibers moving in the roll. Move your hand to where you saw the fiber movement. Hold firmly and tug again. Stop as soon as you see fibers moving. Repeat this firm gripping and gentle pulling along the roll, keeping one hand stationary and moving the other hand to where the fiber moves. Continue until the moving hand has worked two-thirds of the length of the roll, then stop.
8. *Now reverse your hand actions.* Use the hand that has been moving and pulling to hold the other end of the batt against the table. Starting from that end now, use the other hand to grip and gently pull the roll. Stop when your moving hand has worked about two-thirds of the way along the roll. The roll won't look much longer yet, but be persistent and don't hurry.
9. *Grip one end of the roll with one hand, and place the other hand near the center.*

Hold firmly and pull a little. The rule is still to stop pulling as soon as you see the fibers move. Repeat as before and move the hand closest to the fiber movement after each pull. Your hands will get progressively closer (but no closer than about ten inches). When it becomes hard to pull, stop.

Repeat on the other half of the roll by switching hand positions and moving in the other direction. This time the roll will definitely be longer. If there are thin spots in the roll, simply skip them and work on the next portion of the roll.

10. *Starting at either end of the roll, place your hands about eight inches apart and pull gently.* As before, as soon as you see the fibers move between your hands, stop pulling. This time, both hands will be moving along the length of the roll. The hand that is closer to the fiber movement will move to where the fibers moved. The other hand will follow, staying about eight inches away. Pull the roll gently.

    Repeat the moving and gentle pulling along the entire length of the roll. The distance between your hands should stay fairly consistent. The hand placement for each pull should overlap the hand placement of the previous pull to keep the colors pulling out as ribbons, not blobs. (If your hand placement "leapfrogs" and does not overlap, that makes areas of color that stop and start and do not flow.) The roll now looks like a very large roving, about three to five inches in diameter.

    When you reach the other end, reverse your hand actions and go back in the opposite direction. Do not try to pull too much on each pass across the roving. You should be pulling much less than the staple length of the fibers with each pull. If you try to pull faster, the colors will not be consistent for spinning and the yarn will be striped. At the end of this step, the diameter of the roving will be about one inch smaller than it was after the previous step.

    It is much better to work slowly back and forth along the roving, making many passes, than to hurry. The roving should be much easier to pull now. As the roving becomes thinner, your hands will work progressively closer.

11. *Starting at either end of the roll, place your hands about six inches apart and pull gently.* This time keep the inside hand against the table and move the hand closer to the end of the roll. Stop when you see fibers moving. Move your hand an inch or so closer to the stationary hand and pull again. If it is still easy to pull, keep the stationary hand in the same place and move your other hand another inch closer and pull gently again.

    When it is difficult to pull, it is time to move on. Don't forget to overlap your hand positions. Move the hand that's holding the roving against the table back three or four inches, and move the pulling hand forward to where you last saw the fibers moving. Repeat the gentle pull, move your hand an inch, and pull again. Repeat this sequence along the whole roving, then reverse.

    Continue working back and forth along the roving until you have pulled it down to the desired thickness, which depends on the size of yarn you plan to spin. The thicker the yarn, the thicker the roving, and vice versa. The goal is to have the roving thin enough for easy control of the color order in the drafting triangle as you spin. I typically make rovings about the size of a pencil.

12. *Roll the pencil roving loosely into a ball.* While winding, keep your thumb in the ball so you won't wrap the roving too tight. Do not deliberately add twist to the roving. You can spin from the ball right away or store it for future use.

Rolling and pulling a stack of batts.

1. Place the dowel approximately one-third of the way lengthwise into the stack.

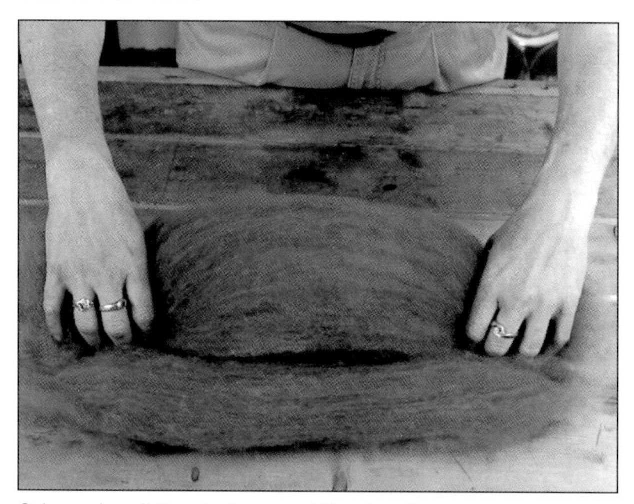

2. Loosely roll the stack around the dowel.

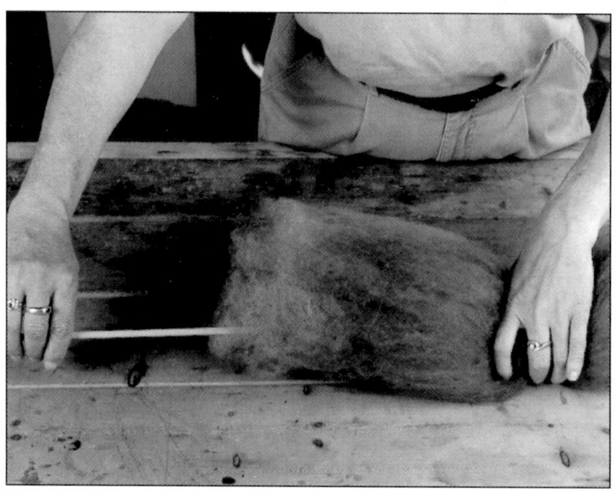

3. With the open edge against the table, pull the dowel out of the roll.

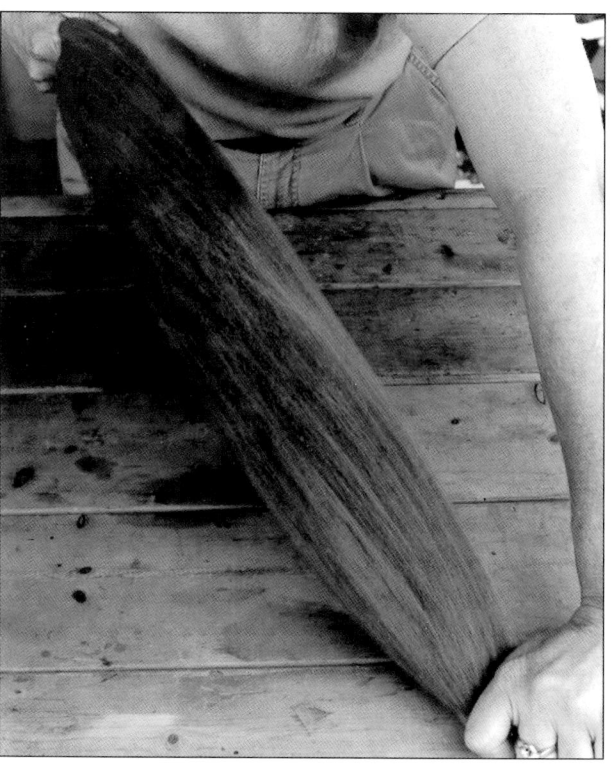

4. Hold one hand steady against the table and gently pull the roll. Stop pulling as soon as you see fiber movement.

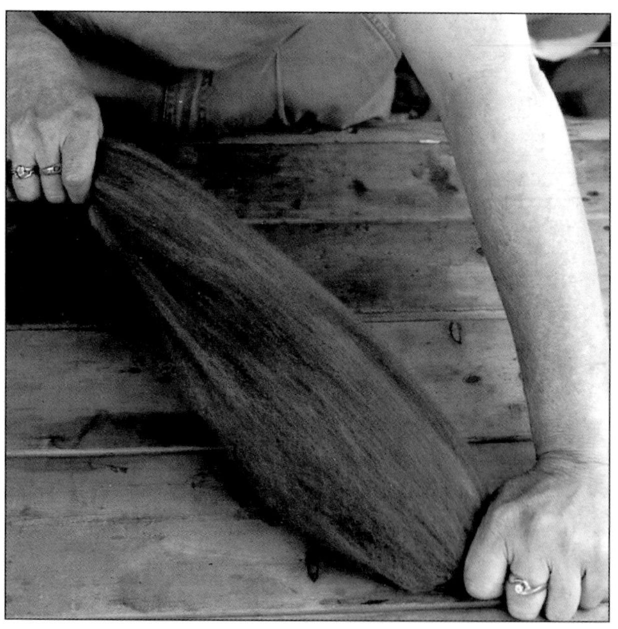

5. Move your hands and gently pull the roll again. The thinner the roll becomes, the closer your hands can be. Alternate the hand that is on the table and the one that is doing the pulling. This will even out any differences.

6. Work back and forth along the roving. Remember to overlap your hands to ensure even distribution of colors. Colors should look like "ribbons" in the roving.

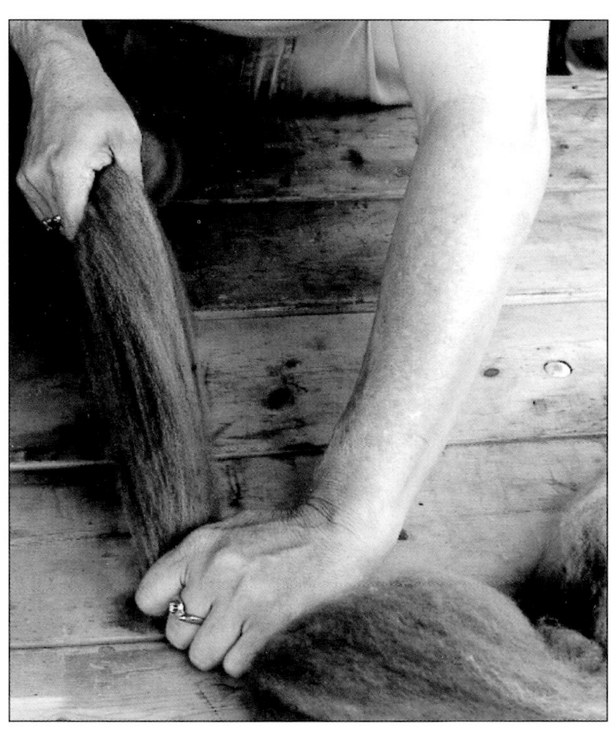

7. Now pull with the other hand and move back along the roving in the other direction.

8. When the roving is thinner, it can be pulled without the support of the table. Do not pull too much each time. Better to pull too little than too much.

9. Go back and forth along the roving several times. You may need to make a dozen passes to get the roving as thin as a pencil.

10. Loosely wind the pencil roving into a ball until ready to spin.

STACKING AND PULLING MULTICOLORED BATTS THAT CONTAIN LUXURY-FIBER BLENDS

Batts containing luxury-fiber blends tend to be a little harder to control as you pull them into roving. This is because the fibers vary in feel and staple length. To keep control of the stack color order, you can split the stack into a continuous strip—a "Z-strip"—and then pull it out into roving. Although you prepare the batts in the same way, making long stripes, short stripes, or thin layers, splitting a stack of batts into a Z-strip dramatically changes the way the colors appear in the yarn. The stack of batts is split into one continuous roving that will be further pulled out to a pencil-size roving for spinning.

Long stripes. Now each stripe color will appear in the yarn for many yards, but once it is gone, it will not reappear in the skein unless there is another long stripe in the batt. Using long stripes is a way to make color or value changes over the length of the skein. The changes will be more subtle if adjacent long stripes are slightly overlapped. The thinner the long stripe, the faster the color changes occur in the roving and yarn. (The length of each color in the skein also depends on how the stack is split.)

Short stripes. The colors in short stripes are still the boldest in the yarn. In Z-stripping, short-stripe colors act as accents that repeat regularly throughout the length of the skein. (In the rolling method, each short stripe only appears for one portion of the skein.) It is still important not to use too much fiber at once when loading a color for short stripes onto the drum, or the fiber will migrate and the short-stripe effect will be lost.

Thin layers. Thin layers set the background for the final yarn whether you Z-strip or roll the stack of batts. The thicker the layer, the more obvious the color. It is easy to get too subtle and blend colors too much. Using thin layers is a way to tone down very bright or highly contrasting colors and give the yarn a subtle excitement.

Along with how you choose and arrange colors in each batt, you can create different effects in the yarn by how you stack and Z-strip the batts. Here are some possible variations:

The number of batts in the stack. Make fiber-blended stacks smaller than all-wool stacks. The differences among fibers, even when they are well blended, reduce your control when you are Z-stripping the stack. The total weight of the stacked batts should be no more than two ounces. The striped or layered batts that go into the stack should weigh no more than a half-ounce each. The batts do not have to be the same size.

When Z-stripping, you can split the batt into wide or narrow strips. This affects how the colors appear in the skein of yarn. Wide strips produce long sections of each color but few repetitions overall. Narrow strips produce short sections of each color and many repetitions

Different effects with Z-stripping.

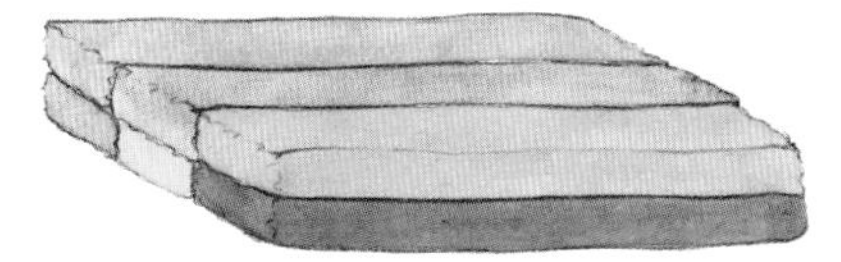

Stack of long-stripe batts.

Stack stripped into fourths. Amounts and proportions of each of the long stripes is different, depending how the stack has been stripped.

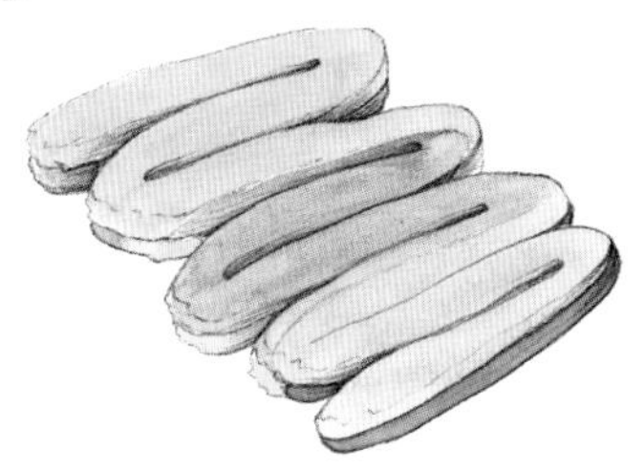

Same stack stripped into eighths. More color interactions can take place.

Stack of short-stripe batts.

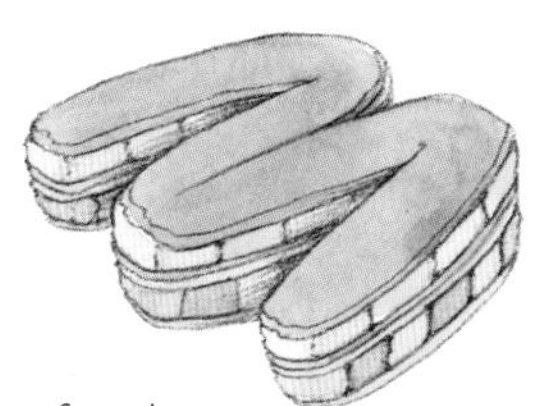

Stack stripped into fourths.

Same stack stripped into eighths. There are more repetitions of the color sequence than when split into fourths.

overall. Having an end use in mind will help you decide which effect you want.

The thickness of the final roving. Once the stack has been Z-stripped, the strips are pulled out into roving. The thickness of the roving should relate to the size of yarn you plan to spin. The thicker the desired yarn, the thicker the roving, and vice versa.

STACKING, Z-STRIPPING, AND PULLING A STACK OF BLENDED-FIBER BATTS

1. *Prepare each carded blend separately,* as described in Chapter 4.
2. *Prepare striped or layered batts,* as described earlier in this chapter.
3. *Stack the batts in the desired order.* Make sure the batts are all spread out to the same size and lined up on top of each other. Remember, the more contrast between layers, the bolder the yarn.
4. *Starting at one corner, begin the Z-strip.* Using both hands, grip one corner of the whole stack and begin to split a strip down the whole length of the stack. Stop short of the end of the stack. You want to divide the whole stack into one continuous strip. The amount left at the end of the stack should be approximately the same width as the strips.
5. *Turn the stack and rip the next strip.* Stop short as you did at the other end. This strip should be the same width as the last strip.
6. *Continue in this manner across the width of the stack.* Split the whole stack into one continuous Z-strip or roving. The thickness and length of the roving will depend on the size of the stack and how you split it.
7. *Starting at one end, slowly and gently pull the roving thinner.* Your hands start out closer with this method. For the first pass, put your hands about six to eight inches apart. Watch where the fibers are moving.

Z-stripping a stack of batts.

1. Stack of color- and fiber-blended batts.

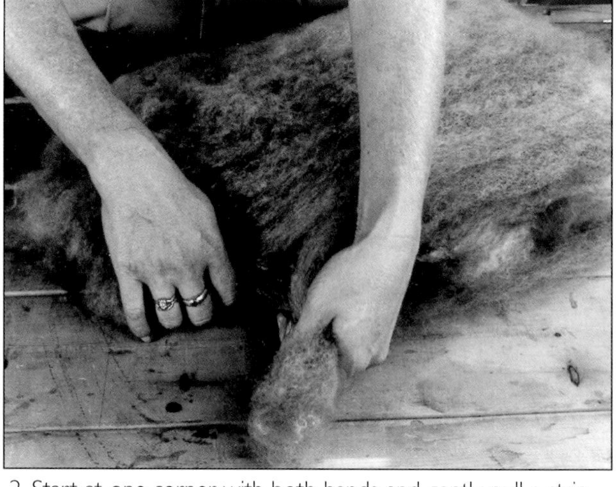

2. Start at one corner with both hands and gently pull a strip of the fiber from the stack lengthwise.

3. Stop short of the end. Leave about the same amount as the width of the strip.

4. Continue on the next strip and stop short of the end.

5. The stack of batts should end up as one continuous strip.

6. With hands six to eight inches apart, pull the strips thinner. Go back and forth several times if necessary to obtain a pencil-size roving.

As before, stop pulling as soon as you see fibers move. Between pulls, your hands will move along the roving, overlapping with where they were before. Grip firmly and be sure the fiber movement is between your hands, not in your grip. Pull no more than one-third of the staple length each time. If you pull out the roving too fast, you will end up with clumps of color, not ribbons of color. You've gotten this far, so be patient during this last step.

8. *Wind the pencil-size roving into a loose ball.*

COLOR AND DESIGN CONSIDERATIONS FOR MULTICOLORED BATTS

The color principles from Chapter 1 apply to choosing and placing colors for multicolored batts. I cannot emphasize too much that when you understand the color principles, making choices becomes much easier. One way to choose colors for a yarn is to use any of the color harmonies as the base for the palette. Keep in mind the variables of hue, value, and saturation within the harmonies.

For a yarn to have a dominant color, choose at least half the weight of its fibers from the dominant hue family, but choose colors that vary in undertone, saturation, and value. The final results are much richer if you use a range of related colors instead of just one. Remember that to dominate a yarn, it takes more of a cool color than a warm.

To liven up a yarn, put accent colors somewhere in the stack. Accents can be brighter, contrasting, or just stripes from a different range. To add spark to a yarn, include a small amount of the complement of the dominant color(s). The complement will highlight and intensify the dominant color.

For quieter yarns, keep your hue and value choices reasonably close. The more contrast, the livelier the yarn. Pay special attention to the color values because they are the first thing you perceive from a distance. To avoid the barber-pole effect, bridge the extremes by using a range of values. When extreme dark and light values are placed side by side, the darks make the lights look lighter and the lights make the darks look darker. Such strong contrasts dull your perception of hues.

When both warm and cool colors are present in a yarn, the warm colors tend to pop out and the cool colors tend to recede. The warm colors are more aggressive and the cool colors are more shy. By manipulating the saturation, quantity, and values of warm and cool, you can achieve a balanced effect.

How you arrange colors in the stack also affects how each color looks. Review the discussion of contrasts in Chapter 1. By knowing what will happen beforehand, you can design and predict your results, thereby increasing your successes. It is important to remember that:

- Colors placed next to black appear lighter and a little brighter.
- Colors placed next to white appear darker and a little duller.
- Complementary colors look more intense side by side than apart.
- A bright color next to a dull color will make the bright more intense and the dull even duller.
- If a color is not working in a combination, it may have the wrong undertone. Choose a related color with a different undertone.

You will not always like how the colors look at the batt or roving stage. Reserve judgment until you've spun some yarn and knitted or woven a sample swatch. The colors you start with need to be lighter and brighter than what you desire in the finished skein. Trust your choices!

Use small batts to keep colors bright in the final stack. Colors are less likely to blur if they don't come together until you pull the batts into roving. Bold effects are possible when hues and values are isolated within batts. For example, to make a six-color blue-violet yarn, putting three blues in one batt and three violets in a second

CARDING MULTICOLORED BATTS FOR A PROJECT

It is not difficult to make skeins of matching multicolored yarn for a project. In fact, it is easier to create consistent multicolored yarns than it is to match skeins of thoroughly blended colors. You'll need to think in terms of many stacks of batts instead of just one stack. Here are the steps to follow: (See example on pages 155–156.)

1. *Decide the total amount of yarn you need.* If you figure in terms of yards, you need to convert to weight. Measuring for fiber preparation is in terms of weight. You can weigh an existing article, such as a scarf or sweater, to estimate how much fiber you will need to make something similar.
2. *Choose the colors you want to include.*
3. *Figure how much of each color you need.* This is easier if you use equal amounts of each color, but you can use different amounts of colors if you prefer. The larger the amount of a color, the more obvious it will be in the yarn. Make sure the total of all the colors is equal to the total amount determined in Step 1.
4. *Card each color separately.* If you are blending colors or fibers, continue through the blending steps now. Make half-ounce batts.
5. *Decide how much each stack will weigh.* A stack of wool batts can weigh from two-and-a-half to three ounces. A stack of blended-fiber batts should weigh no more than two ounces.
6. *Evenly divide the batts, making as many portions as you need for stacks.* If you use equal amounts of each color, the portions will be the same for each stack. The size of the portions will depend on how much of each color you need, and they may be as small as a fraction of a batt.
7. *Decide how many batts will be in each stack.* Remember to limit the size of each batt, and use no more than five batts per stack. Decide where each color will appear. Figure how the colors will be arranged into batts, and how the batts will be arranged in the stacks.
8. *Prepare the first batt for each stack.* Set these aside. Prepare the second batt for each stack, and lay these on top of the first batts. Continue until you have prepared all the batts for every stack.
9. *Roll or Z-strip the stacks of batts.* Then pull the batts into rovings and roll the rovings into balls for spinning.

batt creates a bright effect, while putting both blues and violets in each of two batts makes a heathered effect. Another way to make a bold yarn is to segregate values within a batt. The more you segregate the differences, the bolder the yarn. The more you mix hues, values, and saturations, the more heathered the yarn.

Color placement of stripes in the stack also makes a difference in the yarn outcome. Colors can be highlighted, minimized, or hidden by stack placement. Sampling is the best way to explore these options.

The number of colors you choose has a large impact on the appearance of the yarn. Using fewer than six colors usually results in a very striped yarn. Even if the colors are bold, there are too few present to form the complex color relationships that obviate the obvious store-bought ombre effect. Better to start with nine colors. And what's the limit? The sky and your imagination, of course! I usually use between twelve and thirty colors in my multicolored yarns. It's hard to keep track of more than forty.

SPINNING ROVINGS MADE FROM DRUM-CARDED BATTS

After carding, you end up with a batt or stack of batts which you roll and pull or Z-strip and then draft into a pencil-size roving. It is very important to be patient and take your time as you pull the roving thinner and thinner. The pulling stage is more difficult and time-consuming than the spinning stage.

If the pulling has been done properly, the roving will be easy to spin. Any drafting technique can be used, providing you can control the color order. To draw the colors evenly into the yarn, remember to keep all the colors in the drafting triangle and keep the fiber supply free of twist.

Using several rovings together

If you want more colors in a yarn than you can fit in a stack or you want the colors to be even brighter, consider bundling several pulled-out rovings together to spin into one yarn. This is also a way to salvage a roving you absolutely do not like, or one that didn't turn out the way you envisioned. Combining it with another roving that does incorporate colors you want makes it workable. All the design ideas and principles already covered apply to multi-roving yarns, too.

Using more than one roving can extend your design possibilities. For example, to knit a scarf in which the colors slowly change from one end to the other, I made one stack of batts which included all the colors I wanted to appear throughout the scarf, and a series of other batts which encompassed the changing colors. The colors remained clear because I waited until the roving stage to put them together.

Another reason to combine several rovings after stacking is control of multi-fiber blends. These blends can be slippery and hard to hang onto. By pulling stacks and strips together at the last stage, you give slippery blends less chance to misbehave.

Before you try to spin a group of rovings, first lay them side by side, then predraft the bundle by pulling the fiber gently but deliberately between your hands. Pull a short distance—about one-third the average staple length—then move your hands and pull again. Work back and forth along the group of rovings until it is only about two to four times as thick

Carding multicolored batts for a project.

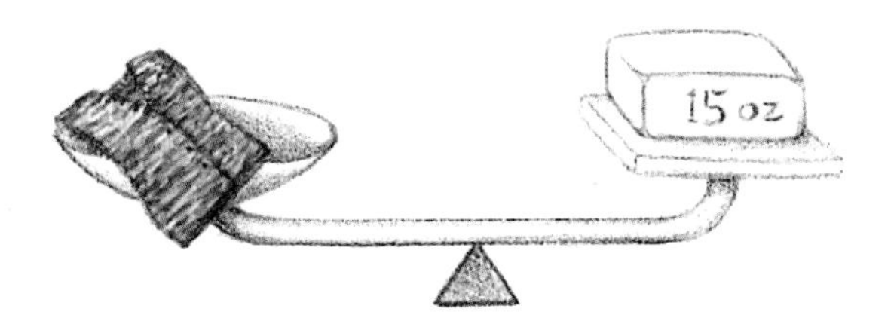

1. It will take fifteen ounces of fiber to make a multicolored vest.

2. Weigh out one ounce each of fifteen colors.

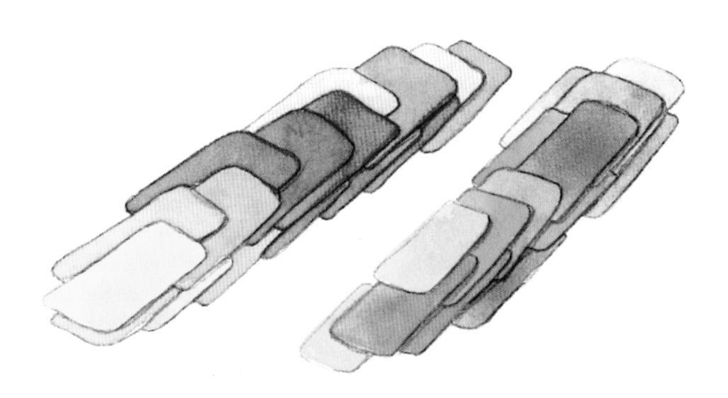

3. Card each of the fifteen colors into solid-color batts. There will be two half-ounce batts of each color.

4. There are going to be six stacks that weigh two and one-half ounces each. Divide the fifteen colors into six stacks. Put the same amount of every color into each stack.

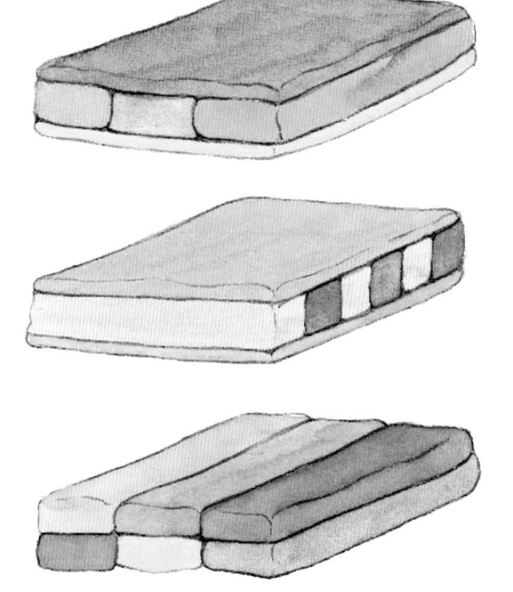

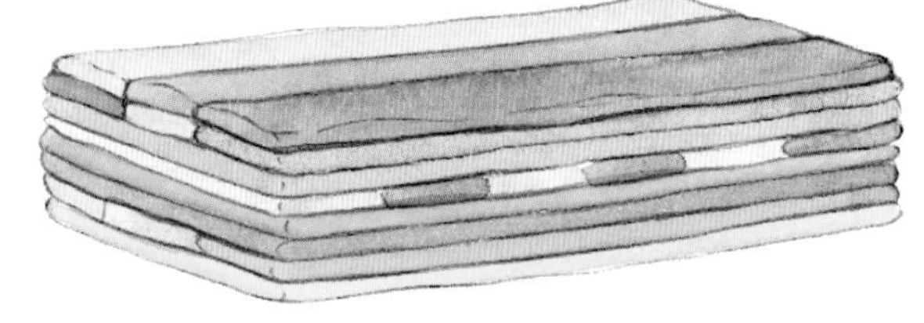

6. Stack the bottom, middle, and top batts. Repeat this for all six stacks.

5. For each stack, the fifteen colors are arranged into three separate batts. Five colors in the top batt, four colors in the middle batt, and six colors in the bottom batt. Card all six of the top batts, then all six of the middle batts, then all six of the bottom batts. Each stack will have the same batts.

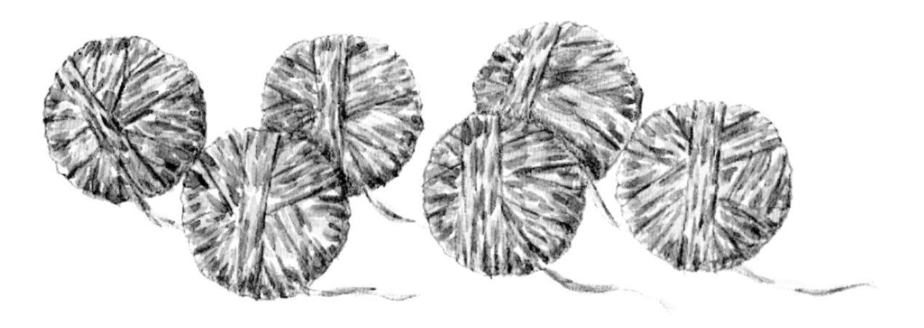

7. Roll and pull the stacks into roving. Repeat for all six stacks. There will be six identical balls of roving to spin for the vest.

Two rovings were combined and spun together for this scarf, which is knitted from singles. One stack used subtle colors that changed slowly from one end of the scarf to the other. The other used the same colors throughout the scarf. Accent colors appear different because of the changing main color.

as the yarn you plan to spin. Predrafting serves to hold the strips of roving together, lets the colors draft evenly into the yarn, and makes spinning easier.

SELF-STUDY EXERCISES

The purpose of the exercises in this chapter is to familiarize you with the process of stacking batts and arranging colors in the stack, as well as with pulling. Pulling is really the key to making the stacked batts work effectively, so it's the first thing to practice. After you work on pulling skills, going through the color exercises will show you clearly how the placement of colors in the different stripes affects the outcome of the yarn. These sample skeins can be used as reference for designing your own skeins.

Making wool batts

1. *Analogous colors.* Choose six analogous colors that have different values. Weigh out half an ounce of each color. Card each color separately, then divide each batt in half lengthwise. You will have two piles of six colors.

   Now make a batt by using the three darkest colors to make three long stripes. Make a second batt containing the three lightest colors. Use one color to make thin layers on the top and bottom, and alternate the other two colors in a series of short stripes. Stack these two batts on top of one another. Roll, pull into roving, and spin.

   Make a second pair of batts, mixing dark and light colors in each. Again, make one batt using three colors in long stripes, and the second batt using three colors in thin layers and short stripes. Roll, pull into roving, and spin.

   Compare how the colors appear in the two yarns. If you have done your pulling carefully, the colors will flow. If you pulled too much too fast, there will be more areas of single colors. Do you see a difference between the segregated-value skein and the mixed-value skein? There should be some difference. If there isn't, practice your pulling again.

2. *Analogous colors.* Choose nine colors in an analogous range, using a half-ounce of each. Tear the nine single-color batts in half, making two piles of nine colors each. You will make stacks of three batts each, with three colors in each batt.

   First separate the colors by value, grouping the three lightest, the three darkest, and the three mid-range values. Put three colors in each batt, making one batt with long stripes, one with thin layers, and one with short stripes sandwiched between thin layers. Stack, roll, and pull. Next, mix the colors, putting light, mid-value, and dark colors together in the batts and changing their locations in each. Stack, roll, and pull. Observe the differences between the two rovings, then spin them into yarns.

3. *Complementary colors.* Choose a total of nine colors from two complementary hue families. Use a half-ounce of five of the colors and a quarter-ounce of four colors. You have an odd number of colors, so one hue family must be dominant. You also have different amounts of colors. This time I want you to think about color dominance and the relationshop of complementary colors in the stack.

   Split all the carded batts in half. For your first stack, segregate the colors either by value or hue. Repeat the layering as in exercise 2, making three batts containing three colors each. For the second stack, change the color arrangement, but keep the three colors per batt as before. Roll the batts, pull into roving, and spin. Observe the differences. How do the complements work together?

4. *Split complementary.* Choose a total of nine colors from the three hue families. If you want to make a balanced effect, choose three from each hue family. If you want a dominant color, then choose more colors from that family. Use a half-ounce of each color. Split each carded batt in half.

   For the first stack, segregate hues or values in the same three-batt configuration as the last two exercises. For the second stack, mix up the colors and values. Roll the batts, pull into roving, and spin.

5. *Triad.* Choose twelve colors from the three hue families. Use a quarter-ounce of each color. Split the batts in half as before. You will make two stacks, each containing four batts with three colors apiece. To arrange the colors, make one batt with three long stripes, one with three thin layers, one with long stripes sandwiched between thin layers, and one with short stripes sandwiched between thin layers. In the first stack, segregate the colors and values. In the second stack, mix them up. Roll the batts, pull into roving, and spin.

6. *Double triad.* Choose twelve colors from the six hue families. Use a half-ounce of four colors and a quarter-ounce of eight colors. There will be dominant colors and accent colors, so choose accordingly. Card and split the batts, arranging the colors as follows:

   Batt 1: Use a half-ounce of a single color.

   Batt 2: Use four colors, making three long stripes and one thin layer.

   Batt 3: Use four colors, making long stripes of two colors on the top and bottom, and short stripes of the two other colors in between.

   Batt 4: Use three colors, making two long stripes and one thin layer. Stack and roll the batts, pull into roving, and spin.

   The purpose of this exercise is to learn how to combine different stripes and a variety of colors in a batt. Experiment with color arrangements. If you do not like the first arrangement, figure out why. Switch colors around with a purpose in mind and see if they work out the way you plan.

7. *Quadradic.* Choose twelve colors from the four hue families. Make sure there is a

dominant hue family. On your own, experiment with the number of batts and arrangement of colors. Try the same colors several different ways and observe the differences.

8. *Picture inspiration.* Choose a picture that you like, and pick out ten colors from it. They will comprise the palette for your stack. Use equal amounts of each color; don't worry about the proportions for now. Think about how you want the colors to appear in the skein and arrange the stripes and batts accordingly.

   Repeat, using the same picture for inspiration, but choosing colors in proportion to those in the picture. Use as many colors as it takes to obtain the results you want. See how different the two yarns are.

9. *Value keys.* Take any color harmony or inspiration, choose colors, and focus on their values. Keep the values very close by using one of the minor value keys from Chapter 1. Make batts, stack, roll, pull, and spin. Observe the yarn.

   Now take the same hues, but change the values for this stack. This time choose one of the major keys. Make batts, stack, roll, pull, and spin. See the difference in the final yarn?

10. *Saturations.* Choose a palette of colors. For the first stack of batts, choose colors that are similar in saturation. Make batts, stack, roll, pull, and spin. Make a second stack of batts, keeping the hues the same, but varying the saturations to include a range from very intense to very dull. Stack, roll, pull, and spin. Compare the two skeins.

11. *Warm and cool colors.* Choose a palette of colors, picking half from the warm side of the color wheel and half from the cool side. For one stack of batts, put the cool colors and warm colors in separate batts. For the second stack, combine them. Roll, pull, and spin. Compare the two skeins.

12. *Balancing colors.* Use the same colors as in exercise 11, but change the proportions so the yarn appears to be balanced. It may take a couple of tries to get the proportions right.

13. *Adding black or white to the stack.* Choose a palette of colors. Add black to one stack, add white to the other. Roll, pull, and spin. Compare the two skeins to see the effects of black and white on the surrounding colors.

14. *Add naturals.* Mix some natural colors of wool with dyed colors. Be careful of the value choices. Make a stack of batts, roll, pull, and spin.

15. *Color progressions.* Choose a palette of colors for a yarn that includes an analogous range with accent colors. In the stack, arrange the analogous colors in the short stripes. For example, one end of a batt would start with blue, then have a short stripe of a blue that has some green in it, then proceed to turquoise, and so on to the other end of the batt. Place the accent colors in thin layers and long stripes in other batts and make a stack. Roll, pull, and spin.

    Instead of a color progression in the short stripes, you could change values or intensities. The idea is to make some kind of progression from one end of the batt to the other.

Making batts of blended fibers and Z-stripping the stacks

All the above exercises can be repeated using blends. In this case, you should Z-strip the stacked batts rather than roll them. Pull out the rovings, spin them into yarns, and compare the final results with the all-wool yarns to see the differences between these two techniques. For more insight into the effect of Z-stripping, try the following exercises.

16. *Width of the Z-strip.* Use any color palette and stacking order. Make three identical stacks. Zigzag back and forth four times as

you Z-strip the first batt, six times for the second batt, and ten times for the third batt. Pull out the rovings, spin three skeins of yarn, and compare them to see how the placement of colors is affected by the number of times you split the batt lengthwise for the Z-strip.

17. *Number of long stripes.* Choose a palette of colors and prepare three stacks of batts. In the first stack, include one batt with two long stripes, in the second, one with four long stripes, and in the third, one with six long stripes. Z-strip the stacks, pull out the rovings, spin three skeins of yarn, and compare to see how the number of long stripes affects the appearance of the yarn.

18. *Using more than one roving at a time.* This is an easy way to increase the number of colors in a single yarn. Choose a total of twenty-four colors and make two stacks with twelve colors each. Z-strip the stacks and pull out the rovings, then put the rovings together for spinning. The two stacks could feature complementary colors, or one stack could be cool colors and the other warm. Your imagination is the limit.

chapter 6

Producing multicolored yarn with combing techniques

—6—

Producing multicolored yarn with combing techniques

Combing is a traditional way of processing wool for spinning. The combing process removes noils and short fibers and produces a continuous, uniform strand of longer fibers called a combed top. Combing produces more waste than carding does, but a top is a top-quality preparation. Only the best fibers are included; everything else is eliminated.

Producing a multicolored top is a several-step process that begins with dyeing the fibers and combing each color separately. Then you place combed fibers back onto a comb in a specific color order and pull them out into a top. The methods explained in this chapter are not based on tradition. Instead, they expand upon tradition and offer exciting new ways to obtain repeatable multicolored yarns.

These new techniques offer unique color possibilities, plus excellent yarn quality. Yarns that are spun in a worsted manner from hand-combed top are smoother, and knitted designs and colors appear crisper when you use combed rather than drum-carded fiber. Adding combing to your repertoire of fiber-preparation techniques means you can make multicolored yarns appropriate for any project.

There are two main variables in producing repeatable combed multicolored yarns. The first is the arrangement of colors on the comb: in horizontal layers or vertical stripes. The other main variable is the size of the diz used and how the fibers are pulled off the comb. This chapter will cover all the options for both variables, explaining and illustrating the many ways each can be handled and how it will affect the final yarn. Of course, the use of color in each variable will be part of the discussion.

CHOOSING COMBS, RELATED EQUIPMENT, AND FIBER

You don't need a lot of equipment for combing, and many tools can be adapted for the task. The basic ones are combs, a wool hackle if possible, C-clamps or a base for attaching a comb to a table, several sizes of dizzes, and a threading device to pull fiber through the diz.

Combs

Combs are sold in pairs, like hand cards, and come in several styles: hand-held combs, traditional English combs, and Russian paddle combs. Each style can be adapted for some portion of the combing, layering, color arranging, and pulling off that is done here.

Hand-held combs with one or two rows of teeth are inexpensive, easy to use, and readily available. Several companies produce them. All models seem to work adequately. Some are aesthetically more pleasing than others. The weight of the combs, the woods used, and the workmanship vary. Choose whichever type is most comfortable and pleasing for you. You'll need a way to hold one comb still while you attach or pull off the fibers. Usually a C-clamp will do.

English combs typically have two to five (sometimes more) rows of teeth. The number of rows is sometimes referred to as the "pitch"; for example, a five-pitch comb has five rows of teeth. The more rows, the finer the fiber you can comb. English combs produce the smoothest tops with the fewest neps or noils remaining. To use English combs, you mount one comb in a stationary base and hold the

Wool-combing tools.

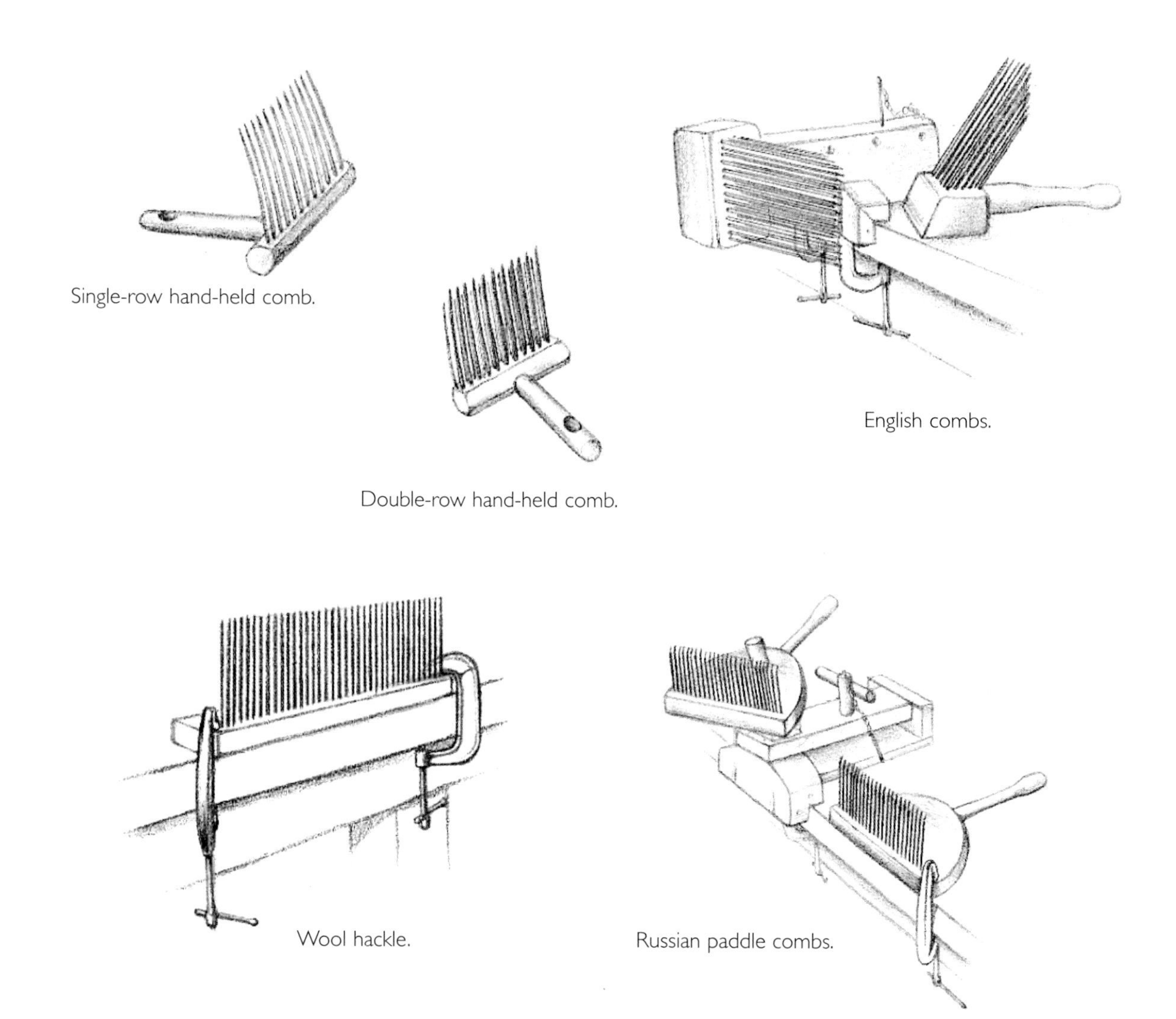

Single-row hand-held comb.

Double-row hand-held comb.

English combs.

Wool hackle.

Russian paddle combs.

other in your hand. Normally a base or mounting system is included when you buy a pair of English combs. A disadvantage of these combs is their heaviness, which makes them somewhat awkward to use. The weight can also be an issue if you have hand, wrist, or arm problems.

Russian paddle combs are wider than other combs and have one or two rows of teeth. There is more waste with the two-row kind, and it's a little harder to pull off the fiber, but the resulting tops have fewer noils than tops from one-row combs. I don't necessarily use paddle combs for the initial combing of dyed wool, but their width does make them handy for arranging colors in the final step of preparing a multicolored top. Russian combs come with a clamp or base so you can mount one comb to a table.

A *wool hackle* can substitute for a paddle comb for the arrangement of colors in the final step. Wool hackles are sold singly, not in pairs, and have one or two rows of teeth mounted in a wooden base that you can clamp to the edge of a table. They come in different widths, ranging from about six to eighteen inches wide. For making multicolored top, get the widest hackle you can find.

Dizzes

A diz is a small, disk-shaped piece of wood, plastic, bone, or shell with a hole in the center. Using a diz helps you pull fiber off the comb into a smooth, uniform top. As long as it's sturdy enough to resist abrasion, the material does not matter. What's more important is the size and shape of the hole.

I use different dizzes for different steps in the combing process or to create different effects in the tops and yarns. For the initial combing and blending, I use a diz with an oval opening approximately one-half inch wide by one-quarter inch high. For pulling off fibers at the final step, I use dizzes with round holes ranging between 0.06 inch and 0.18 inch in diameter. These holes look small, but they are the right size-range for this technique. With them you can produce a top that is thick enough to incorporate all the colors at once, but thin enough that you can control the drafting triangle as you spin. Having a range of sizes is important because a small hole gives blended colors, while a large hole produces bold effects.

A threading hook of some kind helps you pull fibers through the diz. It can be a crochet hook or a hook especially designed for this purpose. A hook saves time when you're using a small-hole diz.

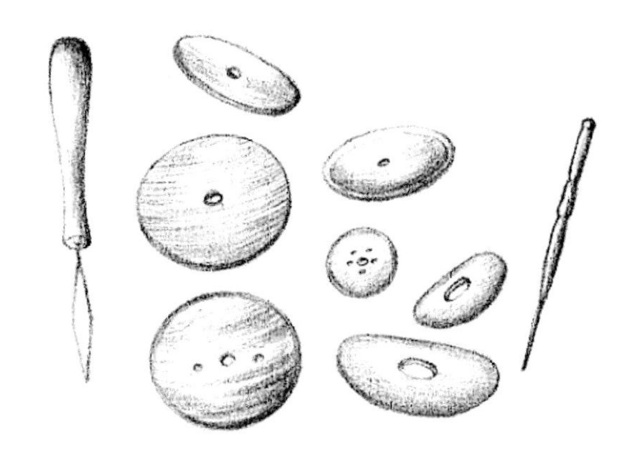

Assortment of dizzes and threading hooks.

Fiber

Wool is the pre-eminent fiber for combing, although you can also comb other medium or long fibers with varying success, depending on the fiber and the combs. You can also blend fiber on combs, but the staple length of all the fibers must be the same or they will pull off the combs separately in the last step. I usually comb wool from Corriedale and similar breeds, starting with raw fleece and washing and dyeing it as described in Chapter 2.

Another option, if you want to save time, is buying commercial wool tops. A good assortment of solid-color dyed tops is available. By using these, you can skip the initial steps of dyeing and combing and begin at the color-blending stage.

COMBING SINGLE COLORS

It is important to thoroughly comb each color of wool by itself before placing colors together. When single colors are already combed, you can blend faster and more consistently. Also, it is necessary that the fiber used in the last step of making multicolored tops be thoroughly combed.

My method of initial combing is not strict or purist, but it removes short fibers and makes a smooth top. The directions below explain how to use hand-held combs. I like to start with one-row combs and switch to two-row combs partway through the process, but if you have only one pair of hand-held combs, you can use them throughout. If you have only English combs, use one comb mounted in a stationary position and the other held in your hand.

In preparing wool for combing, I don't try to keep the locks intact through the washing and dyeing processes. If the locks get disorganized or come apart, I may incur a little extra waste, but since I save time working this way, it's a trade-off.

Step-by-step directions for the initial combing of dyed wool

1. *Load the left comb with fiber.* Hold one comb in your left hand with the teeth facing upward. Hold some dyed wool in your right hand and with a quick downward motion, catch the last half-inch or so of the fiber behind the teeth. Pull down and away. A staple-length of wool will be caught in the comb's teeth. Repeat this catching and pulling until the comb is filled with wool approximately halfway up the length of the teeth. Don't try to comb too much wool at once—you'll end up with a tangled mess instead of a neat parallel arrangement. It's faster, easier, and better to comb many small batches instead of a few big batches.

   If you do have intact locks, you can load them onto the teeth the same way as open fleece. I don't worry about which end of the locks (butt or tip) to lash onto the combs, because I think either way works okay.

2. *Begin combing, transferring the fiber from the left comb to the right comb.* Support the left comb on your left knee, with its teeth pointing away from your body. Hold the right comb in your right hand, with the teeth pointing down. You will move this comb in a circular, counterclockwise motion. Gently swing the right comb down, catching the tips of the teeth into the tips of the fiber, and pull the comb down and away. Some of the fiber will be transferred onto the right comb. Raise the comb and swing it down again, catching more fiber. Repeat. With each pass, the teeth of the right comb should swing closer to the teeth of the left comb, until they are almost touching. Continue until most of the fiber has been transferred to the right comb. (Some short or tangled fiber will remain on the left comb; you can discard that now or wait until later.)

Initial combing with hand-held combs.

1. Loading a single-row hand-held comb with fiber.

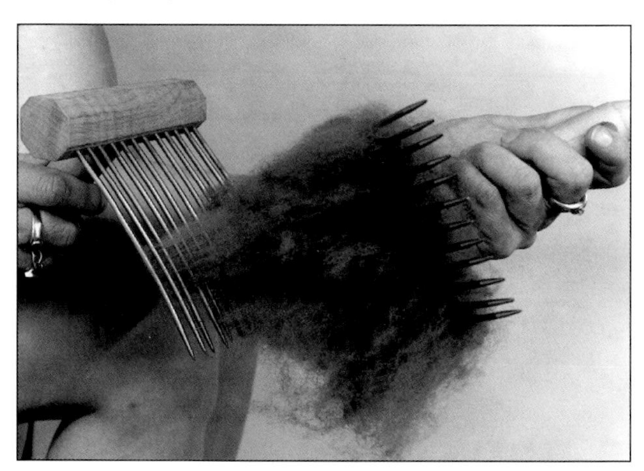

2. Holding the left comb stable, swing the right comb moves in a downward motion, catching the tips of the fiber to be combed.

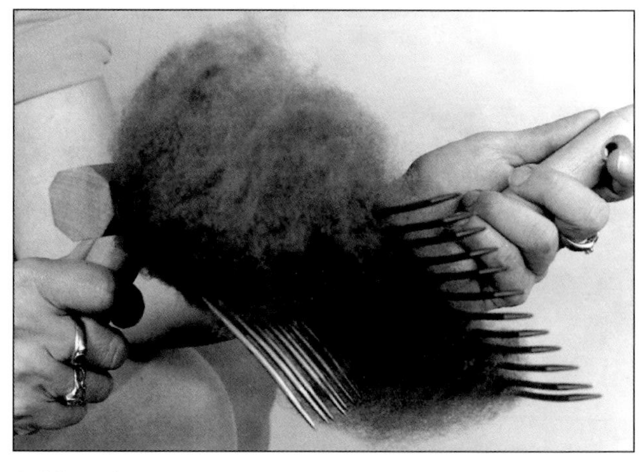

3. After a few passes, the right comb moves closer to the tines of the left comb to catch the remaining fiber. Note that most of the fiber has been transferred to the right comb.

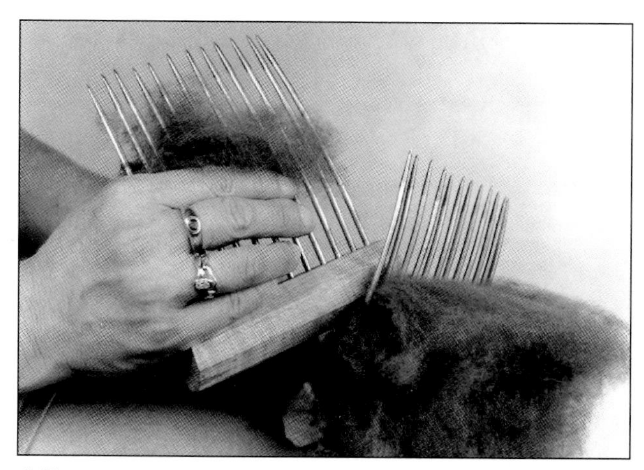

4. If you want, remove short fiber from left comb before continuing.

5. Now hold the empty, left comb steady, and swing the loaded, right comb parallel to the floor and toward the body, catching the tips of the fiber in the left comb.

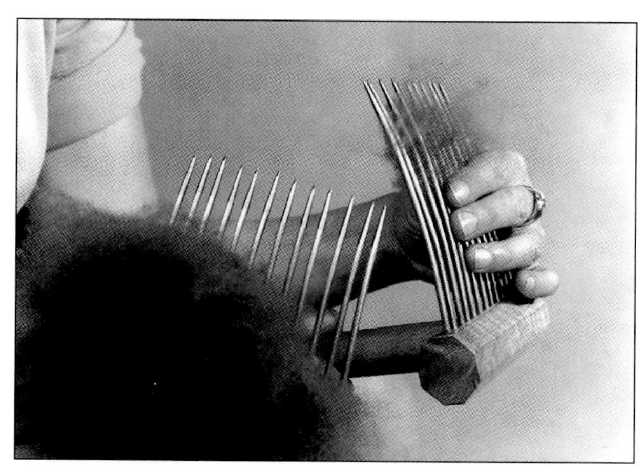

6. After most of the fiber has been transferred back to the left comb, remove the short fiber remaining in the right comb. Repeat the transferring of fiber back and forth until it has been adequately combed.

3. *Continue combing, transferring the fiber from the right comb back to the left comb.* The positions of both combs stay the same, but the *movement* of the right comb changes. This time, the right comb, which is filled with fiber, will move toward you and catch the tips of the fiber into the teeth of the left comb. The movement is a circular shape that moves parallel to the floor in a counterclockwise direction. Keep swinging the right comb around and around, catching deeper into the teeth with each pass, until most of the fiber has been transferred back to the left comb. (Again, you can discard or ignore the short fiber that is stuck in the right comb.)

4. *Repeat the left-to-right and right-to-left transfers.* If desired, you can switch from one-row to two-row combs now. (When a one-row comb is empty, set it aside and replace it with a two-row comb.)

   Examine the wool and decide if you think it has been combed enough. If not, transfer it back and forth again. You will end up with most of the fiber on one comb and just short or tangled bits stuck in the teeth of the other.

5. *Pull the fiber off the comb.* This is easier if you clamp the comb to a table first, but you can hold the comb with one hand and pull the fiber with the other. Either way, gently gather the tips of the fiber into a point and feed the point through a large-holed diz. Then pinch the tips of the fiber between the index finger and thumb of one hand and pull the fiber away from the comb, pulling about one-third of the staple length. The diz will follow your fingers back. Push it forward (toward the comb) about the same distance as the fiber was pulled back. Alternate pulling the fibers out and pushing the diz in until all the nice fiber has been removed. There will be some waste. Stop pulling when noils enter the top.

There's a knack to using a diz and pulling off fiber. Thread the fiber into the concave side of the diz, as you would use a funnel. In pulling off top, watch where you place the diz. If you push it too far toward the comb, it's hard to pull out the fiber. Back the diz toward you and try pulling again. But if the fiber supply gets too thin, push the diz a little further toward the comb and pick up more fiber to pull. Meanwhile, watch how you pinch and pull the fiber. If you pinch too close to the comb, it's hard to pull off the fiber and you'll make a thick spot in the top. If you pinch too far away from the comb or pull too far at once, the top will become thin and may slip apart.

6. *After combing*. Take the top you have combed and pull it apart into staple lengths. Set these aside in a pile for subsequent use.

7. Now mount the loaded comb is on a table with a small stand and C clamp. Having it stable helps the pulling-off step tremendously. Thread the fiber tips through a large-holed diz.

8. Pull the fiber through the diz, pinching with your thumb and index finger. Each pull should be about one-third the staple length of the fiber.

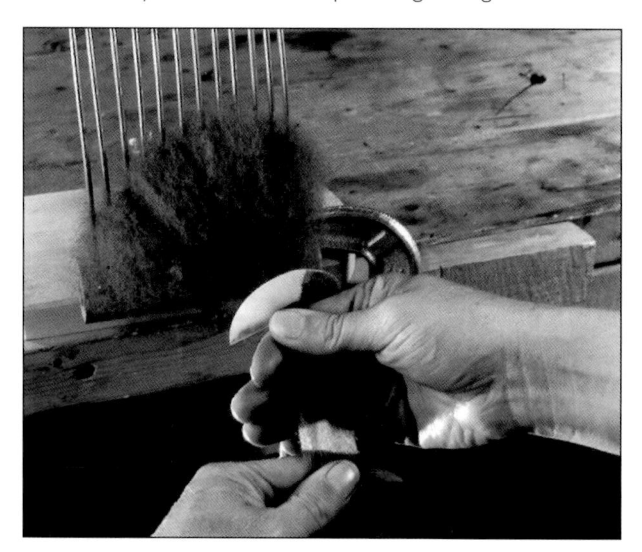

9. Pull alternately with your left and right hands until all of the nice fiber has been pulled off the comb.

10. Discard the short bits and noils that remain in the comb.

Initial combing with English combs.

1. Mount one comb on its stand and lash on some wool.

2. Swing the other comb in a downward motion, so its teeth enter the tips of the fiber.

3. As the fiber gets transferred to the moving comb, the moving comb can swing closer to the tines of the mounted comb. When all the good fiber has been transferred, remove what remains on the mounted comb.

4. With the moving comb circling parallel to the floor and counterclockwise, transfer the fiber back to the comb on the stand. Repeat the combing until the fiber is sufficiently prepared.

5. Thread the fiber through a large-holed diz. Alternate your hands as you pull off the fiber.

Clean the short or tangled fiber out of the teeth of both combs in preparation for combing the next batch.

COMBING TO BLEND COLORS THOROUGHLY

The possibilities for thorough color blending with combs are the same as for blending on a drum carder, and relate back to the color theory described in Chapter 1. A combed color can be changed in the same six ways. You can make it warmer or cooler, darker or lighter, brighter or duller. For specifics on choosing colors for blends, refer back to Chapter 4.

There is one important difference between blending on a drum carder and blending on combs. Carding can thoroughly blend dyed fibers of varying lengths but combing can't. If the fibers of color A are even a half-inch longer than the fibers of color B, color A will pull off the combs before color B, and the result will be a progression from one color to the other, not a uniform blend. This can happen even if you start with two batches of dyed fiber from the same fleece, because fiber length often varies from one part of a fleece to another. Check fiber lengths to be sure they match before you try to blend colors by combing.

Step-by-step directions for blending colors on combs

1. *Choose colors to be blended.* The colors used can be in any proportion. Keep in mind that the more there is of one color, the more it will dominate the blend. Also remember that the values of the colors will affect the appearance of the blend. The greater the value difference, the more heathered the blend. Similar values produce a more solid blend.
2. *Give each dyed color an initial combing before you start to blend.* If you use commercial dyed top, you can skip this step.
3. *Put layers of dyed fiber onto the teeth of a comb.* Using two-row combs blends colors more thoroughly and faster than one-row combs, but you can use one-row combs if that's all you have.

   Hold the left comb as before. Choose one color that's going into the blend, hold some of that wool in your right hand, and catch the fibers onto the teeth of the left comb as you pull down and away. Because this already-combed wool tends to slip

Blending colors on hand-held combs.

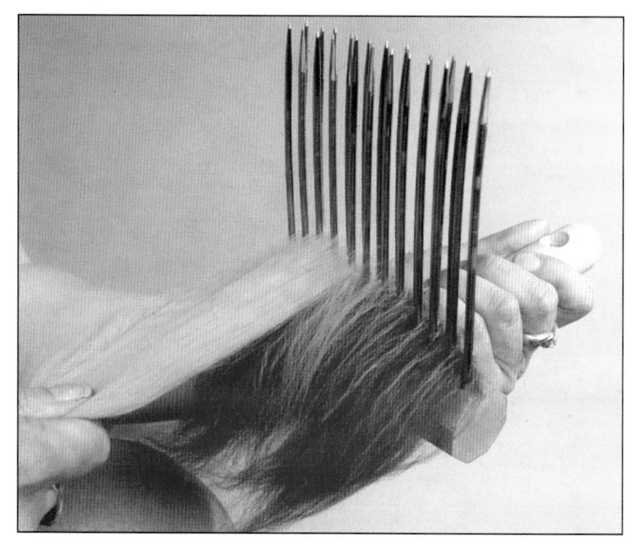

1. For a two-color blend, lash on a thin layer of color A, then lash on a thin layer of color B. Repeat until the comb is loaded.

2. The relative thickness of the layers depends on the proportions of the colors being blended. The number of layers affects how fast the blending takes place.

through the teeth more easily, catch it a little farther (an inch or so) behind the teeth than you did for the initial combing. Distribute a thin, even layer of this first color across the bottom of the teeth.

Now lash on a thin, even layer of the second color. Continue adding colors in alternate layers, or successive layers if there are more than two colors in the blend.

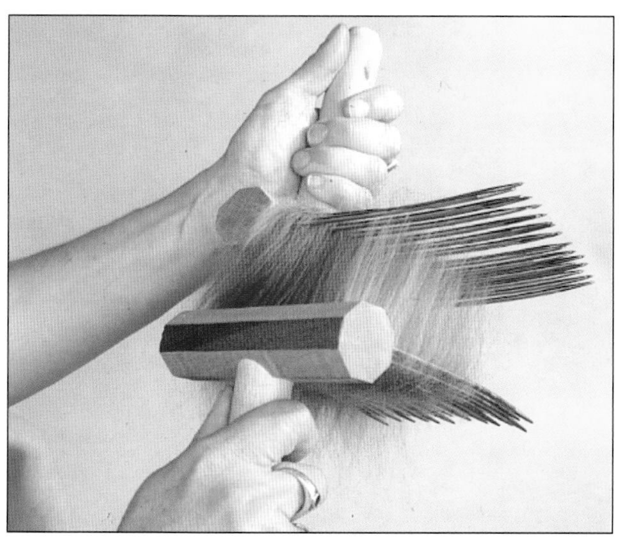

3. The actual combing procedure is the same as in basic combing, but this time the focus is on color distribution.

4. This fiber went through four passes with the combs. A blend is complete when it pleases you. Use a large-holed diz to pull the fiber off the comb.

Making several thin layers instead of a few thick layers means the colors will blend faster as you comb. The combs can be filled until the fiber extends a little over halfway up the teeth. As with the initial combing, don't try to comb too much wool at once—it's too hard and you won't get good results.

4. *Blend the colors.* Use the procedure for basic combing to blend the colors. The colors are adequately blended when you say they are. There is no right or wrong point in this. The less the blend is combed, the more distinctly the original colors appear. The more the colors are combed, the less the individual colors appear.
5. *Pull the fiber off the comb.* Use a large-holed diz and pull the fiber off the same way as in the initial combing.
6. *After combing.* Divide the top into staple lengths as you did after the initial combing and set the colors aside.

Creating multicolored tops

Multicolored tops have distinctly different colors that are not thoroughly blended. All colors to be used, solid or blended, should be combed singly first so they are ready to spin. In this final step of the process, you are simply arranging how the colors will appear in the top and yarn. You can't do any further combing to prepare the fiber at this point because that would muddy the colors.

There are two main ways the colors for multicolored tops can be loaded on the combs: in *horizontal layers* or *vertical stripes.* Let's look at each method and explore its variables. Later, you can try combinations of the two.

Horizontal layers

A horizontal layer uses one color across the entire width of the comb. Successive color layers are placed on top. Layered colors appear regularly in the yarn if pulled through the diz consistently. There are several ways you can

Variations on horizontal layering.

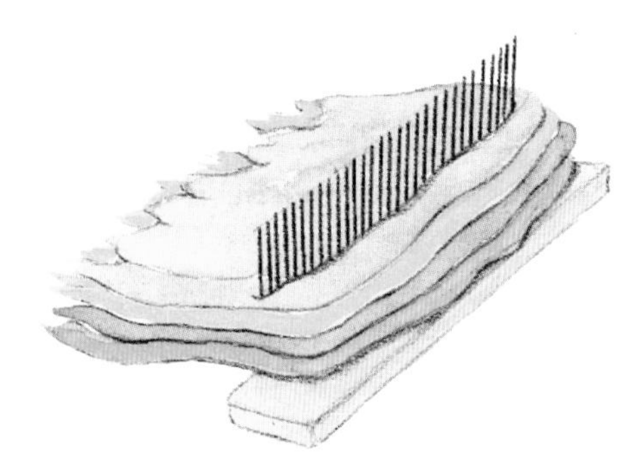

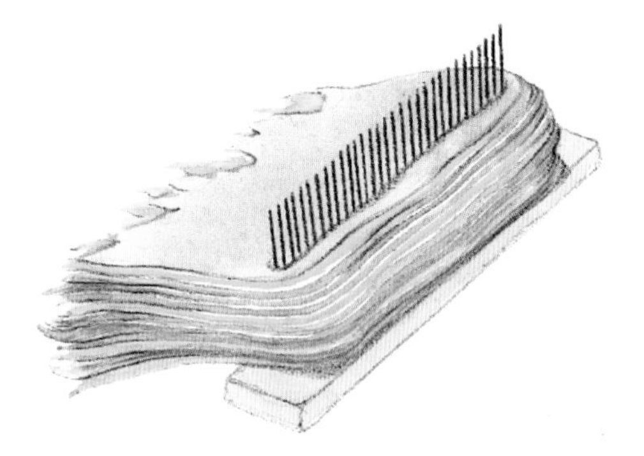

Thickness of layers. Using the same four colors, the left example shows one layer of each color. The right example has two separate layers of each color.

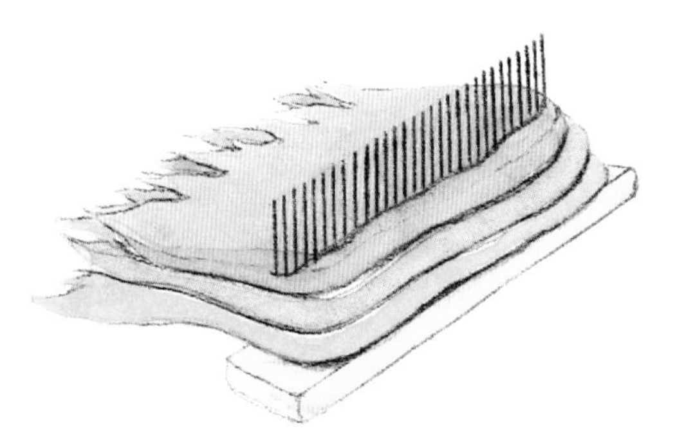

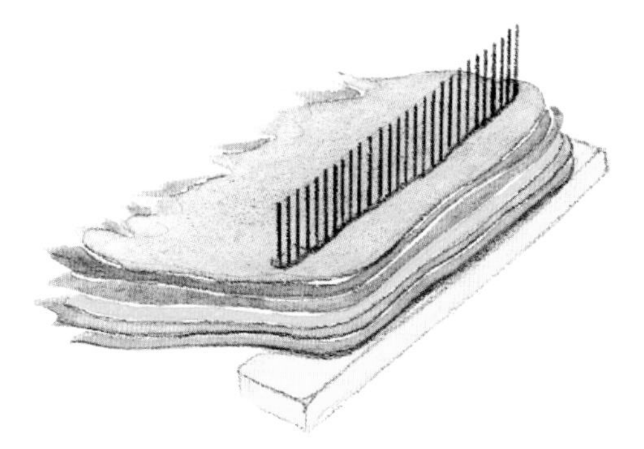

Number of colors. The left example has three colors. The right example has six colors. Using more colors makes a less stripey yarn.

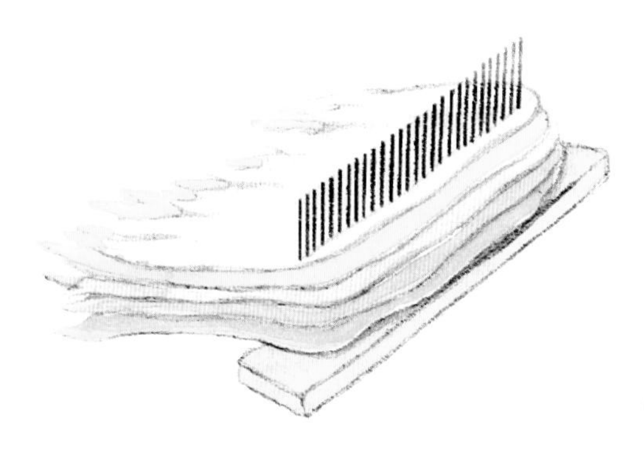

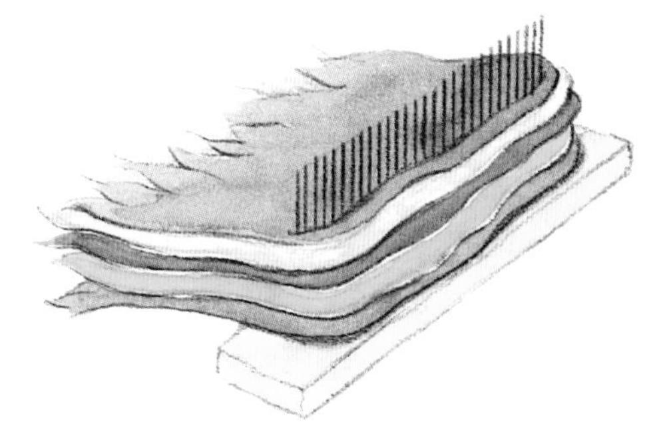

Contrast between colors. The left arrangement has little contrast of hue or value. The right example has high contrast of color and value.

arrange the layers to fine-tune the appearance of the yarn. Variables that affect horizontal layers are:

The thickness of layers. The thicker the layer, the more prominent the color in the yarn. And vice versa. Thin, cheesecloth-like layers can introduce a color so subtly that it isn't obvious in the final yarn. This is a good way to include hard-to-use colors—colors you are not sure you even want in the yarn.

The number of colors. More colors make yarns look less striped. With more colors competing for your attention, each color has less chance of being dominant. To minimize striping, use ten or more colors. (You don't have to put them all in one top, though—you can hold two or more tops together as you spin a yarn.)

The number of layers. This is different from the number of colors. Each color in a yarn can appear in more than one place. To minimize the boldness of a final yarn, the same color can appear in several thin layers instead of one thick layer. If boldness is what you want, then concentrate a color in one place.

The amount of contrast between colors. This can be contrast of hue, value, and/or saturation. With hue, analogous colors placed side by side yield less contrast than complementary colors placed side by side. With value, combining colors of similar values results in a subtle yarn; a wide-value combination produces bold effects. With saturation, similar saturations yield minimum contrast and subtle effects. Combining fully saturated colors with dull ones makes the bright colors more intense and the dull colors duller.

The size of the hole in the diz. This affects the amount of blending that takes place when you pull the top from the comb. The smaller the hole, the more blended and subtle the yarn. The larger the hole, the less blended, and bolder the yarn. The dizzes I use at this stage have round holes ranging between 0.06 inch to 0.18 inch in diameter. They create different color effects, but they all produce tops that spin easily with a minimal amount of drafting so you can preserve the color order you have so carefully arranged.

Step-by-step procedure for making horizontal layers

For the color arrangement steps, I prefer using the widest equipment available. My first choice is a wide wool hackle, C-clamped to the edge of a table. My second choice, again because of its width, is a Russian paddle comb. For extra width, you can fasten two Russian paddle combs side by side. If you don't have either of these tools, you can use one-row or two-row hand-held combs, C-clamped side by side to the edge of a table. This works fine; it just means you'll prepare less fiber at a time.

1. *Load the first layer onto the comb.* Take a handful of fiber and lash on as you did before, using a quick downward motion with a crisp pull at the end to leave only a staple length in the teeth. Repeat loading the fiber across the entire width of the comb. Because the fiber has already been combed, be sure there is enough length (an inch or so) behind the teeth to hold the fiber in place. Otherwise, the fiber will come out in clumps as you pull off the top.
2. *Place further layers on the comb.* Repeat the lashing-on for each color or layer. Remember that the comb is fully loaded when the fiber reaches approximately halfway up the teeth.
3. *Gently pull the fiber tips together and thread the diz.* When all the colors are loaded on the comb, gently pull out the tips of the layers together across the comb. Starting at one side, incorporate all the colors with the threading hook, and pull a few fiber tips through the hole in the diz. The concave side of the diz should be facing the comb.

Creating horizontal layers on combs.

1. Load the first layer onto the comb. Remember the fiber has already been combed; this process simply arranges fiber according to the desired color order.

2. Continue loading layers of color onto the comb. Do not load higher than halfway up the teeth of the comb. Tease the fiber tips so that all the layers are in the fringe and can be caught in the diz.

3. Pull the top off the comb with a diz. Move the diz back and forth across the comb. Be sure all the layers of colors appear in the top.

4. *Pull the fiber off the comb, making a multicolored top.* As before, pinch the tips of the fiber between your thumb and index finger and pull away from the comb about one-third of a staple length. Because the hackle is wider, you need to work back and forth across the comb to pull the top off. Rather than pulling straight off the hackle, the pulling should be angled diagonally to the hackle. Push the diz back toward the comb the same distance as you pulled the fiber out. Pinch and pull again. Repeat until all the fiber has been pulled off the comb. Roll the top loosely into a ball for spinning.

Vertical stripes

Single or blended colors that are placed side by side across the width of the comb form vertical stripes. The number of stripes possible is determined by the width of the comb or hackle used—the wider the comb, the more vertical stripes it can hold. Colors that are arranged in vertical stripes come and go in the yarn. They can act as accents or appear as color transitions or color variations that are regular or random, depending on the colors and arrangement chosen. Variables that affect vertical stripes are:

The number of colors. Each color appears as a vertical stripe every time the diz makes a pass across the comb. How many stripes you can make depends on the width of the comb. Russian paddle combs can hold four or five stripes. A wider hackle can hold more. The more stripes you make, the narrower they must be. The narrower the stripes, the faster the color changes take place. The wider the stripes, the slower the color transitions.

The thickness of each stripe. Viewed horizontally, a stripe can be narrow or wide. Vertically, a stripe can be thin or thick, depending how much fiber you attach at that position on the teeth. The thinner the stripe, the less obvious that color will be in the yarn. The thicker the stripe, the more prominent the color.

The proportions of the stripes. Vertical stripes do not all need to be the same size. Dominance in a yarn can be created by making larger vertical stripes of a specific hue family, value, or saturation.

The number of layers of vertical stripes. Colors will appear choppy in the yarn if you use only one layer of vertical stripes. To smooth out color transitions and create more complex interactions, vertical stripes can be layered vertically on the combs. It takes at least three layers of vertical stripes to create complex color interactions. Layering also makes it possible to use more colors in a skein.

How the layers are positioned. If the vertical stripes line up from layer to layer, the color changes are obvious, clear, and abrupt. Lining up the vertical stripes accentuates the striped quality of the multicolored yarn. Complex interactions begin to occur with the third layer of lined-up stripes. On the other hand, staggering the layers of vertical stripes makes for more subtle color transitions. The same colors will not always interact at the same time, nor will they stripe so much. When you stagger the layers instead of lining up stripes, you need fewer layers and colors to achieve complex yarns.

The amount of contrast between colors. As it does with horizontal layers, using colors with more or less contrast in hue, value, and saturation creates bold or subtle effects in the yarn. With vertical stripes, however, the color changes occur repeatedly throughout the skein.

The size of the hole in the diz. A small hole blends colors and a large hole keeps the colors clear.

How many times the diz moves back and forth across the comb as you pull off the fibers. A Russian paddle comb or hackle is typically

Variables for vertical stripes on combs.

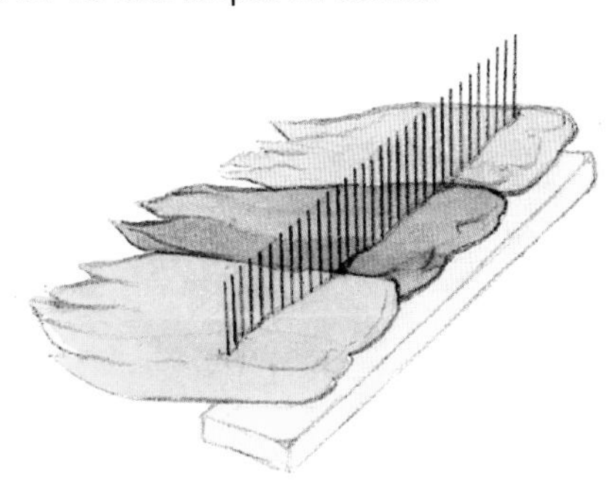

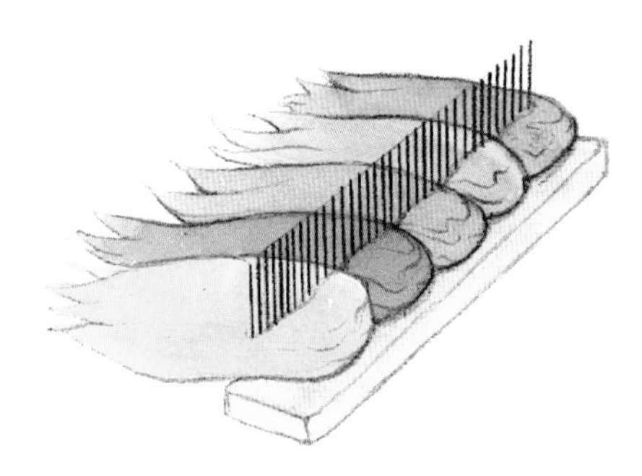

Number of colors. The left example has three vertical stripe colors, the right has five vertical stripe colors. The more colors, the narrower each stripe must be.

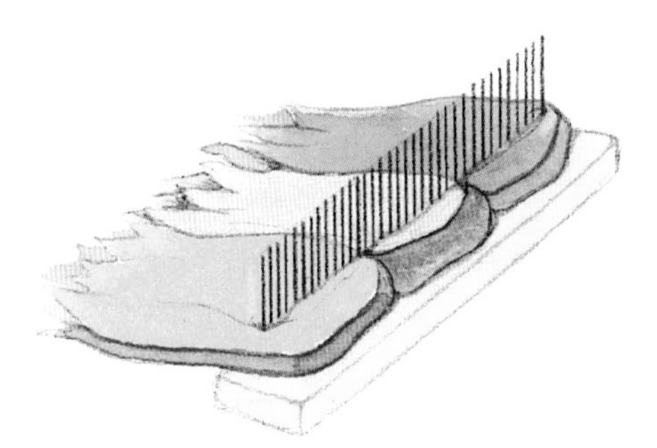

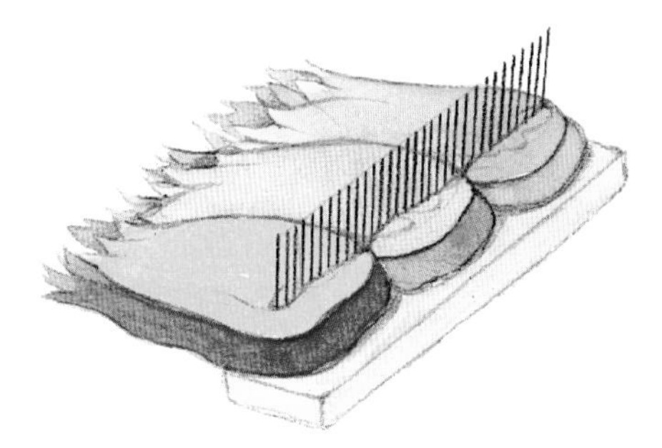

Thickness of each stripe. The left arrangement uses uneven amounts of six colors. Colors used in smaller amounts will show up less in the yarn. The right arrangement uses equal amounts of all colors, so they appear evenly in the yarn.

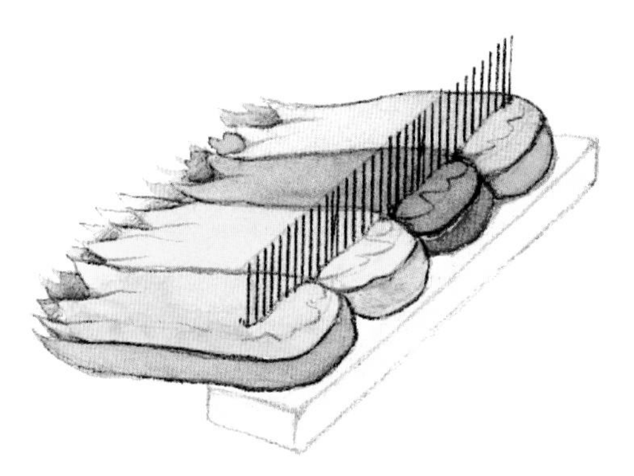

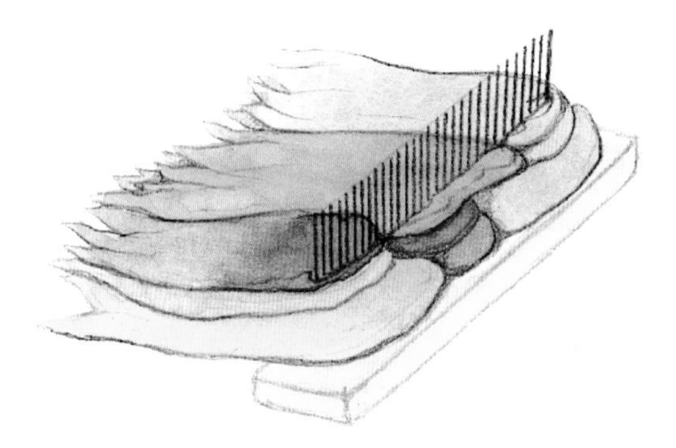

Proportions and width of stripes. The left example shows equal amounts of eight colors with stripes lining up vertically. The right arrangement uses the same eight colors, but changes proportions and staggers the vertical stripes into layers. This arrangement will produce much more complex yarn that has more different color interactions.

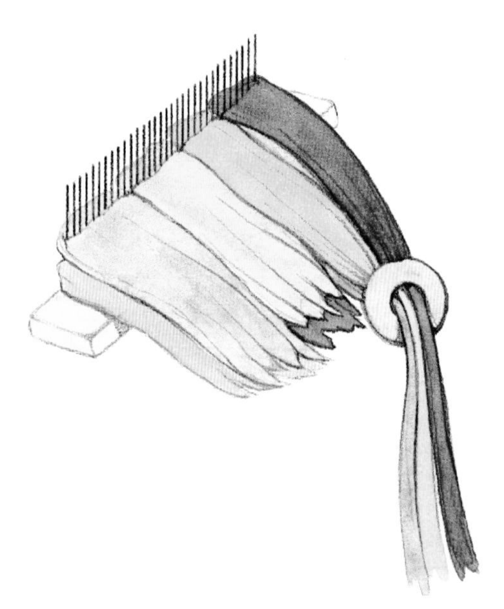

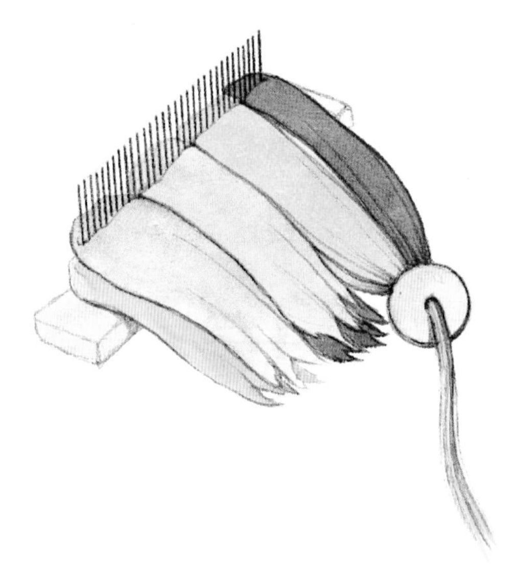

Diz hole size. Both of these arrangements use the same colors on the comb. Using a diz with a large hole, produces bold effects. Using a small-holed diz makes the top look much more subtle.

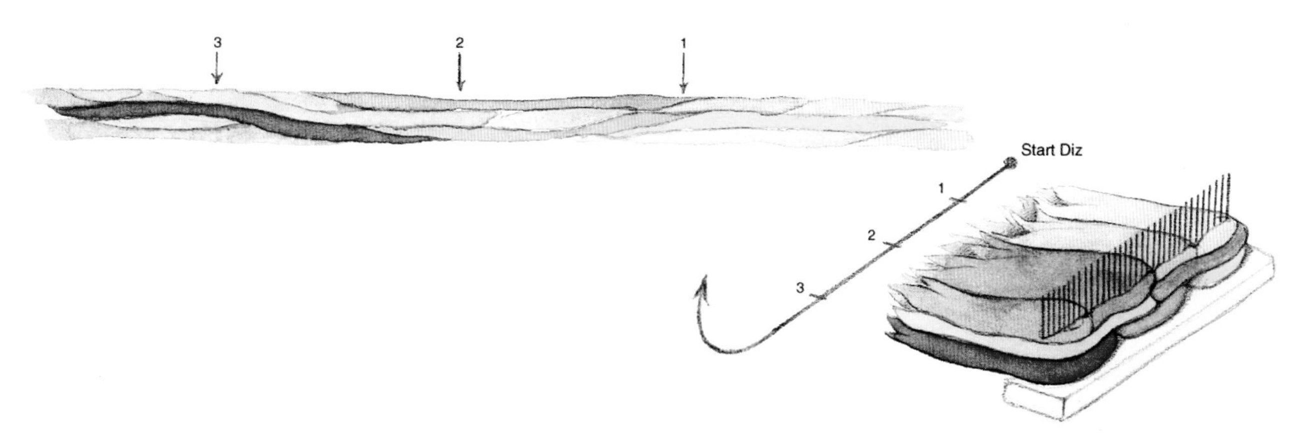

How the diz is moved. The comb shows the colors in layers and stripes. The diz begins across the comb at the top dot and progresses with each pull (the intersecting short line indicates each pull). Shown above is a cross section of the pulled top. From right to left, the top shows the colors that come out from each pull. The arrows indicate where each pull occurred.

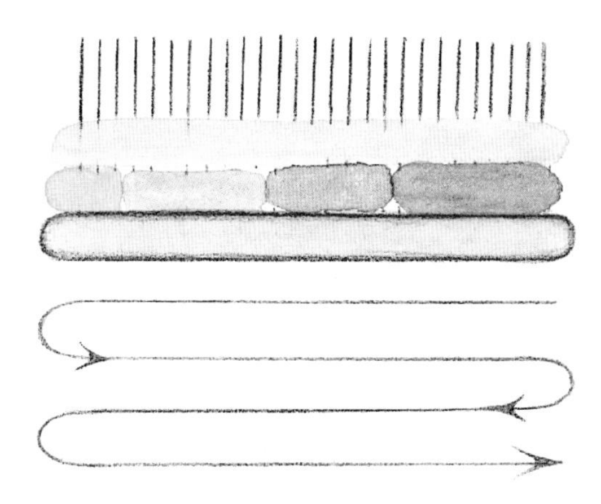

Head-on view of a comb. The arrows below show how many times the diz traveled back and froth across the comb. In this drawing there are four repeats of the color sequence.

about eight to twelve inches wide, so you can't pull all the fiber at once. Instead, the vertical stripes come off one area at a time as you move the diz across the comb. The number of times the diz moves back and forth across the comb determines the number of repeats of the vertical stripe pattern in the top and yarn. The faster the diz moves across each color, the shorter each repeat and the more repeats there are. This is the most important design feature to consider when making tops and yarns from vertical stripes.

Step-by-step procedure for making vertical stripes

1. *Mount a Russian paddle comb or a hackle onto a table.* Either tool works okay. You won't be using the tool to comb fiber—simply to arrange colors. The wider the tool, the better; extra width allows you to make more stripes.
2. *Make the first layer of stripes.* Start at one side of the comb or hackle and lash on some fiber to make the first stripe. Continue across the comb, adding colors in the

Making vertical layers on combs.

1. Load vertical stripes onto a comb or hackle. In this photo, more of the color being loaded needs to be added to make it even with the other colors.

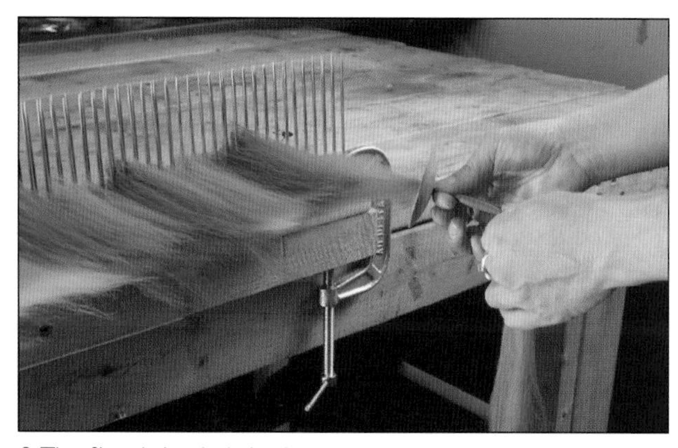

2. The fiber is loaded, tips have been pulled together, diz has been threaded, and top is being pulled. Moving from left to right, pull out about one-third of a staple length at a time. With each pull, move across the hackle. Be sure to include all layers of colors.

3. Now the diz is moving from right to left and is incorporating different colors in the top. Continue moving the diz back and forth across the hackle until all the fiber has been pulled off. Consistency is important for regular repeats of the color sequence.

desired order. Lash on the wool as for other combing techniques.

3. *Add subsequent layers of stripes.* Before starting each layer, look at the previous layer to see if any stripe is thinner than the others. If so, add fiber to level out the layer, using more of the same color if you want the layers of stripes to line up, and using a different color to fill in the stripe if you want the layers of stripes to be staggered. Continue adding layers until all of the stripes have been loaded onto the comb or hackle, but don't fill the teeth past the halfway mark. Make sure the comb is evenly filled, with the same amount of fiber all the way across. If not, add fiber where needed.
4. *Gently pull the fiber tips together and thread the diz.* Start at one side of the comb (I usually start at the right) and thread all of the colors that appear at that edge through the diz. Be sure to include fiber from every layer in the edge stripe, but from that stripe only.
5. *Begin pulling off fiber and making a top.* With diz in place, and the right thumb and index finger firmly pinching the fiber, pull out about one-third of the staple length and stop. Push the diz toward the comb about the same distance as you pulled out fiber. Follow the same guidelines for pulling fiber and using the diz as for other combing techniques.
6. *Begin moving the diz across the comb.* This is what's special about pulling a top from vertical stripes. To obtain an even repeat, you must be consistent in the way you angle the diz and pull fiber from across the comb. Count how many pulls you make from each vertical stripe and try to be consistent with each round. Some blending will take place as you move the diz from one vertical stripe section to the next, but you should keep the colors from each stripe as isolated as possible in the

pulled top in order to preserve the clarity of colors in the yarn.

To angle the diz, point it opposite to the direction you want it to travel. For example, if you start at the right side of the comb and work to the left, pull as many times as you want from the first vertical stripe, then angle the diz to the right at about a thirty-degree angle. Pull again, and fiber from the next area of the comb will automatically start to feed through the diz. Hover in the next stripe area until you are ready to move on, and again angle the diz to the right. Continue this way until you reach the left side of the comb.

When you have reached the left side, you must turn back to the right. To do this, angle the diz to the left and pull. Use the same rhythm and number of pulls in each area. Keep the repeats in the yarn even for each pass across the comb. Gaining control of pulling will take some practice!

Repeat going back and forth across the comb, pulling the fiber and pushing the diz until all the fiber has been pulled off. The number of trips back and forth are up to you. It depends on the number of repeats of color and lengths of each color that are desired in the final yarn.

7. *Roll the top loosely into a ball.*

Tips on making vertical stripes

Be sure that all the colors in a vertical stripe are fed into the diz simultaneously, especially when using a small-holed diz. It's easy to miss the bottom color, so check for that frequently. It will take some practice to evenly include all the colors. Accurately pulling out the fiber with the diz is *very* important for the success of this technique. The color order cannot be maintained if the colors are pulled off irregularly.

Decide how many repeats of the color sequence you want in the skein before you begin to pull fiber off the comb. Advance planning will help you pace yourself and evenly move back and forth across the comb as many times as required.

Think carefully about the placement of colors on both ends of the comb. The end colors will be pulled from twice, as you reach the end and turn around to go back again, so those stripes should be half the width of the others if you want to maintain the same length of each color in the yarn.

Combining layers and stripes on the comb

After you have mastered the layering and vertical-stripe techniques singly, you can combine them to achieve a wide range of design possibilities that will allow you to fit more colors on the comb. It is important to understand how a color will behave in a yarn when placed in a specific space on the comb. When you understand this, you can design yarns without major surprises, or change color arrangements to get the desired results without trial and error. Here are a few ways to combine the layering and striping techniques.

Sandwich a layer of vertical stripes between two horizontal layers. The horizontal layers hold the vertical stripes in place like a sandwich and make it easier to pull the colors out evenly. The layers of colors smooth out the transitions of the vertical-stripe colors which then act as accents in the yarn.

Alternate horizontal layers with vertical stripes. More colors can come and go in a yarn when there is more than one layer of vertical stripes. The horizontal layers provide the background colors and the vertical stripes add complex interest.

Vary the proportions of the two techniques. You'll get different effects when there are more horizontal layers than vertical stripes or vice versa. When the horizontal layers dominate, the yarn has a stable range of background colors on top of which the vertical-stripe colors tend to "float" or interact. When the stripes dominate, the yarn is wilder because there are more color

Variables in combining layers and vertical stripes.

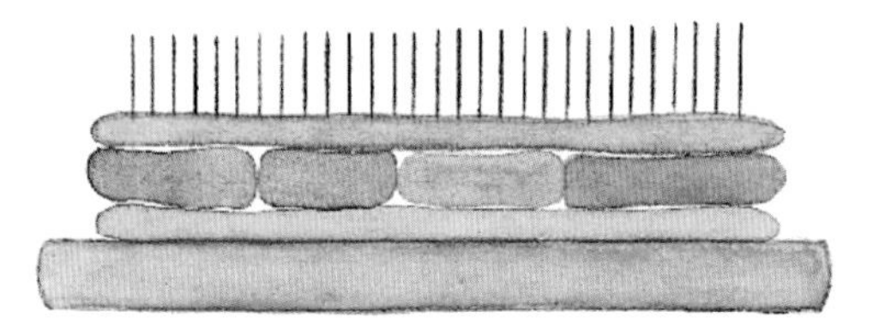

Sandwich a layer of vertical stripes between two horizontal layers.

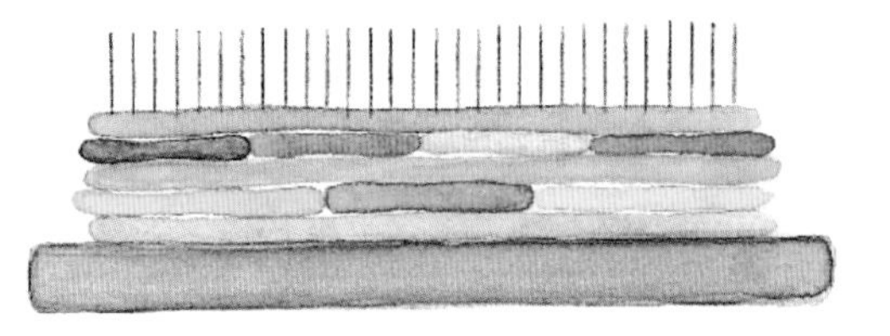

Alternate horizontal layers with layers of vertical stripes.

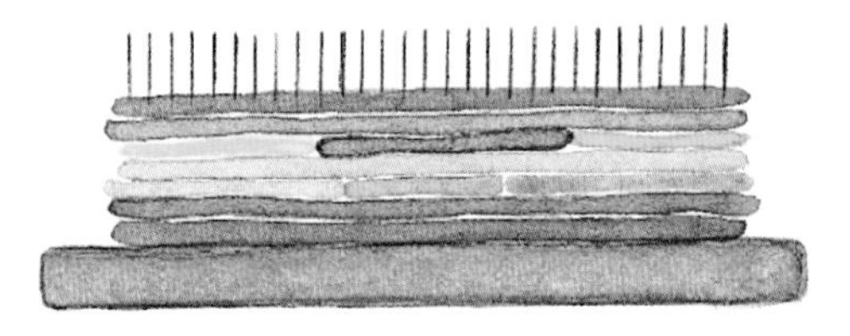

Vary proportions of horizontal layers and stripes. This one has five horizontal layers with two vertical stripe layers.

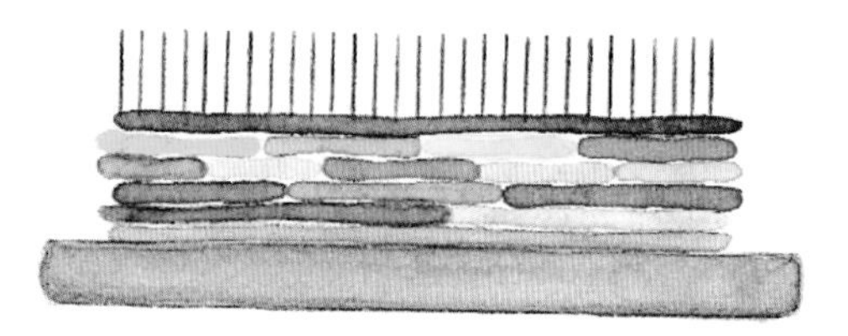

Vertical stripes dominate with four layers of vertical stripes and two horizontal layers.

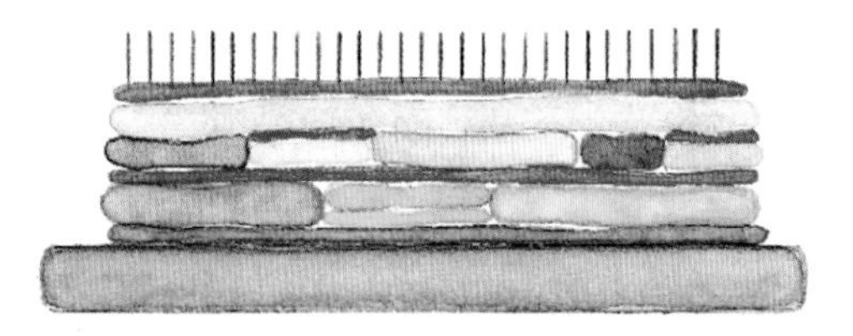

Vary the proportions of stripes and layers. Some of the horizontal layers are thinner than the vertical stripes. At the same time, the vertical stripes are staggered and vary in proportion. Combinations of these effects create the most complex yarns.

changes and more color interactions taking place, and because there are not enough horizontal layers to mellow the stripes' impact. These effects can be dramatically influenced by your color choice.

Vary the placement of colors between the stripes and layers. Placement can maximize or minimize a color's brightness. If the horizontal layers are very bright, vertical-stripe colors will appear dull. If the horizontal layers are dull, vertical-stripe colors will brighten.

Vary the proportions of colors used. By varying the proportions and size of the layers and stripes, you vary the amount of each color in the final yarn. There are infinite possibilities here. Basic color theories apply. When hues are similar, the yarn looks like a solid color; when the hues are very different, the yarn looks heathered. When you use similar values, the yarn is subtle; when you use a range of values, the result is heathered, striped, or speckled.

GROUPING SEVERAL TOPS FOR ONE YARN

Several separate multicolored tops can be used together in a yarn. How does that differ from stacking the colors on one comb, pulling off and spinning from there? First, since there is a limit to the number of colors that can clearly fit into one top, more tops means more colors in your yarn. Also, the colors remain clearer and more distinct when divided among several tops rather than squished into one.

You can incorporate up to five tops in one yarn. Controlling the colors in the drafting triangle as you spin gets "iffy" with more than five tops.

Using more than one top opens up a whole new set of variations, and the design possibilities can be mind-boggling. Here are a few suggestions, and I know you'll come up with many more.

Segregate the color relationships within each top. For example, when you're using two tops,

Combining more than one top in a yarn. From left to right: Top using a combination of layers and stripes; top using only vertical stripes; top using only horizontal layers; all three tops spun together in one yarn.

one could include only warm colors and the other only cool colors.

In a group of tops, the first could include only the dominant color family, the second could include the dominant family with accent colors, and the third and fourth could include variations of the first two.

A group of tops allows long color repetitions. You can alternate tops in the group to extend the length of the color repetition. One could remain the same and the other(s) could change.

You can develop subtle color variations over the course of several skeins by changing one top at a time, or even one color in a top at a time. For example, you can vary color from the bottom of a sweater to the shoulders by changing one top at a time.

Change color interactions by changing the contrast within different tops. Parts of a skein will have distinct and bold color interactions and other parts will look blended and subtle.

Vary the number of tops used at a time, so, for instance, the yarn will appear simple for a while, then complex when you add more tops.

Combine a solid-colored top with one or more multicolored tops. By varying values and hues, you can really change effects.

SPINNING COMBED MULTICOLORED TOPS

Combed preparation calls for a worsted spinning technique, really the easiest way to control colors in spinning. Using worsted technique is a little slower than spinning with a long draw, but the yarn you end up with is wonderful.

Because you pull the top through a relatively small-holed diz, it's usually the correct size for controlled spinning. If you're using multiple tops, there may be too much fiber to maintain control. The solution is to predraft the bundle of tops, thinning it to a controllable size (about two to four times as thick as the yarn you plan to spin).

Another problem you may encounter, due to inconsistencies in the pulling, is variation in the thickness of the top. To correct that, simply stop spinning and predraft any thicker portions of the top down to the desired thinness, then resume spinning. The top must be of even thickness for the colors to appear consistently in the yarn.

SELF-STUDY EXERCISES

The exercises for this chapter will familiarize you with the techniques of using combs for

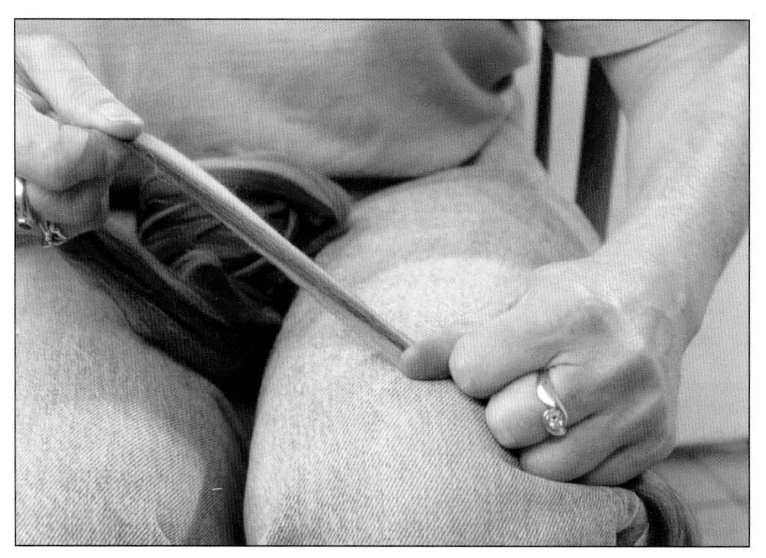

Predrafting. Before you spin, pull a bundle of tops to thin it down to a controllable size.

Worsted spinning. Keep your hands about a fiber-length apart to spin tops into worsted yarns.

multicolored fiber preparations. The variations will be introduced one at a time so you can see firsthand the effects each makes. This will allow you to create complex variations without frustration.

The key to working with combs is learning to evenly include all colors in the pulling process with the diz. It is doubly important when you start to work with vertical stripes where you have to control the pulling while you also count and control how many passes you can make with the diz. Without control, the color arrangement is lost.

Basic combing

1. *Combing practice.* Choose a color and load approximately one-third to one-half ounce of wool onto a comb. If available, start with the one-row hand-held combs and transfer to two-row combs. Comb as instructed. Pull off the top through a large-holed diz or freehand. Experiment with combing a different number of times. Compare the results you get from different kinds of combs.

Thorough color blending on combs

The following exercises are the same as those in Chapter 4, except that you are combing, not carding. To work through the exercises, choose one color of wool and comb five one-half-ounce tops of that color. Split the tops in half, and use one portion for each exercise. Combine the portion with a smaller amount of the color you have chosen to blend with it. The purpose is to alter the original color, not totally change it. Remember that both colors must be combed separately before you start blending them together.

You can use any of these exercises to make a range of blended colors by changing the proportions of the starting colors.

2. *Make a color warmer.* Choose an analogous color warmer than the original.
3. *Make a color cooler.* Choose an analogous color cooler than the original.
4. *Make a color lighter.* Choose any color that is lighter in value than the original.
5. *Make a color darker.* Choose any color that is darker in value than the original.
6. *Make a color brighter.* Choose a color in the

same hue family that is brighter than the original color.

7. *Make a color duller.* Choose a color that is complementary to the original color.
8. *Make a color duller.* Choose a gray that is the same value as the original color.
9. *Make a color duller.* Add black to the original color.
10. *Make a color duller.* Add white to the original color.
11. *Blend close values.* Choose any two colors that are close in value and blend them. Watch carefully to stop carding before they blend too much.
12. *Blend different values.* Choose from the same two color families as in exercise 11, but use two colors that have very different values.

Making horizontal layers

13. *Layering four analogous colors.* Choose four analogous colors that are close in value and put one layer of each on the comb. Pull off using a large-holed diz. Here, I want you to get comfortable with layering and give the diz a try.

    Now choose another four analogous colors, this time with a range of values. Layer each color once on the comb and pull off the top with a large-hole diz. Repeat with the same colors and layering, but this time use a diz with a very small hole to pull the fiber off. Can you see how the size of the diz hole affects the amount of color blending that takes place?

    Repeat, using the same colors, but this time make each layer half as thick and layer the colors twice on the comb before pulling the fiber off. Use a small-hole diz. See how much more subtly you can blend the same colors by making layers thinner *and* using a small diz?
14. *Layering six colors.* Choose six colors in a split complementary harmony. Use each color once and arrange the layers strictly by value, with the lightest on the bottom and the darkest on top. Pull off with a medium-hole diz.

    Now use the same six colors, but this time arrange the layers randomly, mixing up the values. Use the same size diz to pull off the top. The colors should appear differently in the yarn, but you may not be able to see this difference in the top.
15. *Layering eight colors.* Choose four warm colors and four cool colors. Layer each color once in a random order, pull off using a medium-hole diz, and spin.

    Now use the same colors, but this time make two tops—one with the four warm colors and one with the four cool colors. Pull off top using a medium-hole diz and combine the two tops for spinning.

    Compare the two yarns you have spun. The second should look brighter than the first.
16. *Layering ten colors.* Choose ten colors using a double triad. Do not use the same amount of each color—use more of some and less of others. Arrange the layers as you choose. Use a medium-hole diz to pull off. This exercise helps you learn about working with various proportions of colors.

Making vertical stripes

17. *Vertical stripes using four colors.* Choose two sets of complementary colors. Arrange the stripes evenly on the comb, with maximum contrast between colors. Use a medium-hole diz and pull fiber off in one round, pulling from right to left and back again.

    Now use the same colors, the same arrangement, and the same diz, but make two rounds back and forth. There will be more repeats of the color sequence, and each repeat will be shorter.

    These will not be your most wonderful-looking yarns, but there is a purpose here.

I want you to see the difference in repeat length and learn how not to blend the colors too much.(If they blend too much, you are moving across the comb too fast or making the stripes too narrow.) If you use many colors, you will be distracted by other things happening in the yarn and you won't focus on these basic lessons.

18. *Vertical stripes using six colors.* Choose six colors in a triad harmony. Load three colors in one layer, three in a second. Keep values as close as possible. The vertical stripes should end at the same level so the layers line up. Pull off using a medium-hole diz, making two rounds back and forth. In the yarn, you will see that color changes happen fairly abruptly.

    Now use the same colors, but mix up their placement. Pull off using the same size diz and going back and forth twice. Compare this yarn with the first one.

    Finally, use the same colors and whichever color arrangement you have found most pleasing. This time use a smaller-hole diz and go back and forth three times. The smaller hole size will blend colors more and the repeats will be shorter because you are moving across the comb faster.

19. *Vertical stripes using nine colors.* Choose nine colors in a double triad harmony. Make three layers of vertical stripes—bottom with two colors, middle with three colors, and top with four colors. Stagger where the stripes start and stop, so the layers don't line up exactly. Use a medium-hole diz and go back and forth two times. Look for an increased number of different color interactions and more subtle transitions than when all the stripes start and stop at the same place.

    Try this exercise again, using the same colors but changing their placement in the stripes. This time pull off using a smaller-hole diz and go back and forth three times.

20. *Vertical stripes using twelve colors.* Choose any color harmony, and use more of some colors than others. This will affect the stripes because some will be larger than others. Use the diz of your choice and go back and forth as many times as you please.

Combining layers and stripes on the comb

21. *Choose ten colors in any harmony.* Make a color sandwich with one horizontal layer on the bottom, then two layers of vertical stripes with four colors each, then another horizontal layer on top. Pull off with a large-hole diz, going back and forth twice.

    Now use the same colors but change the arrangement. Use a medium-hole diz and go back and forth three times.

    Making these kinds of changes produces dramatic differences in the finished yarns. With practice, you will learn to think through what you are doing and become able to predict what will happen before you pull the fibers off.

22. *Choose twelve colors in any color harmony.* The arrangement will be alternate layers and vertical stripes. At the bottom, make thin layers of two colors, then a layer of vertical stripes using four colors, then a layer of one color, then vertical stripes of three colors, then two final horizontal layers. What I want you to see this time is a series of colors that come and go in the yarn at different times (from the vertical stripes), while at the same time several other colors stay constant (from the horizontal layers). Use a medium-hole diz and go back and forth twice. The yarn should appear complex and interesting.

    Now use the same colors, but rearrange them, putting the stripe colors into layers, and vice versa. Use a medium-hole diz and go back and forth twice. Compare the yarns.

23. *Choose another twelve colors in any harmony.* Vary proportions, using more of some colors than others. Place seven colors in horizontal layers and five in vertical stripes.

Since there are different amounts of the colors, some layers and stripes will be larger or smaller than others. Use the medium-hole diz and go back and forth three times.

Now use the same colors but rearrange them. This time, put five colors in horizontal layers and seven in vertical stripes. Use the same diz and go back and forth three times. Compare the two yarns you spin.

24. *Choose ten colors in a complementary harmony.* Try to accentuate one hue family by using bright values and saturations. Then use duller, darker colors from the complementary family. On the comb, segregate the colors or values to further separate them. Use a large-hole diz when pulling off the top.

    Next, follow the same idea, but choose colors to highlight the other hue family and switch them around.

Grouping several tops together for a yarn

To keep and fit more colors clearly into one yarn, you can group several tops together. I will list some of the many ways to begin to think in this direction. I will not give specific layering or striping ideas—you are ready to do these on your own—but I will give general ideas for each top in the bundle. It should be enough to whet your appetite for carrying on with your own variations.

25. *Choose fourteen colors in a double complementary harmony.* Put the seven colors from each pair in separate tops. Use any combination of stripes and layers and any size diz that is appropriate. When you've pulled off both tops, put them together and predraft them, then spin a yarn.
26. *Choose sixteen colors in a double split complementary harmony.* The first top should have six colors from the dominant hue family in several variations. The second should include six colors from two hue families to act as accents. The third should have four colors from the last two families and one color from the dominant family. Use any combination of stripes and layers in preparing the tops and any size diz that is appropriate. Put all three tops together, predraft, and spin.
27. *Choose twenty colors in any combination.* Make four tops, arranging the colors as you please. To put the colors together, use three at a time, alternating which you include. Change one at a time and keep the other two the same. This will vary the lengths of the repeats and make ever-changing combinations in the yarn.
28. *Choose twenty colors in a wide range of colors and value.* Make four tops, each with a variety of hues and values. Put them together for spinning. In the final preparation, the colors and values will meet up differently, so that some areas will have high contrast and some will blend well. It may take a couple of tries to get this to work well. Take your time and plan it through. Lay the tops on a table and determine how the colors will line up. You can make adjustments at this stage. Finally, predraft the tops and spin into a yarn.
29. *Choose eighteen colors in any harmony.* Make three tops. To combine them for spinning, try using all three tops for a while, then drop one or the other to make a simpler yarn, then add the third one in again for more complexity. You can make a regular repeat or a random one.
30. *Choose fifteen colors in any harmony.* Choose one color that combines well with all the others, and make it into a solid-color top. Make two multicolor tops from the other colors. Put the three tops together, predraft, and spin. The solid-color top will change the appearance of the multicolors that are present.

Good luck! I hope you have as much fun as I've had playing with all the variations on these techniques.

chapter chapter chapter

7

Spinning and plying multicolored preparations

–7–

Spinning and plying multicolored preparations

After all the hard work it takes to create them, actually spinning multicolored fiber preparations is a treat. However, it's well worth taking enough time and care as you spin to ensure that the colors appear in the yarn as you've planned. With that in mind, this chapter starts with general guidelines for careful spinning, then moves on to introduce plying as a design element for multicolored yarns.

Plying is not a necessary part of spinning yarns, but it can be an additional design tool. Plying is an extra step, so make it worth the effort by plying to create more complex and beautiful yarns than you can produce as singles. I have to admit that when I began working on this book, I was not convinced that plying was worthwhile. For many years I was determined to use singles for most of my work. But once I began experimenting with plying multicolored yarns, my mind opened up. Plying has become a whole new avenue of color exploration for me. This chapter goes through the variables for using color in plying and shows how plying different yarns can give a wide range of wonderful results.

SPINNING MULTICOLORED FIBER PREPARATIONS

The main reason to spin any multicolored preparation is the simultaneous inclusion of all the colors in the yarn. To do this, you need to predraft the preparation down to a manageable thickness before you start to spin and you need to monitor the drafting triangle as you do spin. Here are some guidelines to follow.

The thickness of the fiber supply should be proportional to the thickness of the yarn. The fiber supply may be a single roving or top, or a group of rovings or tops. In any case, a good rule of thumb is to predraft the fiber supply until it is only two to four times as thick as the yarn you plan to spin. If you can handle a thicker preparation and still include all the colors in the drafting triangle—*and* keep control of the color sequence—that's fine. But if the preparation is too thick, the colors cannot all be drafted at once, and you'll produce a stripey yarn. On the other hand, if your fiber supply is too thin, you can't do any drafting and you may even have to overlap the fibers to make the yarn thick enough. Again, this process will disrupt the anticipated color sequence.

Different size yarns spun from the same colors will appear very different. The thinner the yarn, the closer you must be to see its distinct colors. The thicker the yarn, the more bright and distinct the colors, even when seen from a distance. The appearance depends on the size of the dots of colors in the yarn. The dots of color in thin yarns are much smaller than the dots of color in thick yarns.

While spinning, keep the twist out of the fiber supply. If the twist goes too far back along one side or the other of the fiber supply, the colors on the opposite side are not included and will appear in the yarn in a totally different place and order. They will tend to appear singly, not as dots of several colors at once. The final yarn will also appear much stripier than anticipated. If the twist does begin to run up one side of the fiber supply, stop spinning. Pull off the fiber supply and draft it a little thinner between your hands, then join on again and resume spinning. As you do, keep the drafting triangle open and make sure that fibers from across the whole width of the fiber supply are pulling evenly into the yarn.

Single versus two-ply multicolors. Both skeins and swatches were spun from the roving shown at left. The bottom skein and right swatch are the singles version and left sample and top skein are the two-ply. Note that the colors in the singles are a little brighter.

Don't be in a hurry. Keep in mind that you have spent considerable time making your wonderful multicolored preparations. Now take the time to spin them well. You'll typically spend two to three times as many hours on fiber dyeing and preparation as on the actual spinning. When you do spin, savor the process. Watch what's happening in the drafting zone. It's okay to spin slowly. Spinning is not a race or competition. Controlling color placement in the yarn takes care and time, but you'll be rewarded in the long run because color effects are the first thing anyone notices when looking at a finished piece.

WHY PLY?

Plying is a choice, not a necessity. Singles yarns can be used with excellent results. Plying should be a planned design element, like color or texture. Plying can dramatically affect the final result of a yarn, so you should design for it from the beginning, not as an afterthought.

Why go to the extra effort to ply a yarn if it is not necessary and might not significantly improve the yarn's performance or beauty? It depends. There are valid reasons for using singles yarns and there are valid reasons for using plied yarns.

The pros and cons of singles yarns

The colors in singles multicolored yarns are clearer and brighter than in plied yarns. The details of the color sequence are more obvious with singles because there's no other distraction. You can use more colors in a singles yarn and they'll be clearly seen.

With singles, it does not take as long to produce the final yarn for a project. The desired size of yarn is produced in one step, not three or more. When you're spinning quantities of yarn, this can be an issue. As a former production spinner, I spun or sold only singles for years. Historically singles yarns have been widely used. Would spinners have taken time to ply their yarns when all the yarn needs of society had to be handspun? They saved plying for specific situations where extra strength was really needed.

The drapability and hand of a well-spun singles is wonderful. To achieve good results, you need to pay attention to how much twist you put in the singles; you also need to keep the yarn size consistent. But once you get comfortable with spinning softer than for plied yarns and learn to maintain consistency, singles yarn is fun to produce and delightful to use.

Avid plyers protest that you cannot knit with singles because it will make your knitting slant. To that, I answer, "Hogwash." I have knitted with my singles for years without that problem. Slanting is caused by overtwisting. If the singles yarn has a twist angle of about twenty-five degrees or less, slanting should not occur. (Check the twist angle of my singles in the photos in this book.) To quickly check the twist in your own yarn as you spin, unwind a little from the bobbin and let it ply back on itself. If you want to use the yarn as a singles, this plied section should look soft and fluffy, not tight. Another way to check a singles is to observe the skein after the twist has been set. If, after the yarn has been soaked, hung, and dried, the skein rotates less than one full turn, the yarn will not skew when knit. I find that spinners who routinely ply put way too much twist into their singles—more than is appropriate or needed.

Another often-heard complaint is that anything knitted from singles yarn will stretch out. My answer again is "Hogwash." If the singles is knit firmly, using small enough needles, the resulting fabric will not stretch out of shape. Wool spun into singles carefully should have enough elasticity for the intended end use.

Finally, spinners fear that anything made from singles will pill. They forget that even plied yarns pill. Pilling is affected by many factors, not just the use of singles. In fact, if a singles pills easily, chances are a plied version of the same wool will pill too.

The pros and cons of plied yarns

Plying increases the strength and durability of the finished yarn. Fibers are anchored more firmly in the yarn and can withstand extra stress. When you're working with very fine fibers, spinning two or more thin singles and making a plied yarn gives better results than using one thick singles.

Plying can even out inconsistencies in the twist or thickness of the singles, but spinning, then plying takes a lot more time than making the same size yarn in a singles. Be clear why you are plying for a project and don't just ply out of habit. Plying to compensate for inadequate singles spinning is not a valid reason to me. If you take the time to learn to spin a good singles, you can design and spin whatever yarn you choose.

Plying opens a whole new arena of color and design possibilities. If color is the focus of your fiber work, don't overlook plying. Plying can dramatically enhance or alter your perception of the colors in a yarn. Plied yarns are richer when more colors are present. If you insist on plying a yarn with itself, at least include more colors in the singles yarn to start with. Plying helps eliminate the stripiness of a yarn and provides washes of color in the final fabric.

DESIGNING PLIED YARNS

Designing plied yarns is not significantly different from designing single multicolored yarns. The color theories from Chapter 1 are still helpful, although they work a little differently. And you have a few more choices to make involving variables that are unique to plied yarns.

Color choices

The variables in this section are consistent with the color theories from Chapter 1 that have been used throughout the book. Let's consider how these same theories work in the context of plying. First, I recommend not using single-color yarns at all because they are too boring. Instead, use yarns that include narrow ranges of analogous colors in similar values. Doing this makes much more interesting yarns.

There are two kinds of color interactions in a plied yarn—the interaction in the singles and the interaction between plies. When plying, the *essence* or overall color of each ply is more important than the exact colors, so in the following discussion, I won't refer to each color included in a multicolored singles but will simply describe the yarn as multicolored or analogous. I will also describe the approximate value of the singles yarn. When you are plying two or more multicolored yarns, don't worry about the separate colors in each ply. Just think about the general essence of each ply. The individual colors will take care of themselves. Trust me.

Choosing hues

To preserve the original color of a quiet, analogous single, ply it with another yarn that also has a narrow color and value range but a slightly different (either warmer or cooler) hue. The plied yarn will appear solid from a distance and look increasingly complex upon close inspection. The colors that both singles have in common will retreat into the background and their different colors will stand out as accents. These hue variations will be even more noticeable when the values are similar. The color effects in the plied yarn will not be too dramatic if you use colors that are closely related or in the same half of the color wheel, especially when values and saturations are close. This is the route to take when you desire subtlety.

You can also use complementary colors. Plied together, complements intensify each other, especially when both yarns have approximately the same value and saturation. Complementary plying doesn't work as well when values or saturations are significantly different.

Plying with multicolored singles offers many exciting possibilities. Yarns with a wide range of many colors make interesting fabrics, no matter what they are plied with. One idea is to ply a "wild" yarn that has a wide range of colors with a quiet yarn whose dominant color is analogous to a color in the wild yarn. In this case, the colors and values that the two yarns share will form a background and the contrasting colors will pop out as accents.

Here's another process: identify the dominant color in one multicolored yarn and ply it with another that includes that color. For example, consider a multicolored yarn with orange dominant. To make the colors other than orange pop out, ply it with another multicolored yarn that includes orange. The oranges and similar hues will blend together, leaving the other colors highlighted. If, by contrast, you want to highlight the orange in the yarn, ply it with a same-value yarn that is mainly blue (the complement of orange). The blue will force the orange to appear brighter, therefore noticeable (see page 194).

An easy way to ply with a multicolored yarn is to choose a singles of the same value and saturation, but with the opposite temperature. If you want to ply multicolored yarns, make one warm and one cool in a similar value range. What is common will fade into the background and what is different will be highlighted.

Given that value and saturation remain the same, there are two main choices for hue selection. The colors you combine can be close or opposite. If they are close, plying will play up subtle differences between them. If they are

Choosing hues for plying.

Plying analogous colors. Here an orange yarn plied with a yellow-orange yarn yields subtle results.

Plying complementary colors. Here a pink yarn is plied with a green yarn. Because values are similar, the colors intensify each other.

Plying yarns that have a hue in common. The two bottom yarns have orange in them. When plied together (top skein), the orange acts as a background and the other colors become accents.

opposite, dramatic interactions will take place. There are no right or wrong answers here. If you create the effect you want, then it's right, and if it's wrong, it is wrong only for that situation. Don't be afraid to try new combinations or ones you think will not work. Usually, those are my favorites. For now I want you to expand your options beyond only plying a yarn on itself!

Choosing values

Of all the design choices you can make, value choices are the most important. Value is seen from a distance, and it overpowers other color interactions. In choosing yarns to ply together, you have two distinct alternatives—low or high contrast in values—and a range of intermediate combinations.

It's helpful to discuss values in terms of keys. Yarns that use a minor key (a narrow range of values) produce quiet, subtle, and coherent fabrics. When the values of the plies are similar—whether all light, all medium, or all dark—then the hues and their saturations become the dominant characteristics of the yarn.

Major keys use the whole range of values. When either light or dark values dominate, the result is a salt-and-pepper or barber-pole effect. From a distance, the yarn takes on a heathered appearance. Colors are minimized, dull, and subtle color variations get lost. Yarns that combine only light and dark values are my least favorite because the colors seem so dead. The light values make the dark values appear darker and duller and the dark values make the light values seem lighter and more washed-out. To avoid the salt-and-pepper effect and make color the featured design element, include some middle values to bridge the gap between lights and darks.

As another variation, consider plying a minor-key yarn with a major-key yarn. The values that the plies have in common will recede into the background, and the contrasting values will stand out as accents. For liveliness, you should use different proportions of the different values in the yarn and the value used in the largest quantity will dominate.

Choosing saturations

Saturation, the brightness or dullness of a color, is a more subtle design element than hue or value, but no less important. Choosing the right saturation for each color can make the dif-

Choosing values for plying.

The top two skeins have a narrow value range and the third skein shows them plied together. The bottom two skeins have a wide value range; the third from the bottom shows them plied together.

Value choice and complements. When the light yellow and dark violet yarns are plied, the result looks like salt and pepper (below). Lighten the value of the violet and darken the value of the yellow and the plied yarn shows more color interaction (above).

ference between a mediocre and a fabulous yarn. The main thing to remember about using saturations in plying is that the most saturated colors tend to stand out. Combining saturated and dull colors, especially if their values are similar, emphasizes the contrast and makes the saturated colors look brighter and the dull colors duller.

If one hue does not work in a combination, try changing its brightness before abandoning it altogether. For one hue to dominate a plied yarn, make the values similar and the dominant color the brightest. To further intensify this brightness, include a duller, same-value version of the color's complement in one of the plies.

When plying analogous colors, the brightest ones in the yarn dominate, especially if the overall values are similar. When colors are on the same side of the color wheel and values are similar, subtle color undertones come out and are most noticeable in the light-value range. If two analogous yarns are plied, one being a little darker than the other, the darker colors make the lighter ones appear lighter and brighter than they are.

When plying complementary colors, the results are most intense if the saturations and values of all plies are as close as possible. If you want only the complementary colors to pop out, make sure that the other colors in each ply are duller than, but the same value as, the complementary colors. This makes the duller colors less conspicuous and the complementary colors more prominent.

What can you do with dull colors? To make a dull color appear brighter, ply it with a color that has the same value but less saturation. Choose a color mixed with its complement or a neutral gray. Making a dull color appear duller is much easier. You can make it become part of the background by plying it with analogous, brighter colors of the same value. Another approach is to ply the dull color with a multicolored yarn whose brighter colors have varying saturations and a wide range of values. The values and saturations that are similar to the dull-colored yarn will fade into the background, and the other colors will act as accents.

Choosing saturations for plying.

A bright green yarn is plied with a dull red yarn. The red intensifies the green in the plied yarn.

When the violet yarn is plied with a dull yellow/gray yarn, the violet looks bright. The same violet plied with a bright multicolored yarn looks duller and the bright colors pop out.

Deciding how many singles to ply together

When considering how many yarns to ply together, ask yourself:

- What is the end use of the yarn?
- What is the desired end size of the yarn?
- What fiber(s) do I plan to use?
- How do I want the colors to appear?
- How much time do I have to devote to this piece?
- Will a singles yarn be adequate? Do I need to ply at all?

All these factors are important, and your final decision will vary from project to project. Sometimes plied yarns are better than singles, sometimes singles yarn work just fine. Sometimes a two-ply is appropriate, sometimes you'll choose a three-ply. The lesson here is that no one kind of yarn is perfect for every occasion. Be flexible and think about each project individually. This will keep your designing and spinning more varied and exciting.

Two-ply yarns

This is the most common approach to plying. A two-ply evens out irregularities in the thickness and twist of singles yarns. A two-ply lets you use twice as many colors. A two-ply can change the appearance of a singles yarn you do not care for.

Basic three-ply yarns

The basic three-ply yarn twists three separate singles together. Compared to a two-ply yarn, it takes a lot more spinning time to end up with the same yardage in three-ply, and if you want to end up with the same size yarns, you have to spin the singles for the three-ply finer, too. But three-ply yarn feels great and is stronger than two-ply. In terms of color, more complex effects can happen with three plies. It is important to include at least one multicolored yarn in the mix, or a yarn that has a high contrast of some kind. Without contrast, the colors seem flat. Try combining yarns that are all distinctively different. The results are much more exciting. Fabrics knitted from three-ply yarns do not look striped. Dots and washes of colors appear, but no solid-color stripes.

Using a range of values in a three-ply yarn is also successful. Major keys produce pleasing results that look quite different from the salt-and-pepper effects you get with two-ply yarns. Minor keys produce small dots of color whose differences are subtle. Changing only one ply can make a dramatic change in the final yarn. That means if you don't like one combination of plies, you can try another! That is the purpose of sampling.

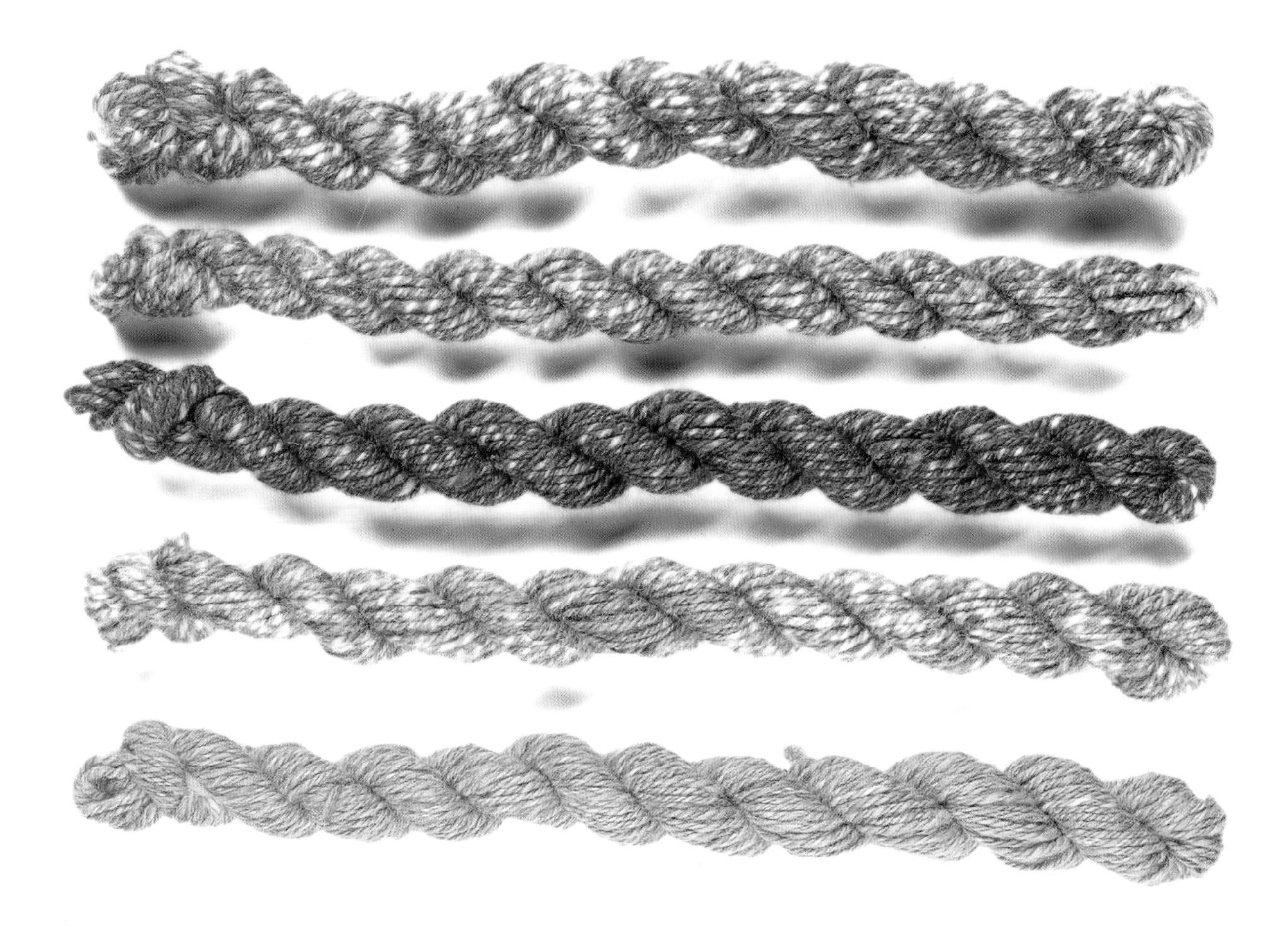

Three-ply yarns. From bottom to top: three plies with high minor values; three plies using extended middle minor values; three plies using low minor values; one light value, one medium value, and one dark value plied together; three plies that have different value keys.

Navajo three-ply yarn

This yarn takes one ball or bobbin and turns it into a three-ply via a simple looping technique, similar to making a chain in crochet. The result is distinctly different from a basic three-ply made from three separate singles. Spinners like Navajo plying because it "comes out even", with no singles left over. However, unless the plying is carefully done, a Navajo three-ply yarn can have messy loops and snarls, and unless you're fluent at making the loops, it's easy to overtwist the yarn as you ply.

In terms of color, Navajo plying can produce bold effects but the colors tend to show up as stripes in the finished fabrics. It takes many colors and contrasts in the singles yarn to make a comparably complex yarn using Navajo plying. By varying the length and placement of the loops as you Navajo-ply, you can create certain color effects. For instance, making the loops coincide with the color changes in the singles yarn isolates colors and creates bold stripes. Arranging the loops so that colors are plied together reduces the striping.

Navajo three-ply yarns. In the top skein, the looping was arranged to blend the colors as much as possible; in the bottom skein, the colors were isolated as much as possible to make them appear bold in the yarn.

Basic four-ply yarn

The basic four-ply yarn twists four singles together in the direction opposite to how they were spun. (Another approach, making a cabled yarn, involves two steps: first you make a two-ply yarn, then you ply two two-plies to make a four-ply.) Spinning a four-ply yarn takes even more time than spinning a three-ply yarn, but you may find it's worth the effort. I've learned to appreciate four-ply yarns for their color possibilities. Combining four multicolored plies that share a dominant hue makes fabrics that almost sing! It is surprising how much each of the plies changes the overall effect. Fine tuning these yarns to obtain one you like is easy.

In terms of value, four-ply yarns that have both very light and very dark values can take on a "marled" appearance that reduces the richness of the hues. Minor keys are more successful than major keys. If the values are close, even dull colors can become iridescent. Using medium- and dark-value colors together almost imitates stained glass.

Four-ply yarns. (All singles used are multicolored.) Bottom to top: three light, one medium; two light, two medium; one light, two medium, one dark; one light, three medium; one medium, three dark; two medium, two dark; one light, three medium.

The thickness of the singles yarns

The thickness of the individual plies and the final plied yarn affects how colors appear. The thinner you want the final yarn and the more plies you want to include, the thinner each ply must be. But the thinner you spin, the brighter and more contrasting the colors must be to show up in the fabric. Otherwise, even from a relatively short distance, the colors will be indistinguishable.

Multicolors show up well in plied yarns of a thickness that compares to commercial sportweight or worsted-weight knitting yarns. I have included up to four plies in a worsted-weight yarn and the colors were readily visible. Experiment with different sizes to see what works for you.

The plies in a plied yarn do not all have to be the same size. Varying their thickness will change the proportions of different colors. That's another design element that you can experiment with.

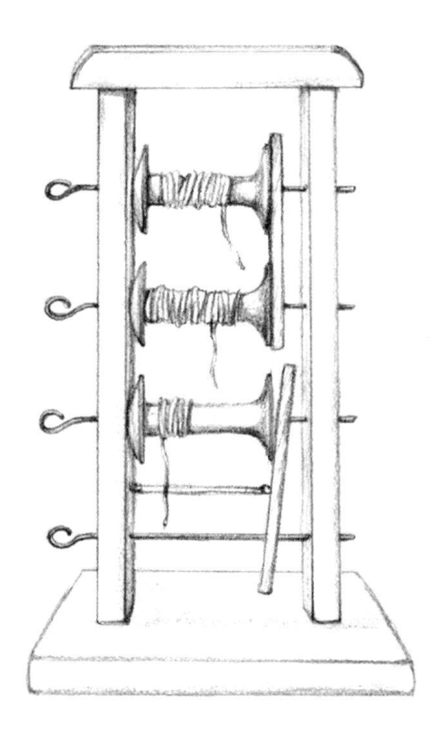

An example of a Lazy Kate with braking device.

The twist of the singles yarn

The amount of twist put into each single determines the amount of twist appropriate for plying. The more twist in the singles, the more twist you can introduce for plying. As you can see from the pictures in this chapter, my personal preference is to ply firmly, at a twist angle of thirty to thirty-three degrees, because I think the yarn looks most interesting and attractive that way. Loosely plied yarns look like separate yarns that are simply stranded, instead of twisted, together.

HOW TO PLY

Before you can ply, you need to spin the appropriate number of singles, then put the filled bobbins on a *lazy kate.* Most spinning wheels come with a lazy kate of some kind, but some are much better than others. Ideally a lazy kate should have a braking device to control how fast yarn unwinds from the bobbin and maintain even tension on each of the singles. If your lazy kate gives you trouble, it may be easier to wind the yarn into balls and put each ball in a box or mixing bowl on the floor beside you. Then improvise a tensioning system: arrange a few dowels or knitting needles in parallel positions in a shoe box or wooden frame and feed the yarn under and over the dowels or needles.

Adjust your wheel so it pulls more firmly on the yarn. You need a stronger take-up for plying than for spinning. You can attach the singles to the wheel by simply knotting them to the leader. Turn the wheel in the direction opposite from how you spun the singles. Most spinners turn their wheels clockwise (Z-twist) for spinning and counterclockwise (S-twist) for plying.

To regulate tension, position a yarn between each of the fingers of the hand further from the orifice. Firmly hold all the yarns with the hand closer to the orifice. Hold back the yarns and count the appropriate number of treadle strokes, then wind the plied yarn on the bobbin. Pull out another arm's length of yarns and repeat the treadling and feeding onto the bobbin. The job of the hand closer to the orifice is to keep tension on the yarns and keep them from tangling. The job of the other hand is to insure the tension is even as the twist enters the yarn. Your treadling and hand movements should be as even as possible to make sure the twist in the yarn is consistent.

For Navajo plying, the singles yarn must be under tension as it comes from the lazy kate or ball. Make a loop at the end of the yarn and tie it onto the leader. Now your hands will do different jobs. The hand that is closer to the orifice guides the twist into the yarn as you treadle. The other hand makes loops one at a time by reaching through one loop and pulling up the next one, like a chain in crochet. You can make the loops as long or short as you choose, all the same or varied. As you're learning to Navajo-ply, treadle very slowly so you don't overtwist the yarn.

Plying is not any harder or more mysterious than this, and it's a technique that can greatly extend your design possibilities. Follow the self-study exercises to explore the possibilities of plying multicolored yarns, and have fun learning these techniques.

Plying techniques.

Plying two yarns together.

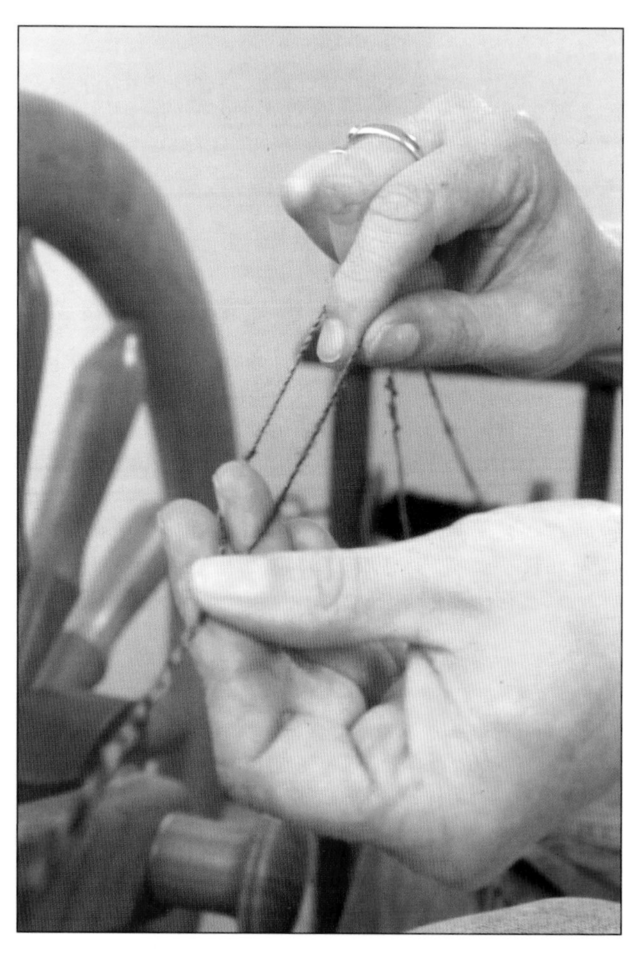

Right hand keeping yarns separated and left hand guiding the yarn into the orifice.

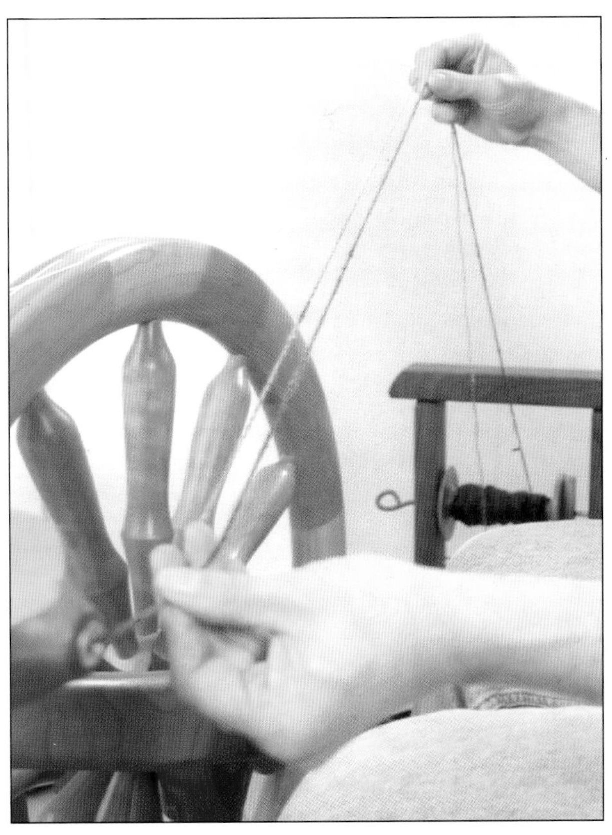

Second hand position when pulling out an arm's length of yarn to ply.

Navajo plying. Both hands put tension on the yarn while the twist is moving up the plies. Right hand brings the yarn closer to the left so the yarn can be pulled through the loop with the left index finger. (Another method is to use one hand to control the twist and the other hand to make loops.)

Pull each loop as far as you want. Loops can be short or long.

SELF-STUDY EXERCISES

These exercises will help you see how the colors in plied yarns affect each other and how you can take any color and create something wonderful with it. You can use a wide range of yarns here, so go into your stash and get out some of the fibers you've been saving. This could be the time to use them. Work with all wool, wool blends, or whatever fibers you prefer, and choose any preparation technique—make painted rovings, drum-carded batts, or combed tops.

For each exercise, you'll start by spinning singles yarns that use at least six colors, or at least eight colors for yarns described as multicolored. In each case, choose and combine colors as needed, so that the essence or general effect of the singles yarn fulfills the description.

Two-ply yarns

1. *Plying one yarn with many other different yarns.* Spin about three ounces of a singles yarn, using six to eight analogous colors that are close in value. Choose any preparation technique you want to use. Spin the singles with medium twist and a thickness of about twenty to twenty-four wraps/inch.

   You will ply this yarn with a variety of other yarns, listed below, to obtain different effects. To make each of these other yarns, prepare about a quarter ounce of fiber and spin it as you did the base yarn. Each two-ply sample will provide enough yarn for you to prepare a small skein and knit a swatch.

   a. Ply the original yarn with itself.
   b. Ply with an analogous color of similar value, but warmer.
   c. Ply with an analogous cooler of similar value, but cooler.
   d. Ply with an analogous color that is much lighter in value.
   e. Ply with an analogous color that is much darker in value.
   f. Ply with a complementary color of the same saturation and value.
   g. Ply with a complementary color that is much duller and has a different value.
   h. Ply with a complementary color that is brighter and has a different value.
   i. Ply with a multicolored yarn that has a narrow range of values and the opposite temperature (e.g. if original color is warm, multicolor should be cool).
   j. Ply with a multicolored yarn that includes the original color and has a wide range of values.
   k. Ply with a multicolor yarn that has nothing in common with the original.
   l. Ply with a darker multicolored yarn.

   You can repeat this series, using different base yarns. Try using a warm color, a cool color, or many different colors and compare the results.

2. *Plying one yarn with yarns of different values.* The purpose of this series is to see the effects of value choices in plying. Again, spin about three ounces of one singles yarn, using six analogous colors of similar, medium values. For the other yarns, spin about one-quarter ounce each, using at least six colors in most cases and at least eight colors for multicolored yarns. Concentrate on values as you work. After working through the series once with a medium-value yarn, you can repeat it with a light-value yarn and then with a dark-value yarn.

   a. Ply with an analogous color of similar medium value.
   b. Ply with another analogous color of a darker value.
   c. Ply with another analogous color of a lighter value.
   d. Ply with a complementary color lighter in value.
   e. Ply with a complementary color with the same value.

f. Ply with a complementary color darker in value.
g. Ply with a light-value multicolored yarn.
h. Ply with a medium-value multicolored yarn.
i. Ply with a dark-value multicolored yarn.
j. Ply with a multicolored yarn that has light values and a wide range of hues.
k. Ply with a multicolored yarn that has medium values and a wide range of hues.
l. Ply with a multicolored yarn that has dark values and a wide range of hues.

3. *Plying one yarn with yarns of different saturations.* Again, spin about three ounces of one singles yarn, using six analogous colors of similar values and medium intensity. For the other yarns, spin about one-quarter ounce each, using at least six colors in most cases and at least eight colors for multicolored yarns. Concentrate on intensity as you work. After working through the series once, you can repeat it using yarn of a different hue or yarn that is lighter, darker, brighter, or duller.
   a. Ply with an analogous color of the same value and intensity.
   b. Ply with an analogous color that has the same value but is duller.
   c. Ply with an analogous color that has the same value but is brighter.
   d. Ply with an analogous color that is lighter and duller.
   e. Ply with an analogous color that is darker and duller.
   f. Ply with an analogous color that is lighter and brighter.
   g. Ply with an analogous color that is darker and brighter.
   h. Ply with a complementary color that has the same value but is duller.
   i. Ply with a complementary color that has the same value but is brighter.
   j. Ply with a complementary color that that is lighter and duller.
   k. Ply with a complementary color that is darker and duller.
   l. Ply with a complementary color that is lighter and brighter.
   m. Ply with a complementary color that is darker and brighter.
   n. Ply with a multicolored yarn that has the same value but is brighter.
   o. Ply with a multicolored yarn that has the same value but is duller.

Multi-ply yarns

4. *Traditional three-ply yarns*

   Again, choose whatever fiber and method of preparation you prefer. Combine at least six colors in each singles yarn. Spin a variety of value ranges and color ranges. I will only specify which values to put together. You can choose the hue families. The variations are endless.
   a. Ply three light-value yarns.
   b. Ply two light values with one medium value.
   c. Ply two light values with one dark value.
   d. Ply three medium values together.
   e. Ply two medium values with one light value.
   f. Ply two medium values with one dark value.
   g. Ply three dark values together.
   h. Ply two dark values with one light value.
   i. Ply two dark values with one medium value.
   j. Ply one light value, one medium value, and one dark value.

   More variations are possible when you combine analogous and multicolored yarns. Other variations include using yarns with a wide range of values and yarns with a narrow range of values.

5. *Navajo three-ply yarns*

   Spin samples of several different multicolored yarns, using about one ounce of fiber for each. Spin quiet yarns using analogous colors, multicolored yarns with narrow value range, and multicolored yarns with wide value range. With each of these:

a. Try making short, medium, and longer loops.
b. Loop irregularly, trying to match colors and make the effect bolder.
c. Loop irregularly, trying to blend the colors as much as possible.

6. *Four-ply yarns*

Again, you can choose whatever fiber and method of preparation you prefer. Combine at least six colors in each singles yarn. Spin a variety of value and color ranges. I will only specify which values to put together. You choose the hue families.

a. Use four plies of similar value—all light, all medium, or all dark.
b. Use three plies of one value and one of another value; for example, three lights and one dark.
c. Use two plies of one value and two plies of another value; for example, two lights and two mediums.
d. Use two plies of one value and one each of the other values; for example, two lights with one medium and one dark.

7. *Other plying possibilities*

There are many other options to try, such as starting with singles of different thickness to see how that affects the colors. You can experiment with novelty yarns or cabled yarns. The possibilities go on and on. Your imagination and your daring are your only limits. Have a ball!

chapter

8 chapter

chapter

A gallery of finished pieces

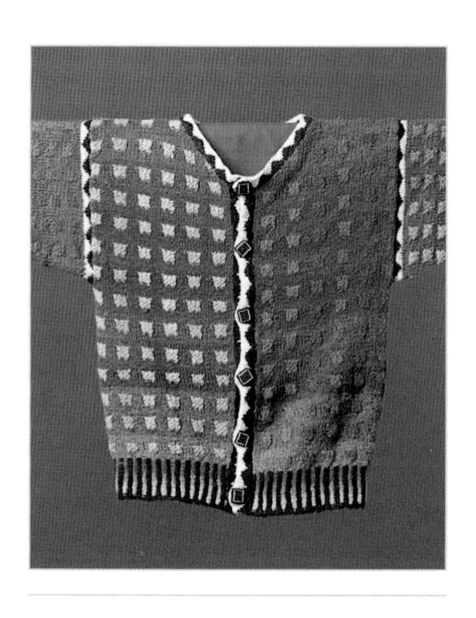

Garments

Accessories

Tapestries

—8—

A gallery of finished pieces

Painted Roving Sample Coat. 90% wool, 10% alpaca. Singles yarns. The painted rovings came from samples from several workshops I taught. The multicolored stripes illustrate the possibilities for yarn design with painted rovings. Black was used to separate the multicolored yarns. The coat was knitted from sleeve to sleeve.

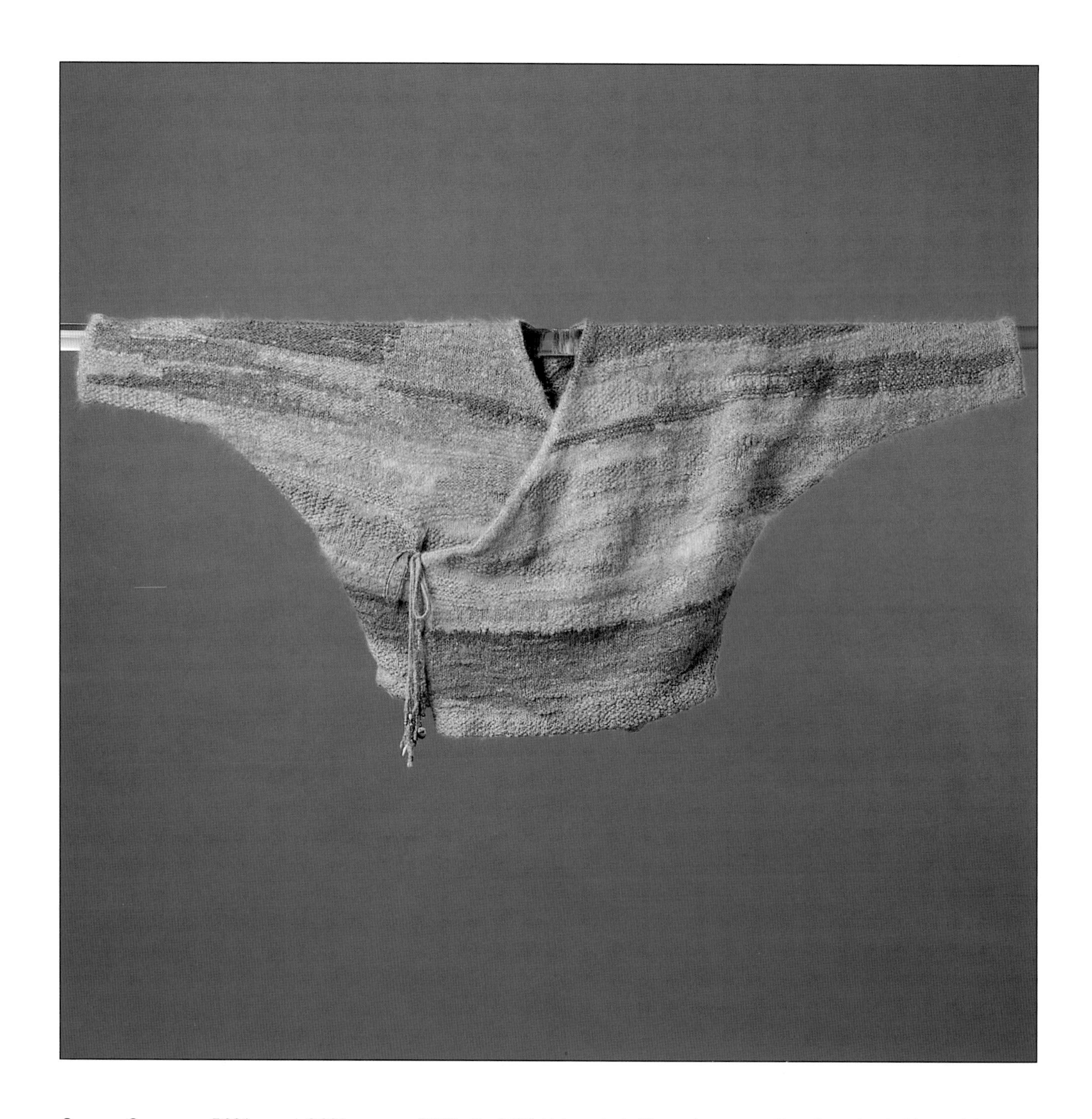

Sunset Sweater. 50% wool, 20% angora, 20% silk, 10% kid mohair. Two-ply yarns. One hundred thirty-eight different drum-carded blended batts were used to create twenty-nine singles yarns that were then plied to create the twenty-eight plied yarns used in the design. Wool was the base for all the blends. Luxury fibers were added for texture and color effects. The design was created as a knit tapestry and was inspired by a beach vacation. The design was charted and the sweater knit from bottom to top with the sleeves included. Edges are faced, not ribbed. Baubles at the ends of ties were found at the beach.

Monet-Inspired Sweater. Wool, camel, alpaca, silk, and angora. Two-ply yarns. The shape of this sweater is the same as the Sunset Sweater. This time, the different-textured multicolored yarns are more isolated. Thirty-two different rovings were painted to create fifteen different singles yarns. The fifteen singles yarns were plied with each other to create thirteen two-ply yarns used to knit. The yarns in the center of the sweater are wool blended with alpaca and camel, the sections over the shoulders are wool blended with silk, and the yarns for the sleeves are wool blended with angora. This sweater positions multicolored texture to create distinct areas within a sweater.

This card was used as the color inspiration for the following three vests. The colors were interpreted differently in each piece.

Lily Vest #1. 100% wool. Singles yarn. This is the first in a series of three vests using the same picture as a design source. This design incorporates all twenty-six colors of the picture into one multicolored yarn. The vest is knit in simple knit/purl patterns selected as the vest was knitted.

Lily Vest #2. 100% wool. Singles yarn. Using the same picture for design inspiration, thirty-two dyed colors of wool were drum-carded and used to create sixteen subtle multicolored singles yarns. The design was knit from side to side and uses variations of patterns in the Bohus style.

Lily Vest #3. Wool, alpaca, and silk. Singles yarn. Using the same picture for design inspiration, the same thirty-two dyed colors of wool were drum carded, along with a little alpaca and a little silk, to create fifteen subtle multicolored singles yarns. The design was knit from bottom to top using a predesigned chart to graphically interpret the picture.

Vest Game. 100% wool. Singles yarn. Nine subtle yarns were created by drum carding and layering the colors in batts. The knitting technique uses various Fair-Isle patterns that are no more than five stitches wide. The design was created as the vest was knit.

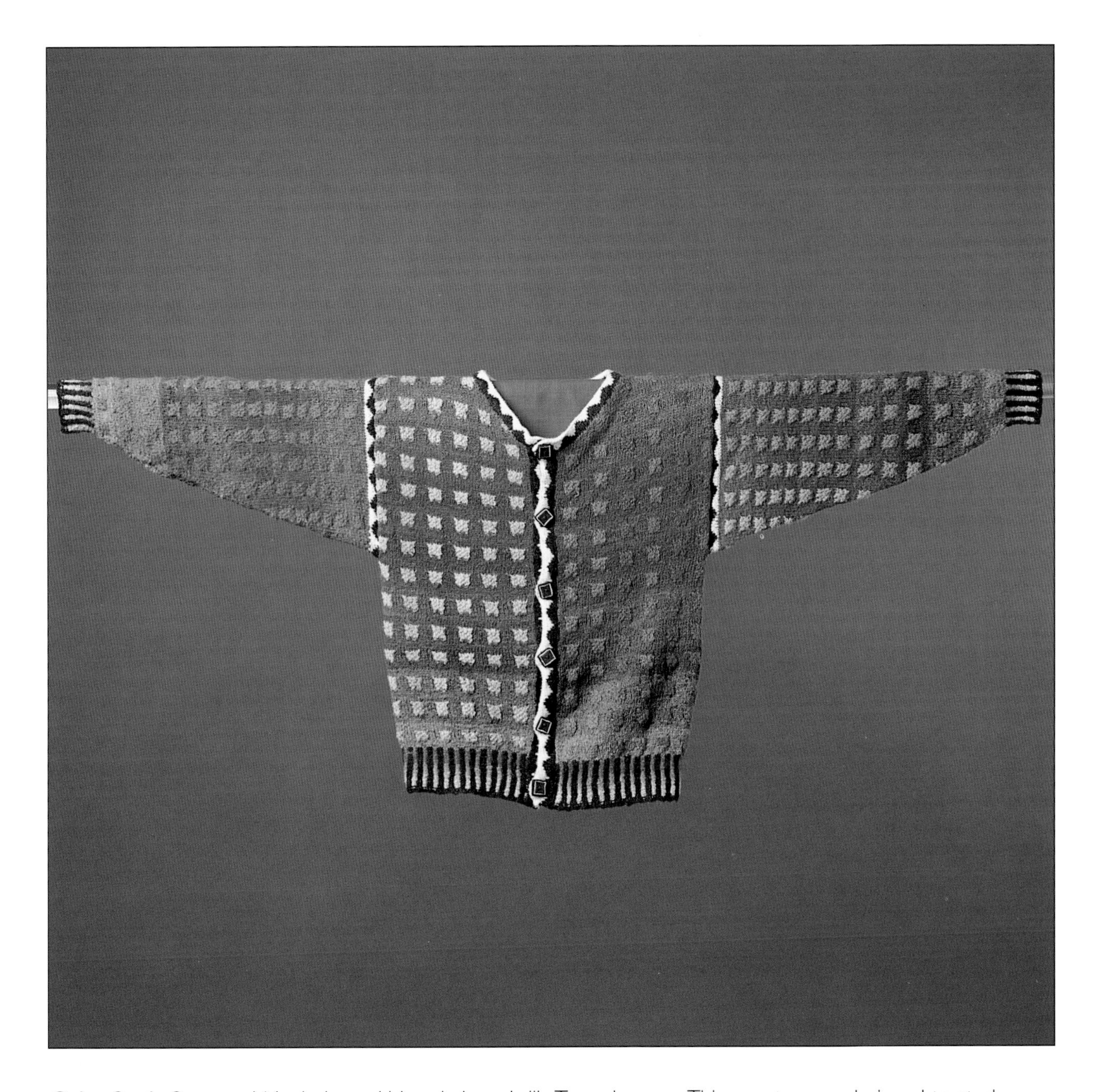

Color Study Sweater. Wool, alpaca, kid mohair, and silk. Two-ply yarns. This sweater was designed to study color interactions within a garment. It is also a study in thorough color blending. The horizontal stripes of the sweater are fourteen cool colors that range from yellow-green to red-violet. The squares are twenty-four warm colors that range from a yellower green to a redder violet. Vertically, the squares remain the same color and progress around the sweater beginning with red-violet on the right front and ending with yellow-green on the left front. The black-and-white trim is an accent. This sweater is worked opposite from a typical Norwegian sweater where the body is black and white and the trim is colorful. The fibers were thoroughly carded on a drum carder. There are three to six colors in each of the yarns. The ribbing is corrugated, with one row of each color.

Eccentric Multicolor Vest. 100% wool. Singles yarn. There are twenty warm multicolored yarns and twenty cool multicolored yarns in this vest. It is knitted with a slip-stitch pattern, using the cool yarns as the background and the warm yarns on the surface. The purpose of this piece was to use lots of very obviously multicolored yarns together in one piece. The closing is off center and the left front piece was knitted on the diagonal. Trims are facings, not ribbings.

Spring Cleaning. 100% wool. Singles yarn. One yarn was used in this vest. It was created from the leftover colors in my studio at the end of a teaching year. There are small amounts of approximately forty colors in the yarn. The fiber was prepared on a drum carder, arranging the colors in both stripes and layers.

Celia's Cotton Top. 100% FoxFibre cotton. Two-ply yarn. The FoxFibre cotton was painted in roving form. One ply used white cotton and the other ply was painted over either green or coyote (brown) cotton; that is why there are both bright and dull colors in the yarn. The piece was knitted in moss stitch.

Multicolored Scarf. 100% wool. Singles yarn. The fiber was combed, then the colors were arranged on a hackle. Two different tops were drafted and spun together. One top had very slow color progressions and moved from blue-greens at one end to red-violets at the other. The second top had many accent colors that appeared throughout the yarn. The stitch is a simple knit/purl pattern.

One-Shot Lace Shawl. 100% wool. Singles yarn. Lace is not my first choice for knitting, but I wanted to try the lace shawl featured in the Winter 1996 issue of *Spin·Off* magazine. Twenty colors were combed separately, then layered on a hackle for color arrangement.

The Afghan Project. Mostly wool with a little alpaca blended into some squares. Singles yarns. This project started as a way to use up small amounts of yarns created during demonstrations. Students and friends volunteered to knit squares for me using variations of seed stitch and moss stitch. I sent them yarn, they returned knitted squares for me to arrange and sew together. An I-cord edging was added after assembly.

Warm/Cool Tam. Wool blended with angora. Two-ply yarn. Colors and fibers were blended on a drum carder. One ply slowly changed colors from warm to cool. The other ply has short areas of accent colors. The colors in the tam flow from warm colors around the face to cool colors at the top.

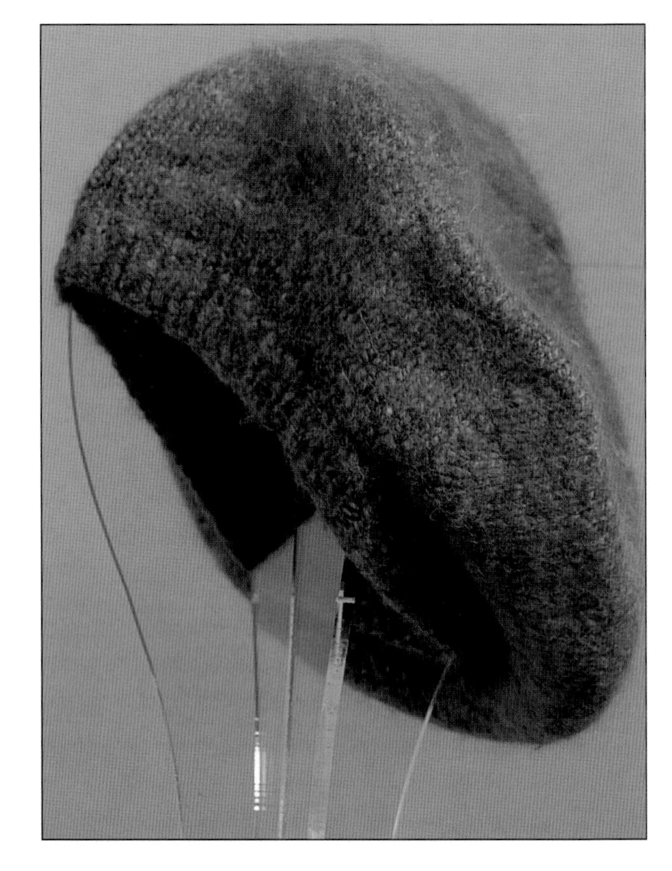

Scarf and hat. 100% wool. Singles yarn. The same yarn was used for both pieces. The yarn was created by layering multicolored batts and pulling them out. These pieces show that a multicolored yarn will appear differently when knit back and forth versus in the round.

Fish Fetish (left). Silk and wool. Singles and two-ply yarns. A 3-D tapestry-woven fish with knitted sea anemones. The fish was woven in pieces, assembled, and beaded. The yarns were spun from carded batts and painted rovings.

Under the Rainbow (right). Silk and wool. Singles and two-ply yarns. A 3-D tapestry-woven fish, woven on a foamcore board in pieces, then assembled and beaded. The fibers were both painted and carded to achieve the desired effects.

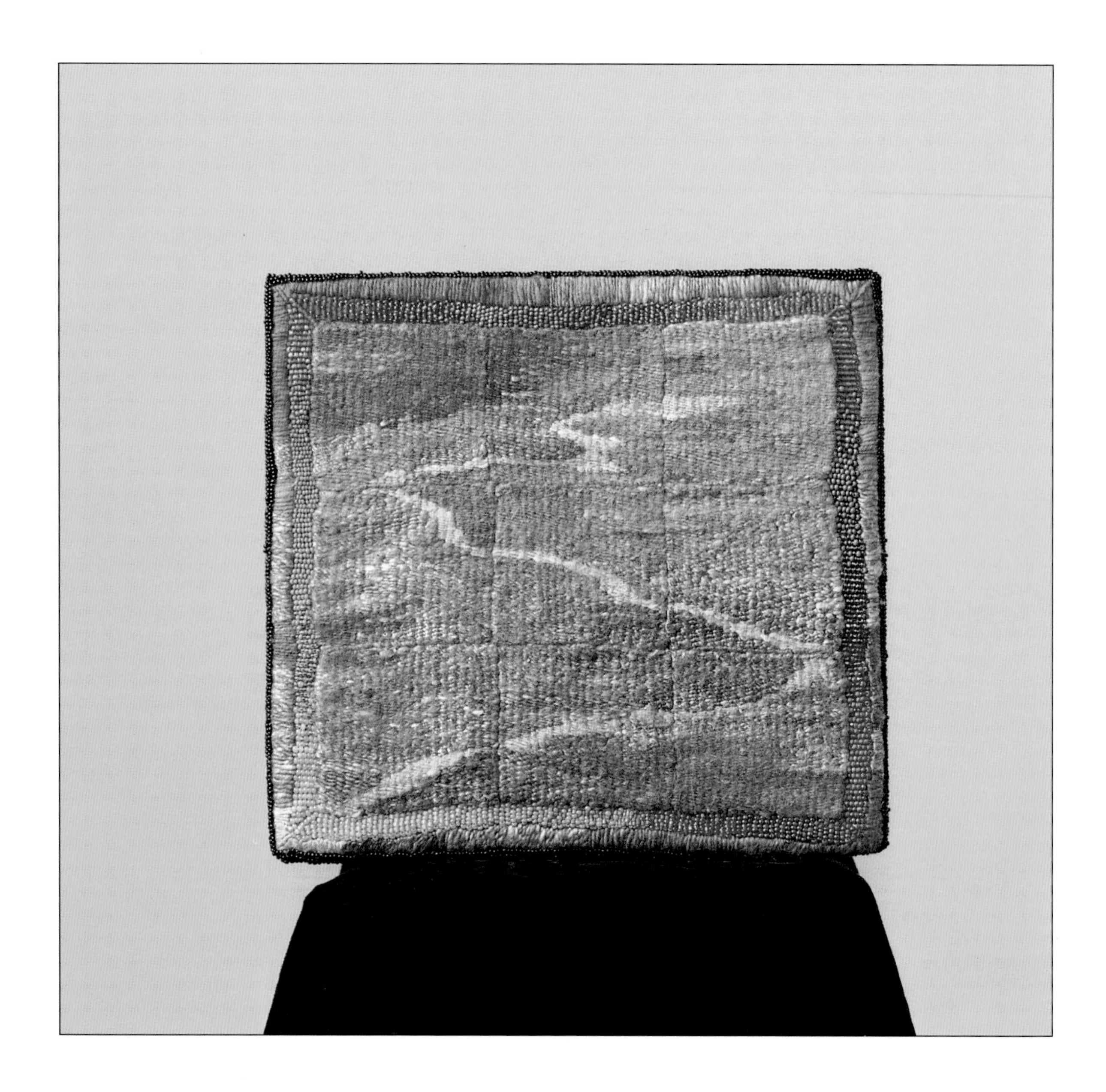

The Yellow Road to Somewhere. Silk and wool. Singles and two-ply yarns. Nine separate tapestries sewn together, then embroidered and beaded. The yarns were all spun from painted rovings.

A Parrotly Speechless. 100% silk. Singles yarn. A shaped tapestry woven in pieces on a foamcore loom, assembled, then embellished. The beak and claws are made from Fimo. The yarns were all spun from combed silk top which had been painted.

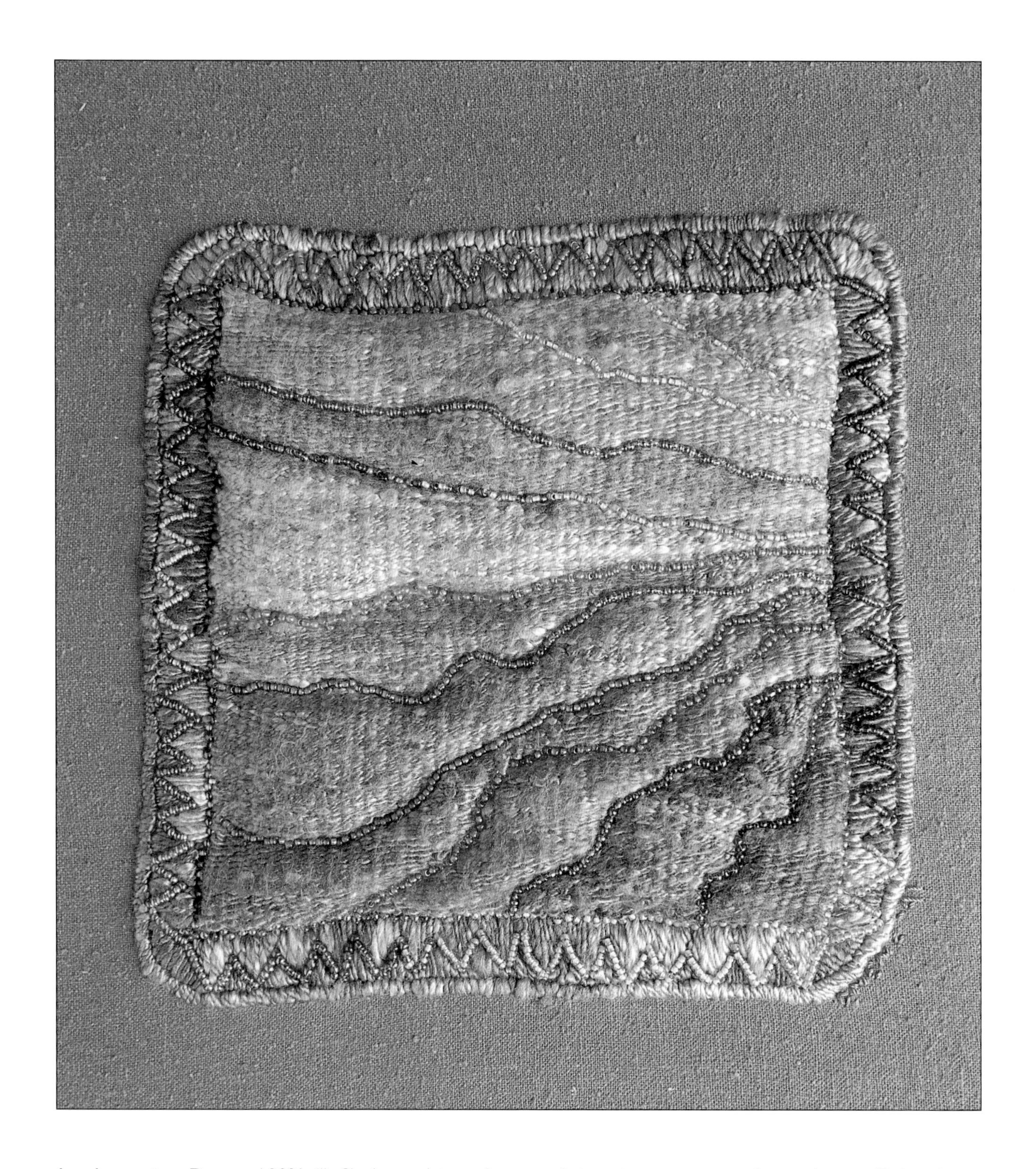

Landscape in a Dream. 100% silk. Singles and two-ply yarns. A tapestry woven on a loom, then stuffed and embellished with beads and embroidery. The yarns were spun from painted rovings.

Appendix A: Dye Worksheets

Sabraset Immersion Dye Worksheet		
Color		**DOS**
ml of dye	dyestock colors	percent
	Mustard yellow	
	Sun yellow	
	Deep red	
	Magenta 338	
	Scarlet	
	Magenta	
	Violet	
	Royal blue	
	Navy	
	Turquoise	
	Black	
	Total	100%
	Plain Salt–10%	
	Acetic Acid–4%	
	Albegal SET–7%	
	Sodium Acetate–1%	
	WOF=	

Sabraset Painting Worksheet		
Color		**DOS**
ml of dye	dyestock colors	percent
	Mustard yellow	
	Sun yellow	
	Deep red	
	Magenta 338	
	Scarlet	
	Magenta	
	Violet	
	Royal blue	
	Navy	
	Turquoise	
	Black	
	Total	100%
	Chemical water to add	
	Acetic Acid–4%	
	Sodium Acetate–1%	

Sabracron F Immersion Dye Worksheet		
Color		**DOS**
ml of dye	dye colors	formula
	Sun yellow 11	
	Golden yellow 14	
	True red 33	
	Fuchsia 35	
	Flame scarlet 31	
	Royal purple 83	
	Brilliant blue 42	
	Deep navy 47	
	Turquoise 40	
	Rich black 61	
	Earth brown 53	
	Total	100%
	Salt ___% WOF	
	Soda Ash–10% WOF	
	WOF=	

Sabracron F Painting Dye Worksheet		
Color		**DOS**
ml of dye	dye colors	formula
	Sun yellow 11	
	Golden yellow 14	
	True red 33	
	Fuchsia 35	
	Flame scarlet 31	
	Royal purple 83	
	Brilliant blue 42	
	Deep navy 47	
	Turquoise 40	
	Rich black 61	
	Earth brown 53	
	Total	100%
	Salt ___% WOF	
	Soda Ash–10% WOF	
	WOF=	

Appendix B: Metric Conversions

Note: These conversions are approximate—metric equivalents have been rounded to the nearest half-unit.

TEMPERATURE

Fahrenheit	Centigrade
110	43
115	46
120	49
125	52
130	54
135	57
140	60
150	65
155	68
160	71
165	74
170	77
175	79
180	82
185	85
190	88

LENGTH

Inches	Metric
1/16	2 mm
1/8	3 mm
1/4	6 mm
3/8	9 mm
1/2	12 mm
5/8	1.5 cm
3/4	2 cm
1	2.5 cm
2	5 cm
3	7.5 cm
4	10 cm
5	12.5 cm
6	15 cm
7	18 cm
8	20.5 cm
9	23 cm
10	25.5 cm
11	28 cm
12 (1 ft)	30.5 cm
36 (1 yd)	91.5 cm

VOLUME

Teaspoons	Milliliters
1/8	0.5
1/4	1
1/2	2
3/4	4
1	5
3 (1 tbsp)	15

Cups	Milliliters
1/4	60
1/3	80
1/2	120
2/3	160
3/4	180
1	240

Fluid Ounces	Milliliters
1	30
2	59
3	89
4	118
5	148
6	177
7	207
8	237
9	266
10	296

WEIGHT

Ounces	Grams
1/4	7
1/3	9.5
1/2	14
1	28.5
2	56.5
3	85
4	113.5
5	142
6	170
7	298.5
8	227
9	255
10	283.5
16 (1lb)	453.5

Glossary

Acetic Acid: a colorless liquid that is the active ingredient of vinegar. It is used in some dye processes to adhere dye to fiber with the assistance of heat.

Acid: optimal pH range (below 7) of solutions for dyeing protein fibers.

Acid Dye: a chemical dye that works in an acid environment. Well suited for protein fibers.

Albegal SET: a liquid that is used to assist in the immersion dye process with Sabraset dyes.

Alkali: optimal pH range (above 7) of solutions for dyeing cellulose fibers.

Analogous Colors: colors that are closely related on the color wheel. Primary analogous colors are the colors between two primaries. Otherwise, analogous colors fit within approximately a one-quarter-wedge of the color wheel.

Balance: the perception that a yarn or piece looks "right" because all elements of the design are in harmony, displaying pleasing proportions.

Barber-Poling: striping that results from dark- and light-value colors side by side in a yarn.

Batch: the amount of fiber that can be dyed at once.

Batt: a rectangular arrangement of fibers that have been prepared on a drum carder.

Bombyx Silk: fiber from the bombyx silk-worm.

Burnishing Tool: a brush-like tool that is used with a drum carder to smooth the surface of a batt.

Carding: a process for loosening and straightening out fibers, also used for blending colors or fibers.

Carding Cloth: the material on the surface of hand cards or carder drums. It is made from a rubber or leather fabric equipped with close-set wire teeth.

Cellulose Fibers: fibers that come from plants or plant by-products.

Chemical Assists: chemicals used with specific dyes to help complete a dye process.

Chemical Water: a 1% solution of water and acetic acid. It is used to regulate the DOS when painting rovings and using Sabraset dyes.

Citric Acid: acid obtained from citrus fruits, usually lemons and limes. Can substitute for acetic acid in protein dye processes.

Color: a way to describe and locate a hue in the context of a color wheel.

Color Family: see hue family.

Color Harmony: a series of color relationships based on a balanced combination of two or more hue families.

Color Loading: using more than one undertone of each primary color to obtain richer color. Example: using both blue and turquoise in a dye formula.

Color Mixing: an intimate mixing of colors that forms a completely new color and is irreversible. The original colors may not be evident in the final mixture.

Color Wheel: a round image that shows how colors relate to each other.

Combing: a method of fiber preparation that removes short fibers and aligns the longer fibers in a parallel formation.

Complementary Colors: colors that are opposite one another on the color wheel.

Cool Color: any color located on the cool half of the color wheel. With blue being coolest, they range from red-violet to yellow-green.

Crimp: the wavy configuration of many protein fibers, particularly wool.

Depth of Shade (DOS): the relationship between the amount of dye and the weight of fiber being dyed expressed in a number. The higher the DOS number, the more intense the color. Each kind of dye has a unique range of DOS numbers.

Diz: a disk with a hole in it used to regulate the thickness of top pulled off a comb at the end of the combing process.

Doffer Groove: the narrow space on the large drum of a drum carder where you separate the batt prior to removing it.

Doffer Stick: a sturdy, pointed stick used to separate the batt on the drum carder before the batt is removed.

Double Complement: two sets of complements that form a square on the color wheel. Can be called a "square quadratic".

Double Triad: pairs of colors that are equidistant on the color wheel.

Draft: the controlled pulling out of a fiber preparation before the fibers are twisted.

Drafting Triangle: The area occupied by unspun fiber just before it is twisted. This area is immediately in front of the hand farthest from the orifice.

Drum Carder: a simple machine designed to speed up the carding process. It consists of a small drum and a large drum, an infeed tray, and a crank.

Dullness: lack of intensity in a color.

Dye: a substance used to permanently color a fiber.

Dye Class: a way of grouping dye according to chemical assists needed to complete the process and the way that dye molecules attach to fiber.

Dye Formula: a recipe, expressed in percentages, giving the proportions of colors to mix together to form a new color.

Dyeing Assist: a chemical used to alter, assist, or complete a dye process.

Dyepot: a sizable container suitable for dyeing fibers, usually made of stainless steel or enamel and fitted with a lid.

Dyestock Solution: a solution that consists of a measured amount of dye powder in a measured amount of water.

Exhaustion: the process in dyeing that involves the dye molecules moving from the dyebath and attaching onto the intended fibers. When as much as possible of the dye has become attached to the fibers, the dyebath is considered "exhausted".

Fastness: the ability of a dye to remain the same color on the fiber for an unlimited length of time.

Fetling Brush: a brush-like tool that is used to clean off the drums on a drum carder. The cloth of the fetling brush is compatible with the carding cloth of the drum.

Fiber-Reactive Dye: a type of dye that reacts with fiber through a chemical bond. It is well suited to cellulose fibers.

Heathering: the effect of putting different values together in either carding, combing, or plying. The lighter values tend to lighten up the dark values and create a subtle salt-and-pepper effect.

Hexad: a color harmony that uses six hue families (three sets of complements) that are equidistant on the color wheel.

Hue Family: a small wedge in a color wheel that includes one color in all its variations.

Infeed Tray: the tray where you place fibers to be carded on a drum carder.

Intensity: see Saturation.

Lashing On: attaching fibers to combs in preparation for combing.

Lazy Kate: a piece of equipment that holds two or more bobbins of spun yarn for plying.

Level: the evenness of the color on dyed fibers.

Leveling acid dye: an acid dye requiring a long period of heating to complete the dye process.

Licker-In Drum: the small drum that feeds fibers onto the large drum of a drum carder.

Lock: a natural bundle of wool fibers.

Luxury Fiber: expensive, natural fibers somewhat hard to find for spinning that include alpaca, mohair, cashmere, and silk.

Monochromatic Colors: a group of colors that different in value and saturation but belong to one hue family.

Multicolored: the presence of many colors in a fiber preparation and resulting yarn.

Natural Fiber: fiber obtained from plants or animals.

Navajo Plying: a method of making a three-ply yarn from a single strand.

Optical Mixing: when small quantities of two or more colors are placed side by side or intermixed, the result is the impression of a new, distinct color.

Orvus: a detergent without additives that can be used to scour fleece. It is manufactured by Proctor and Gamble.

Palette: a range of colors used to create a yarn or finished piece.

Pass: in combing, a transfer of the fiber from one comb to the other, or a movement of the diz from one side of the comb to the other when pulling off fiber.

Pencil Roving: a roving with a diameter that is about the size of that of a pencil.

Percentage of Color: in a dye formula, the proportion of each dyestock color used.

Pitch: the number of rows of teeth on a comb.

Plying: the twisting together of two or more yarns, usually in the opposite direction from the original spinning.

Pointillist Effect: a term used by impressionist artists that describes the use of optical mixing in their work.

Premetallized Dye: an acid dye with metal ions that has improved washfastness.

Primary Colors: red, yellow, and blue, three hue families that cannot be obtained by mixing, and that form the base for mixing other colors.

Printer's Primaries: a specific set of primary colors used with black to print color images in books and magazines. These primaries are cyan, magenta, and yellow.

Protein Fiber: hairs from an animal such as wool from sheep, angora from rabbits, mohair from goats. Also silk from silkworms.

Pulling: the slow, deliberate thinning of batts or tops into spinnable size.

Quadratic: see tetrad, and double complement.

Rainbow Dyeing: a haphazard and unpredictable way to produce multicolored fibers and yarns.

Roving: prepared fiber that has a slight twist. The fiber may have been carded or combed. Fibers run in a generally parallel direction.

S-Twist: the counterclockwise direction of twist, usually used in plying.

Salt-and-Pepper Effect: the appearance of dots of dark and light values side by side in a finished fabric.

Saturation: the amount of pure color within a color. The higher the saturation, the brighter the color. Also called intensity.

Secondary Color: a color formed by mixing two primary colors.

Set: 1. when a dye is permanently attached to the fiber. 2. when the twist in a yarn is stabilized.

Shade: a color that has had black added.

Silk Noil: the short, silk fibers that are left after reeling or combing silk.

Simultaneous Contrast: the principle that states when two colors are placed side by side, the one used in larger quantity will shift your perception of the second color toward the dominant color's complement.

Singles: an unplied yarn.

Sliver: a consistent strand of carded fibers.

Soda Ash (Sodium Carbonate): a powder that is used with fiber reactive dyes.

Sodium Acetate: a white powder that is used as a chemical assist with Sabraset dyes.

Splitting: dividing a prepared fiber lengthwise into thin strips.

Squishy: the presence of excess moisture in a roving to be painted. The water or dyestock present visibly oozes out of the roving when pressed.

Staple Length: the length of a fiber, such as a staple or lock of wool.

Steaming: heating fibers without immersing them in water, sometimes used to set a dye.

Strike: the moment that the dye molecule actually attaches onto the fiber.

Stripping: see splitting.

Super-Milling Acid Dye: an acid dye that is very washfast, but hard to dye evenly. Works well on protein fibers.

Synthrapol: a wetting agent used to prepare fibers to accept dye more readily.

Tertiary Color: a color formed by mixing a primary and a secondary color beside it on the color wheel.

Tetrad: a four-color harmony; actually two sets of complements that form a rectangle on the color wheel. Also called quadratic.

Tint: a color that has had white added to it.

Top: 1. a commercially-prepared fiber that has been carded and combed to remove the short fibers. 2. a hand-combed preparation.

Tone: a color that has had either its complement or gray of the same value added.

Triad: three colors that are equidistant on the color wheel. The primary colors of red, yellow, and blue are a triad.

Undertone: the subtle quality of warmth or coolness of any color.

Value: the relative lightness or darkness of a color when compared to a gray scale.

Value Keys: particular value combinations. Major keys include a wide range of values. Minor keys include a narrow range of values.

Warm Color: any color located on the warm half of the color wheel. With orange the warmest, they range from yellow-green to red-violet.

Weight of Fiber (WOF): the weight of fiber to be dyed, usually measured in grams.

Wick: the tendency of a dye to move uncontrollably along a roving.

Wool Hackle: a one-piece comb-like tool used to arrange colors for multicolored tops.

Woozled: describes a roving or any fiber preparation that appears in less-than-perfect shape.

Worsted: a preparation and spinning method for yarn. Combing the short fibers out of the preparation and spinning with a short-draw technique are the methods involved.

Z-Stripping: splitting a batt or stack of batts into a continuous roving.

Z-Twist: the clockwise twist in a yarn, usually used when spinning singles.

Bibliography

Albers, Josef. *Interaction of Color.* New Haven, CT: Yale University Press, 1975.

Berent, Mary. "Color Games." *Spin·Off*, vol. XI no. 1 (Spring 1987): 21–24.

Birren, Faber. *Color Perception in Art.* West Chester, PA: Schiffer Publishing Co., 1986.

——*Creative Color.* West Chester, PA: Schiffer Publishing Co., 1987.

Bliss, Ann. "Dyes for Handspun: Fiber to Yarn." *Spin·Off* (Annual 1982): 52–53.

Bliss, Ann. "Hints for Dyeing." *Spin·Off* vol. IX no. 3 (Fall 1985): 53–54.

Blumenthal, Betsy. *Hands On Dyeing.* Loveland, CO: Interweave Press, 1988.

Chevreul, M.E. *The Principles of Harmony and Contrast of Colors and Their Applications to the Arts.* West Chester, PA: Schiffer Publishing Co., 1987.

Deems, Flo. "Pointillist Color Effects In Spinning." *Spin·Off*, vol. IV (1980): 53–55.

Dobie, Jeanne. *Making Color Sing.* New York: Watson-Guptill Publications, 1986.

Dozer, Iris. "Wonderful Worsted." *Spin·Off* vol. VII no. 2 (Summer 1982): 32–38.

Fannin, Allen. *Handspinning Art and Technique.* New York: Van Nostrand Reinhold, 1970.

Field, Anne. *The Ashford Book of Spinning.* Cristchurch, New Zealand: Shoal Bay Press, 1986.

——. *Spinning Wool—Beyond the Basics.* Christchurch, New Zealand: Shoal Bay Press, 1995.

Fournier, Jane. "Elegant and Approachable Cashgora." *Spin·Off*, vol. XVI no. 3 (Fall 1992): 43–45.

Gibson-Roberts, Priscilla. "Woolcombing in the Peasant Way." *Spin·Off*, vol. X no. 1 (Spring 1988): 42–46.

Hochberg, Bette. *Fibre Facts.* Santa Cruz: Bette Hochberg, 1981.

——. "Carders: Hand or Drum?". *Spin·Off* vol. III (1979): 40–43.

Itten, Johannes. *The Art of Color.* New York: Van Nostrand Reinhold, 1961.

——. *The Color Star.* New York: Van Nostrand Reinhold, 1985.

——. *The Elements of Color.* New York: Van Nostrand Reinhold, 1970.

Knutson, Linda. "Getting Started with Chemical Dyes." *Spin·Off* vol. VIII no. 3 (Fall 1984): 39–41.

——. *Shades of Wool for Lanaset Dyes.* Self Published, 1983.

——. *Synthetic Dyes for Natural Fibers.* Loveland, CO: Interweave Press, 1986.

Kueppers, Harald. *The Basic Law of Color Theory.* Woodbury, NY: Barron's Educational Series, 1982.

Lambert, Patricia. *Controlling Color.* New York: Design Press, 1991.

Lambert, Patricia, Barbara Staepelaere, and Mary Fry. *Color and Fiber.* West Chester, PA: Schiffer Publishing Co., 1986.

Marx, Ellen. *Optical Color and Simultaneity.* New York: Van Nostrand Reinhold, 1983.

Menz, Deb. "Using Lanaset Dyes on Fibers." *Spin·Off* vol. XV no. 4 (Winter 1991): 53–58.

Milner, Ann. *The Ashford Book of Dyeing.* Wellington, New Zealand: Bridget Williams Books Ltd., 1992.

Newton, Deborah. *Designing Knitwear.* Newtown, CT: Taunton Press, 1992.

Presser, Fran. "A Closer Look at Cashgora." *Spin·Off* vol. X no. 4 (Winter 1986): 49–52.

Quinn, Celia. "Color Exercises for the Beginner." *Spin·Off* vol. IX no. 3 (Fall 1985): 36–38.

——. "Plying a Balanced Yarn for Knitting." *Spin·Off* vol. XI no. 4 (Winter 1987): 30–31.

——. "Navajo." *Spin·Off* vol. XIII no. 2 (Summer 1989): 50–51.

Raven, Lee. *Hands On Spinning.* Loveland, CO: Interweave Press, 1987.

Reese, Sharon. *Jigging. . . 100% Hand Worsted.* Oregon: Johna and Helen Meck, 1984.

Ross, Mabel. *The Essentials of Yarn Design for Handspinners.* Kinross, Scotland: Mabel Ross, 1983.

———. *Handspinner's Workbook: Fancy Yarns.* Kinross, Scotland: Spinningdale, 1989.

Royce, Beverly. "Three Spun Threads." *Spin·Off,* vol. IX no. 1 (Spring 1985): 39–41.

Shull, Paula. "Worsted Yarns." *Spin·Off,* vol. XVII no. 3 (Fall 1993): 99–109.

Teal, Peter. *Hand Woolcombing and Spinning.* Poole, Dorset, UK: Blanford Press, 1976.

Thurner, Noel A. "Viking Wool Combs." *Spin·Off,* vol. XVI no. 1 (Fall 1992): 44–49.

Varney, Diane. *Spinning Designer Yarns.* Loveland, CO: Interweave Press, 1987.

Wilcox, Michael. *Blue and Yellow Don't Make Green.* Rockport, Massachusetts: Rockport Publishers, 1989.

Wipplinger, Michele. "Lanaset: Protein Fiber Dye." *Color Trends 2,* no. 1 (Fall 1985): 4–5.

———."And More about Lanaset Dyes." *Color Trends 3,* no.1 (Fall 1986): 13–14.

Wong, Wucius. *Principles of Color Design.* New York: Van Nostrand Reinhold, 1987.

Sources of Supply

Ashland Bay Trading Company (wholesale only)
PO Box 2613
Gig Harbor, WA 98335
Commercially prepared fibers

Bullen's Wullens
5711 County Road #13
Centerburg, OH 43011
Good color range of dyed tops

The Clearing
1280 Sexton Hollow Road
Painted Post, NY 14870
Good quality Corriedale fleece

Earth Guild
33 Haywood Street
Asheville, NC 28801
Dye supplies

Patrick Green Carders, Ltd.
48793 Chilliwack Lake Road
Sardis, B.C. Canada V2R 2P1
Drum carders and carding tools

Linda Knutson
15280 Douglas Road
Yakima, WA 98908
Source for Shades of Wool for Lanaset Dyes *(extensive dye notebook)*

Lani Combs
5835 West 6th Ave, Unit 4D
Lakewood, CO 80214
Color-blending hackles and combs

Louet Sales
RR #4
Prescott, Ont., Canada K0E 1T0
Combs, wheels

Maiwa Handprints
1566 Johnson Street #6
Granville Island
Vancouver, B.C., Canada V6H 3S2
Japanese stencil brushes

Linda MacMillan
PO Box 531, Main Street
Putney, VT 05346
Source for Kaleidoscope Dye Formulas for Lanaset Dyes *(dye notebook)*

Norsk Fjord Fiber
PO Box 271
Lexington, GA 30648
One- and two-row hand-held combs and stands

Pro Chemical & Dye Inc.
PO Box 14
Somerset, MA 02726
Dyes and dye supplies

Woodchuck Products
114 Woodside Drive
Clarks Summit, PA 18411
Diz sets, wooden spinning tools

Index